FIREMAN

The Evolution of the Closer in Baseball

Fran Zimniuch

TRIUMPH
B O O K S

Triumph Books and colophon are registered trademarks of Random House, Inc.

Library of Congress Cataloging-in-Publication Data

Zimniuch, Fran.
  Fireman : the evolution of the closer in baseball / Fran Zimniuch.
      p. cm.
  ISBN 978-1-60078-312-8
  1. Relief pitchers (Baseball) I. Title.
  GV871.Z56 2010
  796.357'22—dc22

                          2009043089

This book is available in quantity at special discounts for your group or organization. For further information, contact:

  Triumph Books
  542 South Dearborn Street
  Suite 750
  Chicago, Illinois 60605
  (312) 939-3330
  Fax (312) 663-3557
  www.triumphbooks.com

Printed in U.S.A.
ISBN: 978-1-60078-312-8
Design and page production by Patricia Frey
Photos courtesy of AP Images unless otherwise indicated

*This book is for the father of baseball, whether it was
Alexander Cartwright, Henry Chadwick, or Abner Doubleday.
Whoever created baseball created the greatest game in history. This
book is for the starters, mop-up men, long relievers, left-handed
specialists, set-up men, short relievers, and closers who have
made the game so much fun and so interesting.*

*This book is also for my sons, Brent and Kyle, whom,
much like baseball, I consider the greatest in history.*

Contents

Foreword

Major League Baseball has changed a lot since I broke into the big leagues with the Chicago Cubs back in 1980. In those days, baseball was not nearly as specialized a sport as it is in 2010. Way back then, starting pitchers were expected to complete most of the games they started, and bullpens were completely different. Relievers were like utility players who weren't good enough to start. The term *closer* was out there but was an unknown entity, something like HAL in the movie *2001: A Space Odyssey*. Well, 2001 has come and gone, but the closer is here to stay in the grand old game of baseball. And I was there for the start of it.

The thing that struck me about *Fireman: The Evolution of the Closer in Baseball* is how the book speaks to both starting pitching and relief pitching. After all, before the relievers and the closer can do their thing, it is the starters who set the tone of the game. In *Fireman*, Fran Zimniuch not only goes into an in-depth treatment of relief pitching throughout the years but starting pitching as well. This book takes the reader inside the dugout, inside the clubhouse, and, most important, inside the minds of big-league players, managers, coaches, and front-office personnel to better understand the role of relief pitching. It was during my career that pitchers such as myself and a number of others redefined the role of the relief pitcher and closer. Managers started to use us differently, and when we succeeded, a whole new strategy entered the game.

Many former players often take an interest in the history of the game we love. I know I have. Because of my appreciation for the players who came before me, I found the historical aspects of this book fascinating. I always wanted to be a starting pitcher, like Don Newcombe. But I was actually one of the first black guys to have the chance to finish games, an honor a lot like the first black quarterback in football. I had that in my mind in addition to just being a good pitcher.

The first black guy to really act as a closer was Hilton Lee Smith, who pitched with the Kansas City Monarchs in the Negro Leagues from 1937 until he retired in 1948. He was a great pitcher who may have had the best curveball ever. He was a teammate of the great Satchel Paige. Satchel would pitch the first few innings, and then Smith would come in and finish the game, saving the win for Paige. So there is a lot of history in the game and in this book.

Fireman takes you out to the pitcher's mound and helps you understand what we're thinking about out there, what motivates us, and how we get outs in the ninth inning. Not everybody can get those outs in the ninth inning. Of course, when I played we pitched a lot more than just the ninth inning. We'd come into a game anytime from the seventh inning on. And, being like the equivalent of the first black quarterback, I always felt like there was a little more expected of me. It seemed like I was critiqued a little bit more, with people wondering if I could handle the pressure. I had tremendous pride in the way I carried myself. My good friend and former teammate Fergie Jenkins helped me with that part of the game. He taught me how to act on and off the field.

But what Fran really accomplishes in this book is giving an understanding of what changes have taken place on pitching staffs throughout baseball, particularly in the last generation of players, and why these changes have occurred. A lot of the changes to the game didn't occur until I was pitching for the Cubs. So I saw it firsthand, was part of the experience, and, I guess, part of the experiment.

I had always wanted to be a starting pitcher and actually decided to quit the game because the Cubs wanted to make me into a reliever. I had a basketball scholarship at Northwestern State University and was going to go there. But I guess my old manager at Double A ball, Randy Hundley, and the Cubs' great outfielder Billy Williams were right in the way they encouraged me to give relieving a try. I may not have wanted to become a reliever, but having the chance to play every day was a great thrill. Instead of starting and then sitting around for four or five days, I was on call every night. And I wanted the ball. Unlike the guys who close today, 155 of my 478 saves were six-out saves instead of three-out saves. I was so dedicated to saving the game for my starter that I didn't want to ever let any runners that I inherited score, and I wanted my starter to get credit for a win. When I came into the game, being as competitive as I was and still am today, I wanted to totally shut down the other team.

Coming out of the bullpen, I learned a new way of pitching and how to get hitters out and used pinpoint control to do it. I remember when Mike Shannon, who played and announced for the St. Louis Cardinals, said that when he first saw me, every pitch I threw was on the black of the plate. They'd put me in there, and I'd be painting the corners, my control was so good. I learned how to control the baseball when I was a kid. My brother and I would spend hours throwing peaches. He would throw them at the mailbox, but I would throw them at the flag on the mailbox.

Becoming a reliever made it possible for me to pitch for 18 years in the major leagues. It's like nothing else you'll ever experience. I always tell these kids in the minor leagues that there is nothing better than making it to the majors. You don't realize just how few people have played Major League Baseball. If you look at the total population, it's not many that get to play professional baseball in the big leagues. I was one of a micronumber of people lucky enough to do it. And to be in an elite group inside of that elite group—being considered for the Hall of Fame—is even a greater honor.

A lot has been said and written about me getting into the Hall of Fame. It would be the honor of a lifetime, the topping on the cake. But just to be considered good enough to be part of that incredible group of players—and being mentioned in the same breath as them—gives me goose bumps.

It's all about how you handle yourself, whether it's on the mound, in the clubhouse, or just living your life. Fergie helped me out a lot with that, and I try to pass that along to the young players in the minor leagues whom I work with now.

Baseball becomes your whole life, and I love and respect the game. What I like about *Fireman* is that it treats our game with that same degree of respect.

Up to now, all we've been able to do is look at all of the changes involved in major league bullpens and shake our heads in wonder over just how much has changed in such a short period of time. But thanks to Fran's book, with all the interviews he conducted with so many players, managers, and executives who lived through the changes, we now have a much better understanding of how and why all those changes have come about.

The game is very different from only a generation ago, particularly when you are thinking about pitching. But even considering all those changes, it's still the game we all grew up with and came to love. And I am thrilled to have been a part of it. No matter what happens with the Hall of Fame, I just hope that people will remember me as a good player and a good human being.

—Lee Arthur Smith
Fall 2009

Acknowledgments

As anyone who has ever undertaken the task of writing a book will tell you, the number of people who deserve a word of thanks for their inspiration, help, support, and solace during the life of such a project is pretty much limitless. As I go through my day-to-day existence, like many people who write, I have a fantastic regular job that takes up my regular work week and more. But in addition to that part of my life, there is usually something going on with me that only those who are close to me know about: I'm either working on a book, trying to sell a publishing company on the merits of an idea I have for a book, or, most alarmingly, attempting to come up with such an idea.

Book ideas with me are never in short supply. If I didn't need to support myself and my two sons, I could have a very happy daily existence researching, conducting interviews, and writing books about my interests in sports. But as Dean Reinke, an acquisitions editor for a publishing company I wrote for in the past, once asked me about an idea of mine that I thought would get me on the cover of *Sports Illustrated*, "Besides you and me, who will read it?"

That conversation gave me a smack-in-the-face reality check that I obviously needed. With self-publishing avenues available to anyone who wants to write a book, anyone can write about just about anything. But

I'm an old-fashioned sort of guy who wants a publishing company to believe in my idea as much as I do. That's the only way I'll take on such a project. And for giving me the proper mind-set in which to decide if one of my 3,657,335 book ideas is actually marketable, I'd like to thank Dean Reinke for his dose of book publishing reality.

Where did the idea for *Fireman* come from? Hard to say, but it was a compilation of ideas that enabled me to write about baseball, learn about pitching, and trace what may be the most important strategic aspect of America's Game from its meager beginnings to the present day. The idea of writing about a history of relief pitching and trying to discover just how we've reached this time of pitch counts, middle relievers, set-up men, and one-inning closers was a challenge that made me feel like a kid on Christmas morning. The first "closers" I remember were Jack Baldschun, the screwballing right-hander of the Philadelphia Phillies, and southpaw Ron Perranoski, of the Los Angeles Dodgers. When those two gentlemen were playing, their roles were very different from the role of a relief specialist today.

To all of the starters, long men, middle relievers, set-up men, short relievers, left-handed specialists, and closers who ignited such a flame of interest on my part, a heartfelt thank-you. Thanks also to a wonderful trio of publishing executives with Triumph Books—Don Gulbrandsen, Tom Bast, and Michael Emmerich—who looked at my proposal with an open mind and a trusting confidence that I could pull it off. You are the men! This is my second book with Triumph, and I sincerely hope it's the second of many. A special thank-you is also in order to Bill Giles of the Philadelphia Phillies' organization, who recommended I contact Triumph.

Asking a person to pen a foreword for your book is a difficult proposition. More often than not, the book is not yet complete, so although you can furnish someone with plenty of samples of what your book is all about, the writer is taking a tremendous leap of faith that you are not some sort of Charles Manson type who will ruin his reputation and make him the subject of ridicule and scorn. Although I have more faults than you can shake a stick at, all things considered I'm an okay guy. At some point during our discussions, the former great closer Lee Smith must have thought that I was deserving of his trust. Thank you, Lee. Your words give me and my book credibility. The only thing better than this would be for me to see you inducted into the Baseball Hall of Fame in Cooperstown, New York, a long-overdue honor that you richly deserve. Also, a special word of thanks to a wonderful person and a great fan of the game, Cheryl Radachowsky, for her efforts in making the foreword happen. And without the help of Hall of Fame pitcher Ferguson Jenkins, Lee Smith would not have been a part of this project. A big thank-you to Fergie.

There are countless other baseball people who shared their knowledge, ideas, opinions, and concerns. That list includes the likes of Maury Allen; Jack Baldschun; Fred Claire; Carl Erskine; Jim Fregosi; Pat Gillick; Jim Gott; Dennis Eckersley and his wonderful wife, Jennifer; Elroy Face; Gene Garber; Peter Morris; Chris Wheeler; Goose Gossage; and many others who helped me understand the topic better. And I can't acknowledge Goose without a resounding thank-you to Andrew Levy, of Wish You Were Here Productions, who made that fantastic interview happen.

To the many wonderful writers I have had the pleasure to read over the years who helped form my own view of baseball and life, I can only hope to do you proud. People who have had an impact on me include great writers such as the aforementioned Maury Allen, Roger Angell, Buzz Bissinger, Jim Bouton, Darryl Brock, Jerry Casway, Fred Claire, Larry Colton, Bill Conlin, Larry Dierker, Mark Fainaru-Wada, John Feinstein, Stan Hochman, Bill James, Roger Kahn, Bill Kashatus, the late, great Ray Kelly Sr., W.P. Kinsella, Tim McCarver, Peter Morris, Cait Murphy, Rob Neyer, Daniel Okrent, Pete Palmer, Mark Turnbull, Mark Whicker, George Will, Lance Williams, and many more. Although they have nothing to do with sportswriting, Robert Ludlum and Tom Clancy are the best novelists I've ever read.

Larry Colton deserves some special praise. He pitched one game in the major leagues prior to becoming a teacher and an incredibly talented Pulitzer Prize–nominated author. Larry never big-times anyone and has been a huge help to me from early in my writing career until this very day. Just being a good guy, he probably doesn't even realize how his encouragement over the past years has helped me. And his advice about book proposals no doubt made this project fly. Thank you, Larry.

To anyone who helped me with this project, you have my thanks. One person in particular who deserves some long-overdue praise is my high school English teacher during my junior and senior years at Northeast Catholic High School in Philadelphia, Professor Fran Ryan, now of LaSalle University. He was the toughest teacher I ever encountered. But he was also by far the best. He was always prepared, fair, willing to offer his wealth of knowledge to his students, and acted in the best tradition of the teaching profession. My life is one string of deadlines and responsibilities after another. Fran Ryan was the first person to really teach me about being disciplined enough to do what needed to be done, in school and in life. Thanks, teach.

Lots of friends offered their constant encouragement. If I had writer's block or a frustrating experience during the process or just needed a break, they were a welcome breath of fresh air, making me laugh, helping me realize that my little project would take care of itself, and putting me in a better place. That list includes and starts with the likes of Lou Chimenti and his lovely wife, Marcia; Dannielle Spivak; Jim Groff; Joe and Janet Nickels; Christina Mitchell; Bob Scott; Elissa Walker Campbell; Dan Kisch; Matthijs Braakman; Trace Shelton; Lenny and Katie Krol (Go Huskers); Jeff Gasman; Howard Gurock; John Warren (my idea tester); and my wonderful late friend from the Napa Valley, Jack Heeger, as well as a host of others.

Some people I had never met before, such as Sean Forman, Bill Deane, and Larry McCray, went out of their way to help me get information I deemed important.

Thanks also must go to my two sons, Brent and Kyle, who live with my daily grind, whether it's selling advertising for *Instore Magazine* or pitching a book idea, researching the project, interviewing sources, and finally writing the manuscript. So much for weekends, huh? They are both fine young men who do me proud every day.

I hope I've done you all proud.

Introduction

The fifth and final game of the 2008 World Series was both as typical and atypical as a baseball game can be in the new millennium. It was typical in the sense that, en route to their championship-clinching 4–3 victory over the Tampa Bay Rays, the Philadelphia Phillies used their bullpen according to baseball's current book on pitching. In fact, to look at a box score of the game, which started the evening of Monday, October 27, would give no hint as to the atypical nature of this contest. But baseball fans will remember that the game took more than 50 hours to complete when inclement weather—cold temperatures and a steady, heavy rain—forced the suspension of play in the middle of the sixth inning, after Tampa scored a run to tie the contest at 2–2.

The conditions in Philadelphia were just as bad the following night, which required the game to be delayed one more day, until Wednesday, October 29. Even that night offered far-from-ideal conditions for baseball. Though the bone-chilling rain had stopped, temperatures hovered in the upper 30s as the Phillies finally came to bat in the bottom of the sixth.

Although Phillies starter Cole Hamels threw just 75 pitches through six innings, he was no longer an option on the mound when play resumed after the extended suspension—but this was not really a

problem for the home team. Like any successful franchise in this generation of baseball, the 2008 Philadelphia Phillies were blessed with a
prototypical bullpen with no missing parts. Closer Brad Lidge had a
perfect season and postseason, not blowing a single save in 2008. But
manager Charlie Manuel also had in his bullpen arsenal what local
scribes called the "Bridge to Lidge": set-up men Ryan Madson, J.C.
Romero, Chad Durbin, and Scott Eyre.

When the Phillies finally came to bat in the bottom half of the sixth
inning, two days after the top half of the inning ended, Geoff Jenkins—
in what was likely his final big-league at-bat—pinch hit for Hamels and
promptly lined a double to right-center field off Rays reliever Grant
Balfour. Jimmy Rollins bunted Jenkins to third base, and he scored on a

Phillies closer Brad Lidge was perfect in the 2008 regular season and postseason, converting every
save opportunity presented to him and leading Philadelphia to a World Series title.

bloop hit by Jayson Werth. The Phillies took a 3–2 lead into the seventh inning.

Madson, a tall righty who had cemented his role as set-up man with a solid regular season and outstanding playoffs, entered the game and fanned Tampa Bay catcher Dioner Navarro for the first out in the top of the seventh. But then Rocco Baldelli promptly tied the contest with a home run. Another hit and sacrifice bunt later, the Rays were threatening to take the lead once again when Manuel replaced Madson with lefty specialist Romero. He promptly induced Akinori Iwamura to hit a grounder up the middle to second baseman Chase Utley, who made a fantastic play to fake out the runner and throw out Jason Bartlett at the plate to preserve the tie.

In the home half of the seventh inning, in what turned out to be his final at-bat for the Phillies, Pat Burrell led off the stanza with a long double off the top of the wall in left-center field, missing a home run by inches. One out later, Pedro Feliz singled home pinch-runner Eric Bruntlett. Philadelphia once again took the lead, 4–3, and was six outs away from its second World Series championship in franchise history.

Romero completed his role as set-up man perfectly, shutting down Tampa Bay in the visitors' half of the eighth inning. The Phillies failed to score in their half, leaving Brad Lidge three outs from finishing his perfect season perfectly.

The first Rays batter Lidge faced in the top of the ninth inning was Evan Longoria, who popped out to Utley at second. But then Navarro singled sharply to right, putting the tying run on base and making things interesting. Fernando Perez pinch ran for Navarro and promptly stole second base—and the Rays were a single away from tying the game and breaking Lidge's perfect streak. At this point, the closer bore down. Ben Zobrist, pinch hitting for Baldelli, lined out to Werth in right field. The Rays' last chance fell to another pinch-hitter, Eric Hinske, hitting for Bartlett. Lidge delivered a nasty slider to strike out Hinske, giving the championship to Philadelphia, four games to one, and earning Brad Lidge his seventh postseason save and 48th save for the year.

That the game ended in a World Series championship for Philadelphia was extraordinary to say the least, but the way the Phillies' pitching endgame was orchestrated was actually pretty ordinary for modern-day baseball. Championship-caliber clubs such as the Phillies have a broad arsenal of pitchers who know their roles and perform them to the highest degree. Phillies relief pitchers had so consistently performed their assigned jobs during the regular season that manager Charlie Manuel and pitching coach Rich Dubee could dial up their numbers in the bullpen without hesitation—even during the high tension of a championship series.

As a result of this bullpen maneuvering, for one cold, damp night in October 2008 Brad Lidge was king in Philadelphia, and the Phillies were the best team in baseball—ironic because Philadelphia is the losingest team in all of sports—and it had been 28 years since the club's last championship. But Philadelphia's climb to the top was appropriate for a sport in which change has become the norm and has been an important factor in maintaining baseball's popularity over several generations of fans. And it is easily argued that no aspect of the game has changed more that the role of the relief pitcher.

As far as relief pitchers are concerned, the terminology used to discuss them has changed along with the strategy for using them. The *closer* is the most visible reliever as far as the casual fan is concerned. The closer normally comes into the game when his team has a lead of three runs or fewer in the ninth inning. Under the current system, should a pitcher protect the lead and ensure the victory for his team, he earns a save. In the past, *short relievers*, precursors to closers, were pitchers who would often come into games as early as the seventh inning, usually with men on base. Their job was to deliver the out or two necessary to close out that stanza before finishing the final innings to secure the win for the team. Old-time short relievers often scoff at today's one-inning closers.

Typically, the closer is one of the most talented pitchers on the staff. But because closers normally face batters but once per game, they don't need the variety of pitches that a starter needs. Many have just two outstanding pitches or one signature pitch that can be nearly unhittable. For example, Brad Lidge possesses an outstanding fastball and a devastating slider that hitters have a hard time not swinging at, even though the pitch often winds up out of the strike zone. It's a strike when they begin their swing, but it swoops down and out of the zone by the time it reaches the plate.

When a talented closer is at his best, he can be "Lights Out," like the moniker that Brad Lidge acquired during the good times in Houston. The top closers seemingly have ice water in their veins, thriving on crucial situations with the game on the line. But no matter what pitches they throw, the best closers maintain their composure and can get out right-handed and left-handed batters with equal regularity.

Though closers get most of the bullpen headlines, the pitchers who act as a bridge to the closer have become increasingly important. With starters expected to pitch only six or seven innings on most outings, *middle relievers,* or *set-up men,* pitch the innings between the starter and the closer. These pitchers might throw an inning or two, depending on which opposing batters are due up at the plate. Although a generation ago teams would carry nine or 10 pitchers on staff, the importance of middle relief has seen the number of pitchers on a team's roster increase to as many as 12 or 13.

There are even specialists within the middle-relief corps. Most teams enjoy the luxury of having a left-hander in the bullpen whose specialty is getting out left-handed hitters. Some managers like to use these lefties against weaker right-handed batters who are vulnerable to southpaws because they see relatively few of them in a sport dominated by right-handers. These lefty specialists usually pitch to one or two hitters before giving way to another reliever.

Going back to Philadelphia's World Series–clinching game in 2008, the Phillies had hoped that Ryan Madson would be the "Bridge to Lidge" after taking a quick lead following the 50-hour weather delay. Although Madson did not fare as well as he had throughout the season and post-season, he is a prototypical set-up man. He has a hard fastball, a breaking pitch, and one of the best change-ups in the game—a pitch that can handcuff even the most talented hitters. As a pitcher who has also started at times during his career, he has no problem pitching two innings if necessary.

Philadelphia's J.C. Romero is another outstanding set-up man, though one with a specialty: he's a lefty. Left-handed batters have a difficult time hitting against him, and he has good enough stuff to get out most right-handers, making him a valuable pitcher in almost any late-inning spot. As a result, he often sticks around for more than the typical batter or two that most southpaw specialists face.

Specialization is the key word in baseball these days, and nowhere is it more evident than in the bullpen. Teams like the Phillies need pitchers on their staff to fill very specific roles. "It's the focal point of the sport now," said Chris Wheeler, a television and radio broadcaster for the Philadelphia Phillies since 1977. "If you don't have a seventh-, eighth-, and ninth-inning guy, you're done. Starters used to pitch complete games. Now you can't win if you don't have these people coming in and out of the bullpen. They need to get people out in the seventh, eighth, and ninth inning. Bullpens are comprised of specialty guys who have an inning to pitch or match up against a particular right-handed hitter or left-handed hitter.

"It really annoys me when people complain about the specialization of baseball. Get over it. That's the way the game is now. I watch a football game and 10,000 guys run on and off the field before every play, and nobody says anything. You have the guy who only plays on first down or third down or the nickel back coming in on passing plays. Basketball has whistles galore, and substitutions are made for specific matchups. Why don't they piss and moan about that the way they do about baseball? It annoys me that people criticize baseball for doing the same thing that every other sport does. It's the way the game is, and it has evolved to this point, so just relax and enjoy it. Clearly, teams that address the situation are the ones that win. If a team doesn't, or guys don't do their job properly, they fail."

Unlike the Phillies' experience in 2008, bullpens can fail in the World Series. Just ask another Phillies closer, Mitch Williams, who served up a World Series–winning walk-off home run to Toronto's Joe Carter in 1993. Or go back in time to the plight of Brooklyn Dodgers right-handed pitcher Hugh Casey.

"My first memory of a baseball game was about a relief pitcher named Hugh Casey," said veteran sportswriter and author Maury Allen, who has penned more than 50 books over his illustrious career. "In 1941 he came in for the Brooklyn Dodgers when they were ahead in the fourth game of the World Series. He was facing Tommy Henrich and had two strikes on him. He then threw a pitch that history has never really explained, whether it was a spitball, a hard slider, or whatever. But it got away from the catcher, Mickey Owen, who was a fine defensive catcher, and Henrich went to first base.

"The Yankees rallied to win the game. From that time on I've related to relief pitching and always worried that the reliever would blow the game. Hugh Casey was famous, a fine relief pitcher. He was a focal point of that game for me. I criticized [Dodgers manager Leo] Durocher about not going to the mound to talk to Casey after Henrich got on first base. But he just said that everyone was sort of stunned after it happened.

"The fascination of baseball is that you can get a play in a World Series game or an All-Star Game that sort of gets exaggerated, and it stays with you over the years. I heard that game on the radio, and I was only eight years old. But that was my first memory of a game. I used to listen to games with my dad. We were big fans."

Just ask Brad Lidge how much his performance in big games has affected how people view him or how quickly the career of a closer can take off—or plummet. The life of a closer is tenuous, probably the most glaring example of "what have you done for me lately?" in sports. Consider that just a year before his World Series glory with the Phillies, Lidge was anything but the confident, consistent pitcher he was throughout 2008. He struggled with Houston in 2007, for the second time in three years, and actually lost his spot as closer for a short time.

Going back to 2005, Lidge was considered one of the premier relievers in baseball. He had a fine campaign that year, helping the Astros to the World Series while establishing himself as one of the best closers in the game—yet not every game he appeared in that year went according to plan. Lidge was called on to close out the St. Louis Cardinals in the fifth game of the 2005 National League Championship Series but instead surrendered a majestic, game-winning, three-run home run to Albert Pujols. Fortunately, Houston won the sixth game and advanced to the World Series against the red-hot Chicago White Sox, so Lidge was forgiven—temporarily.

Then, in the Fall Classic, Lidge gave up a walk-off, game-winning home run to Scott Posednik in Game 2, and the White Sox went on to sweep the Series. As a result, Lidge's fine season—with a 4–4 record, 42 saves, and an ERA of 2.29 in 70 games—was forgotten thanks to two balls that went yard in the postseason. Two pitches conspired to create a question mark as to whether Lidge still had the right stuff.

The questions continued in 2006 as Lidge struggled with a 1–5 record and an alarmingly high 5.28 ERA and 11 wild pitches. He still had 32 saves but blew six while Houston came back to earth after its Series run.

The trend continued in 2007 as Lidge was inconsistent despite a 5–3 record and a 3.36 ERA. He recorded just 19 saves and was demoted to middle relief during the season. The Astros had seen enough. The following November Lidge was dealt to the Phillies along with utility man Eric Bruntlett in exchange for pitcher Geoff Geary, speedy outfield prospect Michael Bourn, and minor leaguer Mike Costanzo.

He arrived in Philadelphia in 2008 with a damaged knee that needed surgery during spring training and a damaged reputation due to his decline in Houston. Which pitcher were the Phillies getting, the outstanding closer or the inconsistent enigma? And how would he react to the demanding Philadelphia fans after his first blown save or disappointing loss?

Amazingly, Lidge never had to face that challenge during his debut season pitching for the Phillies. The man who was anything but invincible over his last couple of seasons in Houston rebounded with as good a season as a relief pitcher could possibly have. In addition to a World Series ring, he nabbed the 2008 National League Comeback Player of the Year Award, the 2008 National League Rolaids Relief Man of the Year, and the 2008 DHL Delivery Man of the Year.

When discussing relief pitching, it is important to remember that there are as many facets to the role as there are relievers. Pitching out of the pen in general—and as the closer in particular—can take a pitcher to the highest of highs or to the deepest valleys from one game until the next...in fact, from one pitch until the next. You are dealing with fragile egos and unsteady psyches. Did Lidge lose his edge in Houston, or did the Astros give up on him too quickly? Was the move to Philadelphia the proverbial change of scenery that the veteran player needed to rejuvenate his career, or would he eventually have rediscovered that marvelous mojo in Houston? Whatever the answer, the Brad Lidge story is just one more reason why baseball fans have become so fascinated with closers.

Today there is an orderly fashion in which the bullpen pitchers are used, and they know what their roles are on a team. It wasn't always that way. The current reliever roles are the culmination of decades of change in the game. Whether the changes have been as obvious as the advent of the designated hitter or as subtle as the incremental increases in time between pitches, they continue to shape and reshape America's Pastime. Who would have believed 50 years ago that there would ever be artificial surfaces or video replay review of near-miss home runs?

One of the most discernable changes to the game along with the specialization of the pitching staff has been an elevation of the role of relief pitchers. Unlike the 2008 Philadelphia Phillies bullpen staff, there was a time, not that long ago, when the typical relief pitcher was either a washed-up veteran trying to hold on, an underachieving starter sent to bullpen Siberia by the manager, or a pitcher with good stuff but lacking the ability to pitch deep into games. How things have changed.

Fireman: The Evolution of the Closer in Baseball bridges the gap between those days and today's game with a historical treatment of pitching out of the pen and the influences and changes in the game that have brought bullpens to their present state.

In baseball generations past, the two- and three-inning save used to be the norm, meaning that pitchers who closed games pitched many more innings during the season and, as a result, more than one pitcher closed games. If Goose Gossage or Bruce Sutter had to pitch three innings one night, odds are that he would have been unavailable the next night. And quite simply there were plenty of nights when there would be no need for anyone to close, because most teams had more than one inning-eating horse on their pitching staff who would think nothing of pitching 25 complete games per year.

In fact, in baseball's previous generation, Hall of Famer Robin Roberts threw 183 complete games in the seven-year period from 1950 to 1956, including 33 complete games in 1953. During that time he averaged more than 26 complete games per season. In 2008 the entire National League Eastern Division totaled 12 complete games pitched. Again, how things have changed!

The complete game has become a lost art in today's brave new baseball world. A "quality" start consists of a six-inning stint in which the hurler gives up three or fewer runs. Old-time, die-hard fans fail to see the quality in such an effort.

Unable to pitch inside because hitters and umpires might object and afraid to pitch to contact in breadbox, hitter-friendly stadiums, today's starting pitchers nibble constantly, which invariably leads to pitch counts over the century mark by the fifth inning. Whereas in years past, that number signaled a time when the starting pitcher might finally be getting loose, now 100 pitches causes the bullpen phone to ring with options ranging from long men to set-up men and, eventually, to closers. That is, of course, unless the game is out of hand early—which might result in some much-needed innings from a swing man who has the ability to start as well as eat innings in a blowout.

These are all changes from the days when relievers were the sweat hogs of the bullpen. They now have specific roles on the team. Should they fail a little too often, there are a plethora of younger pitchers waiting in the wings. And if they seldom fail at all, the end result is sometimes a World Series championship.

As much as the public responds to high-scoring slugfests, it is undeniable that pitching and defense wins titles. And an increasingly important aspect of pitching is the men who strut out of the bullpen in the ninth inning and bring the game to a satisfying close.

CHAPTER 1

Relievers: A Historical Perspective

Early in the history of America's Game, "base ball" (as it was once called) had no use for pitchers, relief or otherwise. The pitcher in those infant days acted as a catapult for the offense, not really trying to get the hitters out. In the first decades of the game, the pitching mound was nowhere near as far from home plate as the current 60 feet, 6 inches. It was, in fact, less than 50 feet away from the dish. More often than not the ball would be thrown—underhanded, of course—rather than pitched. In those batter-friendly times, hitters could direct the pitcher to throw the baseball either high or low, and any sort of trick pitch, such as a curveball, was illegal. A modern-day pitcher who complains about an umpire squeezing him should probably consider himself lucky and keep his mouth shut.

While versions of baseball spread throughout much of the country during the 1840s and 1850s, uniformity became something to strive for. In these early days of the game, teams would often play with different sets of rules, which were decided geographically. Instituting uniform, agreed-upon rules enabled baseball clubs to graduate from practices and what amounted to intramural play to real games against neighboring towns and cities. This uniformity allowed games rather than arguments about rules. But baseball needed visionaries to look at the game and help create worthwhile rules as well as spread news of the game and these rules to the masses.

Enter a pair of bearded gentlemen who each shared a love of the game: Alexander J. Cartwright and Henry Chadwick. Both are sometimes referred to as "the father of baseball." Cartwright and Chadwick both helped move the game of "base ball," also known as "town ball," much closer to the game of baseball that we are all so familiar with today. Which one of the two gentlemen truly merits the "father of the game" title can be debated, but both Cartwright and Chadwick were intimately involved in the formulation of the game we know and love today.

Alexander Cartwright led a group of players who became known as the New York Knickerbockers on September 23, 1845. A bookseller and volunteer fireman, Cartwright named his team after the Knickerbocker Fire Engine Company. The Knickerbockers formulated their own rules, making their version, described as the "New York style" of play, the most

Pioneer baseball writer Henry Chadwick (standing at right in this 1864 photo of the Brooklyn Resolute Base Ball Club) is credited with spreading the popularity of baseball, creating the box score and the earned-run average, and encouraging the use of relief pitchers. *Photo courtesy of Getty Images*

similar to today's game. Up until this point the game was still not necessarily considered an adult pastime, partially because of its similarity to the English game of rounder. The New York style featured a longer distance between the bases: 90 feet. Fielders would tag or force out base runners, as opposed to the former rule of soaking, or plugging, the runner, where the fielder could get the runner out by plunking him with a thrown ball. The game also took on a different look because the field itself was divided into fair and foul territory, which gave the game a more concentrated look and also made it possible to have just nine players patrolling the field. Another Knickerbockers change included the diamond-shaped infield.

The New York style of play was much easier to follow than the rival Massachusetts game, which saw a team win by being the first to score 100 runs. Obviously, Cartwright and the Knickerbockers were early proponents of speeding up the game. But the Massachusetts game was an interesting one, particularly when contrasting it to the game we know today.

To witness a game played under the Massachusetts rules would leave a modern observer in a constant state of wonder and amazement, because the game would be a very different, albeit entertaining, experience. The pitcher was allowed to throw overhand, unlike the New York style. There were four bases, just 60 feet apart. The fourth base was still called home, but the "striker," or batter, stood midway between the fourth and first base. Fielders were allowed to put out runners by soaking them with the ball, there was no foul territory, and base runners did not have to stay within the base lines.

The Massachusetts game was, as you might expect, a much more wide-open game with lots of scoring and tons of base runners, because the striker stood just 30 feet from first base. The absence of foul territory allowed a skillful striker to take advantage of the entire field, including when a striker tipped a ball over the catcher's head. Unlike today's harmless foul tip, in the Massachusetts game, such a tip was in play. There were

10 to 14 players on a side, and outs were so hard to come by that the rule was "one out, all out"—an inning would end when one out was recorded.

It was certainly a different game than we've grown to understand over the years, but it had its proponents. In the *Boston Globe* on July 10, 2005, historian John Thorn wrote, "All that the Massachusetts game had going for it was joy."

Alexander Cartwright was not the only shaper of America's Game. Henry Chadwick moved from England to America with his family at the age of 12 in 1836. He reportedly came across baseball for the first time in 1856 as a reporter covering a cricket game. Chadwick witnessed a game between the Gotham and Eagle clubs of New York and became convinced that he could make the game America's "national game in word and in truth."

The following year, he joined the *New York Clipper* newspaper and focused his attention on baseball, first as a writer and later as a person who had a profound impact on the game. Chadwick also edited various publications about baseball, including *Beadle's Dime Base Ball Player, Spalding's Official Base Ball Guide,* and *Reach's Official Base Ball Guide,* which served to whet the country's appetite for baseball and helped elevate its popularity.

Chadwick's writing and editing skills helped spread the New York game to other cities, such as Philadelphia and Boston, locales that had previously been involved with town ball. New York was a major hub of the publishing industry, not unlike today, and many New York publications were read throughout the country.

Chadwick was one of the most vocal proponents for eliminating the bound catch, where fielders were allowed to catch the ball on a bounce to retire a batter. His feelings about this matter no doubt had their genesis in the game of cricket, which he knew from his childhood in England, as well as covering the game as a reporter in America. In cricket, the fly catch was required. This rule change was a major ingredient in the development of the game as it spread throughout the country.

In the *Beadle* guide of 1861, he included statistical information that was not always part of the early coverage of the game. He had compiled lists of games played, outs, strikeouts, home runs, and other numerical reference points.

Henry Chadwick also created the baseball box score, where knowledgeable fans can access a statistical review of a game. He adapted the box score from a similar scorecard used in cricket and included a grid with nine rows for players and nine columns for innings. The same basic structure is still in use today.

A question often asked in scoring a baseball game is why the letter *K* is the abbreviation for a strikeout. Chadwick used the letter as a symbol for the strikeout because *K* is the last letter in the word *struck*, which is part of the phrase *struck out*.

Another statistic that Chadwick is credited with devising is earned-run average (ERA), which is the average number of earned runs (those directly accountable to the pitcher and not to errors or passed balls) given up per nine innings pitched. It is determined by multiplying the number of earned runs allowed by nine and dividing by the number of innings pitched. So if a pitcher has an ERA of 3.50, he, on average, gives up three and a half earned runs per nine innings pitched. Needless to say, a hurler cannot surrender half of a run, but he who lives by numbers can also die by numbers.

The ERA statistic caught on as a measure of pitching effectiveness after relief pitching came into vogue in the 1900s. Prior to that time—and quite frankly, for many years after—pitchers were expected to pitch complete games, and their won-lost record was a good measurement for determining their effectiveness. But wins and losses could not accurately measure the effectiveness of a reliever. In addition, ERA also gave merit to a particularly good starting pitcher as well as a reliever.

Henry Chadwick may have also been the first real strategist as far as pitching—especially relief pitching—is concerned. Although substitutions of any kind were either difficult or against the rules in the very early years of baseball, there has always been a need for relief pitching, because there are times when a hurler is just not at his best. At such times in the early years, an ineffective pitcher would just switch positions with another player on the field. Quite a few clubs kept this in mind when considering a lineup. Pitcher Tom Pratt was often penciled into the lineup of the Brooklyn Atlantics in the outfield or infield in a game when it seemed likely that a pitching change would be necessary.

The first relief appearance in the major leagues was made by the Boston Red Caps' Jack Manning on April 25, 1876. Substitutions were still not allowed, except in the case of sickness or injury. But on that day, Boston starter Joe Borden had spotted the Brooklyn Mutuals five runs. In the fifth inning, Boston manager Harry Wright had Borden exchange roles with right fielder Manning. Baseball's first reliever surrendered just a single run the rest of the game and was credited with a win as Boston prevailed 7–6.

Henry Chadwick had written about changing pitchers from a strategic point of view several years prior to this. He included a reference to relief pitching on August 22, 1867, in *Haney's Base Ball Book of Reference for 1867*, which was reprinted in *The Ball Player's Chronicle*. "A first-class team always has two pitchers in it, and it is in your management of these batteries that much of your success will lie. Put your swift pitcher to work first, and keep him in at least three innings, even if he be hit away from the start. Supposing, however, that with good support in the field the swift pitching is being easily punished, and runs are being made too fast, if your pitcher is one who cannot drop his pace well without giving more chances at the bat, you should at once bring in your slow- or medium-paced pitcher."

Although ideas about pitching may have been changing in these years, the rules of the game were quite different than today. This was still an era when batters had the right to call for their pitches to be either high or low. Evening things out for the hurlers was the fact that they were allowed nine pitches out of the strike zone before the batter earned a base on balls. But some dramatic changes were on the horizon. In 1884 pitchers were finally allowed to throw overhand, and the batters could no longer call the pitch position.

It wasn't until April 20, 1889, that baseball's first true bullpen appearance occurred, and it happened thanks to a rulebook change. "A rule revision permitted clubs to designate two extra players as substitutes who could be brought in at any time," noted baseball historian Bill Deane. "In an American Association game, Columbus manager Al Buckenberger became the first to utilize this rule for a pitching change. During an 18–3 drubbing at the hands of Baltimore, Buckenberger removed starter Al Mays in favor of John Weyhing. Weyhing thus became a relief-pitching pioneer, ironically, in his final major league appearance."

Around this time, other significant rules affecting pitching were adopted. In 1887 a uniform strike zone was installed. The following year, the three-strike rule was adopted, and in 1889 the number of pitches out of the strike zone ("balls") to earn a walk was lowered to four.

Despite these various changes, pitchers who completed what they started were still the overwhelming rule of the game. From 1876 to 1899, pitchers completed games they started 90 percent of the time. In 1885, 97 percent of all National League games were complete games, while 96.4 percent of American Association contests were finished by the starters. In 1884, one of the great pitching feats of all time occurred. Providence Grays right-hander Charley "Old Hoss" Radbourn chalked up 59 wins while throwing $678\frac{2}{3}$ innings.

"In early baseball, teams could not always afford more than nine players," declares Peter Morris, a baseball historian and author of the books *A Game of Inches: The Game on the Field; But Didn't We Have Fun? An Informal History of Baseball's Pioneer Era, 1843–1879*; and *Catcher: How the Man Behind the Plate Became an American Folk Hero.* "A relief pitcher was one of your backup outfielders. That's when all you could afford was nine. Then it became 10 and 11. And overhand pitching changed how much rest pitchers need, too. You find that in the 1880s teams started using dramatically more pitchers."

In an effort to inject more offense into the game, in 1893 the distance between the pitcher's mound and home plate was increased from 45 to 60 feet, and the pitcher was required to maintain contact with the rubber slab on the mound with his back foot when releasing the ball. Three years later, an additional 6 inches was added to the pitching distance, to its current 60 feet, 6 inches.

The changes had the desired effect—at least for a while. After the distance change the average ratio of complete games dropped to 82 percent. After a couple of seasons, however, successful pitchers were able to stretch their arms out and pitch effectively from the new distance.

"Earlier rule changes—like establishing a uniform strike zone in 1887, permanently adopting the three-strikes rule in 1888, and the four-balls walk rule, along with the aforementioned 1893 changes—exceeded the league's wildest expectations," writes Paul Votano in *Late And Close: A History of Relief Pitching*. "Batting averages increased by the greatest margin in history for a single season—35 points. Almost a thousand more runs were scored. The older pitchers had more trouble with the new rules than the younger hurlers like Cy Young, Kid Nichols, and Amos Rusie, all of whom adjusted rather easily. Older pitchers like Boston's Jack Stivetts dropped from 35 wins in 1892 to only 19 in 1893. Other top pitchers fared just as poorly. While earned-run averages (ERA) were not compiled in that period, historical statisticians have since computed that the league went from a 3.28 ERA in 1892 to 4.66 in 1893 and jumped even more the following year to 5.32, the highest up to that time."

As time passed to the last decade of the 19th century, a common practice was to have one of the outfield positions manned by someone who could come into the game and pitch, should the starter falter or tire. Pitching staffs had expanded, and substitutions were legal, which made it possible for relief pitchers to play a more important role in baseball. But most of the time, the pitchers who were used in the role of reliever were actually starting pitchers between starts.

Chicago White Sox manager Clark Griffith caused quite a stir in 1902 when he announced that he planned to use pitcher Virgil Garvin "scientifically" that season by letting him go as far as he could in games in which he started but relieving him the moment he began to show weakness after the sixth inning.

Suffice it to say that at the turn of the century and for quite a few decades to come, starting pitchers were expected to finish what they started. Robin Roberts was not the only pitcher to boast impressive complete game stats. Three times in one month during the 1903 campaign, "Iron Man" Joe McGinnity of the Giants started, completed, and won both games of a doubleheader. The incomparable Cy Young completed 749 of his 815 big-league starts en route to his 511 victories.

In 1904, Red Sox pitchers had 148 complete games in a 154-game season. The following year, the Cubs had 133 complete games. Of the great Christy Mathewson's 561 decisions (373 wins, 188 losses), 435 were complete games. Around the turn of the last century, being the relief pitcher was easy work. (Sort of like a backup quarterback in the National Football League today.) There was little concern for "overworked" starting pitchers at that time.

While pitching with Buffalo, Jack Lynch completed 215 of 217 starts. He still holds the record for most consecutive complete games with 199.

"As a general thing managers use their judgment as to when the proper time has arrived to replace a pitcher in a losing game, but some use a system of allowing a certain number of hits on a twirler in one or more innings in a game," observed the *Washington Post* on July 31, 1904. "Others figure that a pitcher is or is not in form by the number of batsmen he sends to first on balls. Many close observers are of the opinion that a pitcher should be allowed to remain in and take his medicine, if the score is greatly against his team. Pitchers, as a rule, would prefer to remain in and try to turn defeat into victory. The best-minded class of fans do not care to see a twirler replaced, especially if he is at all popular."

Early relief pitchers were normally starting pitchers coming in to pitch between starts. In fact, most teams had no more than two or three pitchers on their rosters. But more and more teams would use multiple pitchers in games. That change was not something that was embraced by all who loved the game. *The Spalding Base Ball Guide* in 1892 editorialized against the use of too many pitchers.

"The season of 1892 was marked by the presence of too many pitchers in a majority of the 12 club teams. No less than 48 different pitchers were employed during the season by the six leading clubs of the championship campaign while 54 pitchers took part in the games of the six tail enders. Three pitchers—two good strategists and a single cyclone twister—would have amply sufficed to take each club through the season. A batter force of five players—three pitchers and two catchers—should be the lowest for 1893. In the spring, when club teams are being worked into good form, it may do to experiment with several pitchers, but when the team has been got into full fighting trim, three pitchers should be amply sufficient for each club's team."

Before 1889 a pitcher could be replaced only if he was injured. Prior to that, substitutions could be made only during a game in which a starting player was seriously hurt. And the opposing team's captain had to allow the injury substitution. Teams would normally have a player who was capable of pitching play in the outfield. If the situation necessitated, he'd simply change positions with the pitcher.

In 1900, the moundsters got another break when the size and shape of home plate was changed from a 12-inch square to a 17-inch, five-sided shape. The following season, the National League began to count the first two foul balls as strikes, which had not been the case previously.

Although Chicago Cubs skipper Frank Chance and his Washington Senators counterpart Clark Griffith began to use starting pitchers to

New York Giants manager John McGraw at training camp in March 1930. The legendary skipper was one of the early proponents of sitting down his starter and bringing in strong, fresh arms to finish out close games.

relieve other starters to finish games, it was John McGraw of the New York Giants who took relief pitching to a new level.

As a result of this new trend, complete games were not the sure thing that they had been in years past. The frequency of the complete game fell to less than 60 percent in the National League in 1910. But pitchers still felt compelled to complete what they started. Burt Keelley of Washington pitched a complete game in 1908 in which he yielded 18 runs.

Although pitching out of the bullpen was becoming a more regular occurrence, communication and defined roles were not strong points of America's Game early in the 20th century. A comical misunderstanding between Giants skipper McGraw and his great right-hander, Christy "Matty" Mathewson, was one of the highlights of the 1908 season, although it's safe to assume that McGraw failed to see the humor.

The Giants led the Cubs 4–1 with Chicago getting the final at-bats in the ninth inning. With starter Doc Crandall seemingly having the game well in hand for New York, Mathewson decided to get an early start on his postgame shower while Crandall was still pitching. After all, the locker room only had two showers, and long lines often occurred after games.

The situation is recounted in Cait Murphy's outstanding, informative, and entertaining book, *Crazy '08: How a Cast of Cranks, Rogues, Boneheads, and Magnates Created the Greatest Year in Baseball History.*

Crandall had quickly lost his effectiveness, and the Cubs had the bases loaded with just one out.

"Relief pitching as a specialty does not yet exist, but it is common to bring in a fresh arm in tricky situations," wrote Murphy. "[Matty will record five saves this year.] And given the team and the time, it is not surprising that McGraw calls for his ace. The only problem is that the ace is nowhere to be seen. Growing angry, McGraw orders his players to find Matty. Now. They fan out, call his name. Meanwhile, the Cubs are losing their limited patience—what are we playing, hide-and-seek? Let's get the damn game going. Umpire Johnstone tells McGraw to get a pitcher on the mound, pronto, on pain of forfeit."

McGraw brings Joe McGinnity into the game while the reserves continue their search for Mathewson.

"His teammates had found him lathering up and informed him his services were wanted. He pulls on odd bits of uniform—but can't jam his wet feet into his cleats. It is worth pausing here to consider what the scene must have looked like. Dripping, half naked, with his teammates imploring him, the crowd roaring, and McGraw molting in anger, one of America's finest athletes cannot put on his spikes. So he dons his street shoes and races to the rescue. Although Matty is capless, breathless, damp, ill-shod, and undoubtedly chagrined, he is still the last man on earth the Cubs want to see. He takes the mound, flicks two warm-up pitches, and nods that he is ready—an ominous sign."

Mathewson got a ground ball out and then struck out Del Howard on his fadeaway pitch to protect the victory. Following the game, McGraw told his best pitcher, "The next time, damn it, don't take your shower in the middle of a pennant race."

By the time that story occurred in 1908, the game of base ball had evolved into the game of baseball. The game was played differently, and pitching had changed drastically in a single generation. Mathewson decided to take a shower a little earlier than he should have, but starting pitchers were not always waiting until the end of the game for their showers. With more and more regularity, starting pitchers were not completing the games they started.

Surely the instances of that happening were nothing compared to the game of today. But relief pitching was becoming an accepted part of the game. If only the founding father of the game, be it Cartwright or Chadwick, knew where it would all end up.

CHAPTER 2

The Role of the Early Bullpen

The Christy Mathewson shower story is not only an entertaining tale, but it also exemplifies how relief pitchers were used in the early years of the 20th century. In between starts, a pitcher could be used for an inning or two. At a time when more than 90 percent of games were completed by the starter, the first wave of relievers were doing the same thing that Mathewson did. Matty relieved 84 times during his career, earning 28 saves. In fact, he led the league in that category in 1905 with five saves, along with his 37–11 record.

This is a practice that extended well into the 1950s and occasionally beyond. "Managers would interchange starters and relieve in between with them when we didn't have closers," said former Brooklyn and Los Angeles Dodgers pitcher Carl Erskine, who went 122–78 in his 12-year major league career, starting 216 times while coming out of the bullpen an additional 119 times. "So you started every four days. The day after you pitched you didn't throw. But the next day you did. And on that day the manager would send you to the bullpen to pitch an inning, if need be."

So the practice that started early in the 20th century extended well beyond those early years. Christy Mathewson was not simply a phenomenal pitcher of that era. He was also a refreshing change who only enhanced the image of professional baseball players. He was educated, intelligent, and a real gentleman. Matty won 20 games for 12 consecutive seasons and earned 30 victories four different times, including a league-leading 37 in 1908. He also led the league that season in games (56), complete games (34), saves (5), innings pitched (390), strikeouts (259), and ERA (1.43).

As far back as 1875, Boston's Jack Manning had a 15–2 record. Although he started 17 games, he also relieved in 10 other contests, saving seven. The following season Manning was 18–5, starting 20 times and relieving 14 others.

Another Boston hurler, right-hander Jack Stivetts, won 203 games during his 11-year career, starting 333 times. But he also came in out of the bullpen 55 other times, boasting a 19–7 record with four saves.

In addition to his All-World 511 wins, the great Cy Young also relieved 91 times during his brilliant career, earning 17 saves. Young won 30 games five times and surpassed 20 wins on 15 different occasions. At the age of 42 in 1909, Young barely missed a 16th 20-win season—going 19–15 with Cleveland.

Charles Augustus "Kid" Nichols won 361 games during his extraordinary 15-year career, including at least 30 games 7 times and at least 20 wins 11 times. The Hall of Famer completed 531 of 561 starts. But even this talented righty came in out of the bullpen 59 times, saving 17, leading the league on four occasions. His success is even more incredible when you consider that Nichols threw just one pitch—a fastball.

After his stellar career ended, he returned to Kansas City, Missouri, and became a baseball coach. One of his players was none other than Casey Stengel.

Hall of Fame member Big Ed Walsh was a phenomenal pitcher for the Chicago White Sox early in the 20th century, winning 195 games in 14 seasons. But he also relieved 115 times, earning 34 saves. He led the league in saves five times, including his career high of 10 in 1912. That was the fourth and final time he led the American League in appearances with 62, including 41 starts.

The hard-throwing right-hander pitched a minimum of 369 innings five times in the six-year period from 1907 to 1912. But the overuse of his arm was too much, and he never appeared in more than 16 games in a season again, making just 17 appearances between 1914 and his retirement in 1917. To his credit, Walsh retired with an ERA of 1.82, the lowest career ERA of all time.

Walsh joined the White Sox with an overpowering fastball. But in spring training of 1904, teammate Elmer Stricklett taught him how to throw the spitball. Stricklett was supposedly the first pitcher to master the pitch. And Walsh's spitter was literally unhittable.

"I think the ball disintegrated on the way to the plate, and the catcher put it back together again," said Sam Crawford, who hit .309 in his 19-year career.

One of the great pitchers of the game overcame a severe handicap to pitch well enough to be elected to the Hall of Fame. Mordecai "Three Finger" Brown lost the index finger of his right pitching hand after inserting it into a corn shredder on his uncle's Indiana farm. A short time thereafter, he broke the third and fourth fingers on the same hand while chasing a pig on the farm. While his hand healed, his fingers became gnarled, which, along with the stump of his index finger, enabled him to throw a baseball that reacted in a way hitters had never seen before. His grip caused his straight pitches to behave like knuckleballs, and his breaking pitches had an even greater dip. Not blessed with a great fastball, it is believed that Brown would never have made it to the big leagues were it not for his uncle's shredder.

Brown was such a talented hurler that he won 20 games for the Chicago Cubs six straight times, from 1906 to 1911, a feat that fellow Cubs Hall of Famer Ferguson Jenkins would accomplish from 1967 to 1972. In his career, Brown relieved 149 times, earning 49 saves in addition to his

332 career starts. He led the National League with 13 saves in 1911, a year in which he went 21–11.

But his most memorable season might well have been 1908, when he won a career-high 29 games against nine losses and a sparkling 1.47 ERA. He relieved 13 times that season but none more important than the Cubs' playoff game against the New York Giants, which was necessitated due to Fred Merkle's "Boner," a base-running error by Merkle that cost his Giants a game late in the season. Had they won that contest, the playoff game would not have been necessary.

The Giants scored an early run in the first inning against Chicago's southpaw starter Jack Pfiester when Brown was brought into the game

Mordecai "Three Finger" Brown overcame a hand-mangling farm injury to become a Hall of Fame pitcher. During his heyday with the Cubs, he was used as both a starter and a reliever. Over his 14-season career, he earned 239 wins and 49 saves.

with no warm-up pitches and struck out Art Devlin to end the first inning with New York ahead 1–0. But the Cubs rallied against the great Mathewson in the third inning, scoring four runs. Brown yielded just a single run the rest of the way to earn the victory for his Cubs in what may have been baseball's first truly definitive relief appearance. Brown bested Mathewson, and the Cubs won the pennant.

Nine years after Mordecai Brown's playoff game relief effort, the great Babe Ruth was involved in another game that will go down in the annals of relief-pitching history. In addition to being the Sultan of Swat, the Bambino was also on his way to a Hall of Fame career as a pitcher until he stopped pitching on a regular basis following the 1919 season. Ruth sported a 94–46 career mark as a pitcher, including four saves earned in his 15 appearances out of the bullpen.

But on June 23, 1917, Ruth was starting for the Boston Red Sox against the Washington Senators. He issued a walk to leadoff hitter Ray Morgan and then got involved in a heated discussion with home-plate umpire Brick Owens, who ejected Ruth from the game. He was replaced by righty Ernie Shore, a regular starter, to relieve in the first inning. Morgan was promptly thrown out trying to steal second base, and all Shore did after that was retire 26 more Senators in a row for a near-perfect game. Shore pitched out of the pen just 39 times in his 160-game career, but his 1917 combined no-hitter is certainly one of the most memorable games ever by a relief pitcher. (Although Shore was initially given credit for a perfect game, the criteria for such games changed, and his name was removed from the record book.)

Another pitcher included in baseball's hallowed Hall of Fame is Charles Albert "Chief" Bender, a half–Chippewa Indian, who left the White Earth Indian Reservation in Minnesota at the age of 13 to attend school in Philadelphia. Chief Bender jumped from semipro ball to the major leagues. Bender started 334 games but relieved in another 125 contests, saving 34. He led the league in 1913 with 13 saves en route to a 21–10 campaign for the Philadelphia Athletics.

Blessed with a good fastball, Bender also threw what was known as the "talcum" pitch. He would rub one side of the ball with talcum powder until the ball had enough powder on it to drop. The talcum pitch was legal at the time.

The great left-hander Robert Moses "Lefty" Grove had a .680 winning percentage during his 17-year career, boasting a 300–141 record. He won at least 20 games in eight of the nine seasons from 1927 through 1935. But he also amassed 55 saves in 159 relief appearances and led the American League with nine in 1930 while going 28–5 for the Philadelphia Athletics.

While the norm was for starting pitchers to fill in between starts, it could be argued that baseball's first actual reliever was Otis "Doc" Crandall, who pitched with the New York Giants, St. Louis, and Boston during his 10-year career, ranging from 1908 to 1918. While pitching for John McGraw's Giants from 1908 to 1913, Crandall started 77 games but relieved in 132 others. Although never leading the league in saves, he accumulated 25 over his career.

Crandall came out of nowhere to make the Giants' roster in 1908. "...[P]itcher Otis 'Doc' Crandall, an Indiana farm boy whom McGraw purchased mostly for sentimental reasons," wrote Cait Murphy in *Crazy '08*. "A friend from Cedar Rapids recommended the right-hander, and McGraw had a soft spot for Cedar Rapids, where he had played briefly. Crandall was such a long shot that the Giants didn't even have a uniform for him, and he had to play in his street clothes for several days. He pitched well enough to get one."

He had a respectable 12–12 record during his rookie campaign, but Crandall seemed to have difficulty pitching deep into games. It was that inability, coupled with McGraw's inventive ideas about relief pitching, that may have led to Crandall's being baseball's first real reliever.

The great Christy Mathewson wrote about Crandall in his wonderful book, *Pitching in a Pinch*.

"Crandall warmed up, and he didn't have much of anything besides a sweeping outcurve and a good deal of speed. He looked less like a pitcher than any of the spring crop, but McGraw saw something in him and kept him. The result is he has turned out to be one of the most valuable men on the club, because he is there in a pinch. He is the sort of pitcher who is best when things look darkest. I've heard the crowd yelling, when he has been pitching on the enemy's ground, so that a 16-inch gun couldn't have been heard if it had gone off in the lot.

"'That crowd was making some noise,' I said to Crandall after the inning.

"'Was it?' asked Otis. 'I didn't notice it.'

"One day in 1911, he started a game in Philadelphia, and three men got on the bases with no one out, along about the fourth or fifth inning. He shut them out without a run. It was the first game he had started for a while, his specialty having been to enter a contest after some other pitcher had gotten into trouble, with two or three men on the bases and scarcely anyone out. After he came to the bench with the threatening inning behind him, he said to me, 'Matty, I didn't feel at home out there today until a lot of people got on the bases. I'll be all right now.'"

Crandall had ice water in his veins and was one of the earliest examples of the closer's mind-set in the game.

Other pitchers of the era who relieved more than they started include Washington right-hander Doc Ayres, who came out of the pen 159 times, earning 15 saves while starting 140 times. Southpaw Garland Braxton started 70 big-league games but relieved in 212 others over his 10-year career, earning 32 saves, including a league-leading 13 in 1927. Guy Bush relieved 234 times between 1923 and 1945, primarily with the Chicago Cubs, with 34 saves, including a league-leading 8 in 1929.

Right-hander Frederick "Firpo" Marberry is credited with being baseball's first prominent relief pitcher. Marberry, who hated the nickname of Firpo, earned the moniker because of a nasty scowl that always seemed to be on his face while facing opposing hitters. His appearance and disposition reminded observers of boxer Luis Firpo, the Wild Bull of the Pampas, who knocked Jack Dempsey out of the ring.

Marberry may not have liked his nickname, but opposing hitters probably disliked facing him even more. Spending nearly his entire career pitching for the Washington Senators (1923–1932) and the Detroit Tigers (1933–35), the native of Streetman, Texas, appeared in 551 games during his 14-year career, 364 of which were as a reliever.

"Bucky Harris began to use him pretty much the way most managers used their pitchers in this era—as an occasional starter against the weaker teams and as mop-up men during games that were out of control one way or another," wrote Paul Votano in *Late and Close*. "But as time went on, Harris' confidence in Marberry grew, and he began utilizing the 6'1", 190-pounder to 'save' games.

"'Firpo was the type of pitcher who could toss a few in the bullpen, casually saunter to the mound, and then knock the bats out of their hands with his blazing speed,' Harris recalled once. Bill James calls Marberry 'The first true reliever in baseball history who was the first pitcher aggressively used to protect leads, rather than being brought in when the starter was knocked out.... He was a modern reliever—a hard-throwing young kid who worked strictly in relief, worked often, and was used to nail down victories.'"

Marberry led the league in appearances six times, including a career-high 64 games in 1926, all but five out of the bullpen for the Senators. He has also been credited with 101 career saves, a category in which he led the league five times, including 22 in 1926. Historian Bill James has written that, between the years of 1924 and 1934, Marberry was as valuable as any pitcher in baseball except for Lefty Grove.

As Marberry's career wound down in the 1930s, another right-handed reliever came into prominence in the American League. "Fordham Johnny" Murphy went 14–10 for the 1934 New York Yankees, starting 20 games and relieving in 20 games. But he clearly had the right stuff to pitch out of the bullpen, as during the next 11 seasons he appeared in 375 games, all but 20 out of the bullpen. He appeared in at least 30 games 10 times in his career and was credited with 107 saves, leading the league on four occasions.

A curveball specialist, Murphy was sometimes called "Rocking Chair" or "Grandma" because of his rocking pitching motion. But he was also known as "Fireman" because of his ability to put out fires.

An early example of an ineffective starting pitcher who found a happy home in the bullpen was Jack Russell. A right-hander who spent 15 years in the big leagues with Boston, Cleveland, Washington, Detroit, the Chicago Cubs, and St. Louis Cardinals, Russell had little success in his starter's role. From 1926 to 1932, Russell was 46–88 pitching for Boston and for Cleveland for part of a season. That record included a 6–18 mark in 1929 and a 9–20 campaign in 1930. After going a combined 16–32 over the next two seasons, Russell became a relief specialist with much better results.

His final eight big-league seasons saw his record improve to 39–43 with 38 saves. He led the league in that department with 13 in 1933, led the league in appearances the following season with 54, and became the first reliever named to the All-Star team.

Following his baseball career, Russell became the city commissioner in Clearwater, Florida, where he helped construct the Phillies' spring training stadium, which was known as Jack Russell Stadium until it was replaced by Bright House Field in 2004.

Right-hander Hugh Casey was a dependable reliever primarily with the Brooklyn Dodgers through most of the 1940s, with 287 relief appearances and just 56 starts. Casey recorded 55 saves, leading the league with 13 in 1942 and 18 in 1947.

Another influential pitcher of this postwar era was Jim Konstanty, who toiled in the major leagues for 11 seasons with the Reds, Braves, Yankees, and Cardinals. But the bespectacled right-hander made his mark with the Philadelphia Phillies.

Starters would still come in and throw an inning between starts, but relief pitchers who came primarily and sometimes exclusively out of the bullpen were becoming an accepted change in the game. These early relievers set the stage for what was still to come.

CHAPTER 3

The Introduction
of the Closer

After World War II, the respect and appreciation for what became the closer, or short reliever in those days, increased exponentially. Relief pitchers were not just starters pitching an inning between starts or hurlers not good enough to maintain their spot in the starting rotation. They were players with a role on the team. They were certainly not held in the high esteem of the specialized relievers in today's game, but they had taken some small steps toward respectability.

"I think back to following the game even as a youngster, that there were two teams that had a significant impact on relief pitching that happened about the same time," said Fred Claire, former general manager of the Los Angeles Dodgers and author of the book *My 30 Years in Dodger Blue.* "When I think of them, the first successful one was Joe Page of the Yankees. Then, looking at the statistics relating to saves and relief pitching in 1949, Page with the Yankees recorded 27 saves, which was a key mark. I don't think there was a higher number in the history of the American League. At the same time in the National League, Jim Konstanty of the Phillies in 1950 had 22 saves. He even started the first game of the World Series that year.

"It may be that it was the time I first followed the game closely, but the stats kind of relate to that period of time. That was the time of change

The Phillies' Jim Konstanty took relief pitching to unprecedented heights in 1950 when he became the first reliever to win the MVP Award. The crafty veteran appeared in 74 games, went 16–7 with a 2.66 ERA and 22 saves, and led Philadelphia to the World Series.

because it was then that the numbers started to increase and the role of the reliever became more important. The identity of the roles became more established."

While Jim Konstanty was making a name for himself, a knuckleball pitcher, Emil "Dutch" Leonard made a successful transition from an average starter to a better-than-average reliever. After 14 nondescript seasons as a starter, Leonard was traded by the Philadelphia Phillies, along with Monk Dubiel, to the Chicago Cubs in exchange for Eddie Waitkus and Hank Borowy before the start of the 1949 season. After starting 28 games with the Cubs in '49 with a 7–16 record, Leonard became a reliever the following season and responded with a 5–1 mark with six saves and a 3.77 ERA. In the four years he relieved, Leonard had a record of 19–12 with 28 saves.

His greatest thrill in the game was when he was called into a contest with a one-run lead to protect, the bases loaded, and no outs. All he did was protect the lead and win the game…by retiring Jackie Robinson, Gil Hodges, and Roy Campanella, three of the greatest players in the history of the game.

After breaking in with Cincinnati in 1944 and the Boston Braves in 1946, Jim Konstanty was toiling in the minors with manager Eddie Sawyer. When his skipper took over the reins in Philadelphia, he brought Konstanty with him. In 1949 "Gentleman Jim" appeared in 53 games for the Phillies—all out of the bullpen—responded with a 9–5 mark with a 3.25 ERA, and was credited with seven saves. Konstanty looked like a math teacher and pitched like one, too; that is, until he bagged his fastball in the minor leagues with Sawyer. He developed and perfected a new off-speed pitch that he called a "palm ball." With that pitch in his arsenal, Konstanty was able to keep hitters off balance.

"Let me tell you about Konstanty," Sawyer told the *Philadelphia Inquirer*. "I managed him when I had the Toronto club. He's a strange character. He throws a lot of crazy, breaking stuff, and he knows how to pitch and how he wants to pitch. I may start him here or there, but we need a relief man who can hold a one- or two-run lead for a couple of innings. That's going to be his job. Just watch him."

Unlike a flamethrower who gets by with sheer speed, Konstanty was the epitome of a pitcher, as opposed to a thrower. He used guile, guts, and grit to fool hitters. Consider the following comments from his catcher, Andy Seminick, in the November 1950 issue of *Baseball Magazine.*

"Jim wins because he can control the ball, and he knows what he's doing," said Seminick. "He uses his head. When he throws a fastball, he throws it where they can only look at it, not hit it. When they're swinging, they get a slider, screwball, palm ball, or curve—some kind of breaking stuff. He really has those hitters buffaloed."

Dubbed the "Whiz Kids," youthful players such as Robin Roberts, Curt Simmons, Richie Ashburn, Del Ennis, Willie "Puddin' Head" Jones, and a cast of others helped propel the Phillies into the pennant race in 1950. But it was the efforts of Jim Konstanty more than any other that helped earn Philadelphia a World Series berth. By this time Konstanty was 33 years old. He appeared in what was an all-time record 74 games, going 16–7 with 22 saves and a 2.66 ERA. His efforts were rewarded with the Most Valuable Player Award, as he beat out the Cardinals' Stan Musial, to become the first relief pitcher to win MVP honors.

In one of the great pitching feats in the history of the game, after relieving 74 times in the regular season, Konstanty was forced into a starting role in the opening game of the 1950 World Series against the Yankees. Phils ace Roberts had pitched the pennant-clinching finale against Brooklyn three days earlier, and flame-throwing southpaw Simmons had been pressed into military service. So Sawyer called upon his fireman to open the Fall Classic, and he responded with an outstanding effort that nevertheless saw him lose to Vic Raschi and the Yanks 1–0.

"Spectacled, scholarly looking pitcher Jim Konstanty never had the mow-'em-down speed of Dizzy Dean nor the big, sweeping curve of Lefty Grove," wrote in the November 13, 1950, edition of *Time* magazine in an article titled "A Natural." "This year he never so much as started a game for the Phillies until the World Series came along, and he lost that in a 1–0 heartbreaker. But last week big right-hander Konstanty was voted the Most Valuable Player in the National League.

"Konstanty's selection was a natural: without his ever-ready arm, Philadelphia could never have won its first National League pennant in 35 years. As a relief pitcher, Konstanty was called from the Philadelphia bullpen a record-breaking 74 times; he won 16 games, lost seven, saved some 22 more. Unsung and unwanted [by Boston and Cincinnati] as a starting pitcher four years ago, hardworking Jim Konstanty, a middle-aged [33] ballplayer who neither smokes nor drinks, hauled himself up from minor league [Toronto] obscurity to become the best relief pitcher in baseball."

The Phillies slumped in 1951 as did Konstanty, as evidenced by his 4–11 record with just nine saves and an inflated ERA of 4.05. He was eventually traded to the Yankees in 1954 and enjoyed some success there and in St. Louis until his retirement in 1956.

At the same time Konstanty was a force with the Phillies, one of the great rookie seasons in the history of the game belonged to right-hander Joe Black, who came out of the Negro Leagues to earn a spot on the 1952 Brooklyn Dodgers. All Black did was win the Rookie of the Year Award with a 15–4 mark in 56 games, with a miniscule ERA of 2.15 and 15 saves. The 28-year-old came within eight innings of winning the National League ERA title. In addition, he finished third in the voting for the Most Valuable Player Award behind Hank Sauer and Robin Roberts.

Black started the first game of the World Series, beating the Yankees and Allie Reynolds 4–2, marking the first time an African American had ever won a game in the Fall Classic. Black lost Game 4 2–0 to Reynolds and also took the loss in Game 7. But it was a momentous season for Joe Black. It could be argued that he had nowhere to go but down, which, unfortunately, was the case.

In 1953 Black went 6–3 in 34 games, saving five. But he never came close to the incredible season he had in 1952, and he pitched his last major league game with the Senators in 1957.

Another pitcher who made the transition from starter to reliever was lefty Al Brazle, who enjoyed success primarily as a starter in the 1940s with St. Louis. From 1943 until 1949 he sported a 57–34 record, including two 14-win seasons. But in 1950 the side-arm hurler started just 12 of 46 games with an 11–9 record and six saves. His stature as a reliever continued to grow as he led the league in saves in both 1952 (16 saves, 12–5 record) and 1953 (18 saves, 6–7 record). Brazle retired after the following season with 60 saves.

The Dodgers also had one of the premier relief pitchers of the era in the pride of Woonsocket, Rhode Island, Clem Labine. From 1951 to 1961, he was as steady a relief pitcher as there was in the game. He sported a 77–56 career mark with 96 saves and an ERA of 3.63. Labine led the league in appearances in 1955 with 60 and was a league leader in saves in 1956 with 19 and 1957 with 17.

"Clem Labine was a relief pitcher on our team who I thought could be a great starter," said fellow Brooklyn and Los Angeles Dodgers pitcher Carl Erskine. "But he often said he didn't like to start. He liked to come in with the game on the line. I preferred being a starter because you owned the game. Clem pitched a 1–0 game in the World Series for 10 innings. He was an outstanding starter, but Clem just didn't want to start. He liked pitching every day or coming in when the heat was on."

Labine had a reliever's mentality and great stuff. He threw a good fastball, but his best pitches were a devastating curveball and his sinker, which probably resembled a latter-day split finger.

"Clem Labine was one of the best relief pitchers for several years because he had a wicked curve and a terrific sinker," St. Louis outfielder Stan Musial said in *Stan Musial: The Man's Own Story*. "He had powerful forearms. I found it difficult to pick up his curveball, and I tried to pull his fast sinker without much success."

Labine was not the only pitcher who grew to like the concept of relieving. Right-hander Marv Grissom had lots of success in the minor leagues, including a 20-win season. But after a 12–10 campaign with the White Sox in 1952, he got off to a 2–6 start with the Red Sox the following season and was claimed off waivers by the New York Giants.

He was a spot starter with the Giants for the rest of the season, but he relieved more than he started. An exhibition tour following the season opened up a spot in the Giants bullpen. That led to a fantastic 1954 season in which Grissom relieved 53 times with a 10–7 record and 19 saves.

"The reason for the good year in '54 was that the Giants had a 20-game exhibition tour after the '53 season," Marv Grissom told the *Diamond Angle* in an interview. "We played 12 of the 20 games in Japan. We had only six pitchers, and there were times when [manager Leo] Durocher needed somebody to pitch an inning or two to finish a game. He'd look down the bench, and the other guys didn't want to pitch, so they would look the other way. I would look at him and kind of nod like, 'Yeah, I'll pitch an inning.' That gave him confidence that I wanted to pitch, so he started using me in '54.

"We had a pretty good staff, and [Hoyt] Wilhelm was the main man in the bullpen. The first game in '54 I went in and saved it for Sal Maglie. Shortly after that the rotation settled in pretty good, so I asked to be sent to the bullpen."

From 1954 to 1959, Grissom enjoyed his relief role with a 27–21 record and 58 saves.

Relievers had made a name for themselves. Purists would hardly have believed that Jim Konstanty would ever win a Most Valuable Player Award. But something was missing. Relief specialists had certainly become more important cogs in the team's wheel of success, but they didn't dominate the way a hard-throwing starter could. Sure, a number of relievers put together some excellent seasons, but there wasn't a pitcher with a hammer who could punch out an opposing hitter in game situations with any regularity.

The occasional reliever had a big season or two, but he wasn't a game changer. But as the evolution of the game continued, the role of the reliever started to change. There were a handful of pitchers who soon would make a mark on the game. They were the ones who gave bullpen artists respect. And it was their careers and accomplishments that led to the total specialization of the bullpen.

CHAPTER 4

The Groundbreakers in the Pen

As the post–World War II era of baseball continued, the role of relief pitching became more accepted and standardized, with pitchers gradually assuming the role of full-time reliever. In both leagues pitchers made rosters as relief pitchers, although many would still be spot starters when a team would have its rotation foiled by a baseball term from yesteryear—the doubleheader. There was actually a time in the game when fans could enjoy two games for the price of one. At the conclusion of the first game, there would be a half-hour break followed by the nightcap. Now, of course, teams will have a day game, empty out the stadium, then fill it up with a new group of paying customers for a night game just a few hours later.

Although doubleheaders were great for fans who loved the game, they were challenging for managers and pitching coaches who needed to control their pitching staff. More money was infused into the game as attendance soared, so roster spots could be taken by utility position players and pitchers who rarely started.

"The overriding theme is that there is a lot of money in the game, and you can afford to do different things," said author and historian Peter Morris. "Pinch hitting comes in when the Giants had more money than anybody else. [John] McGraw had guys whose job it was just to pinch run.

A good base runner was a pinch runner. Guys who were good at batting and not fielding were pinch hitters. As baseball became incredibly lucrative you have all these specialized roles. A certain guy may not be so good at one thing but outstanding at another. It changed the outlook of the game.

"Now there is a guy who can do one thing well. You can keep him on the 25-man roster and put him in roles where he can be effective. As the game got wealthy, they could put resources where they couldn't before, such as the expansion of the bullpen."

Not every pitcher who came out of the bullpen threw the basic pitches of fastball, curveball, change-up, and slider. As the earliest forms of the specialization that is so prevalent in the game today began to be part of the game, pitchers were always looking for new weapons to get big-league hitters out. Specialty and trick pitches also became more evident in the repertoire of some of the more successful relievers. Pitches such as the knuckleball, the forkball, and the screwball helped revolutionize the game as well as the role of pitchers in the bullpen.

One of the major reasons for the beginning of the specialized roles in the bullpen dealt with trick pitches. Up until the 1950s, with a few notable exceptions, relief pitchers consisted of starters throwing between turns, as well as starters not good enough to break into the rotation, veterans trying to hold on for another summer in the sun, and youngsters not quite good enough to take their place in the rotation. The result was quite often much of the same. Hitters were facing the same type of pitcher out of the bullpen as the one that started the game. They'd feature a fastball, curve, slider, and maybe a change-up, but none of those pitches were as good as those featured by the starter. After all, these guys weren't good enough to crack the rotation. So hitters were pretty much facing the same style of pitcher out of the bullpen, but in many cases his stuff was inferior to the starter's. That being said, at least he was a fresh arm in the game.

But the advent of the relief pitcher who threw an oddball pitch—a knuckleball, forkball, screwball, or some such pitch—made the relief

Knuckleballer Hoyt Wilhelm used his mastery of the trick pitch to become the first relief pitcher to earn a spot in Cooperstown. He pitched for an amazing 21 seasons, appearing in more than 1,000 games for nine different teams.

pitcher a real entity. All of a sudden a reliever was someone who had a pitch that hitters had trouble with. Hell, even catchers had trouble catching a Hoyt Wilhelm knuckler, an Elroy Face forkball, or a Jack Baldschun screwball. Imagine how difficult it was for hitters to try to get good wood on the pitch.

The knuckleball is an interesting phenomenon. It floats toward the plate with moves that resemble a tipsy driver trying to walk a straight line for a police officer. It goes up, down, inside, outside, and back again. It can be thrown at different speeds, which affects the outcome, as do other conditions, such as the wind. Not only is it a difficult pitch to throw and hit, but trying to catch a big-league knuckler is no day in the park, either.

The late Charlie Lau, a renowned hitting guru from a generation ago, was a catcher during his playing career. "There are two theories on catching the knuckleball," he once said. "Unfortunately, neither of them work."

The pitch probably originated with Toad Ramsey, a southpaw who pitched during the 1880s with Louisville and St. Louis. Ramsey sported a drop curve that may well have been a knuckler. An injury to his pitching hand necessitated a strange grip on the ball.

Knuckleballs are all about strange grips and unpredictable movement, so the name of the pitch is probably a misnomer. Although pitchers today use their fingertips to grip the knuckleball, two of the early proponents of the pitch, Eddie Cicotte and Nap Ruker, actually threw the pitch with their knuckles. They accomplished this feat by gripping the ball tightly with their thumb and little finger while the middle knuckles completed the grip. But calling it the "fingertip ball" doesn't exactly strike fear into the hearts of opposing batters.

According to Rob Neyer in "The Dancing Knuckleball," from the book he coauthored with Bill James called *The Neyer/James Guide to Pitchers*, "The origins of the knuckleball are a bit murky, as four different pitchers have been said to have invented a nonspinning pitch thrown off the knuckles, or the fingertips, at roughly the same time.

"In 1907, Nap Rucker arrived in the major leagues with the Dodgers and quickly established himself as one of the better pitchers in the National League. At that time he threw very hard, but before long he also came up with an effective knuckleball.

"In 1908, the *New York Press* described Phillies right-hander Lew 'Hicks' Moren, pitching in his second season, as the knuckleball inventor.

"Also in 1908, Eddie Cicotte reached the majors for good—he'd pitched briefly for the Tigers in 1905—and quickly got hung with the nickname 'Knuckles.'

"Also in 1908, Ed Summers became known for a pitch called a 'dry spitter,' but a photo shows a pitch gripped with the first knuckles of the index and middle finger; that is, a knuckleball in the most literal sense."

In fact, according to a report in *Sporting Life* in 1908, Summers' manager in Grand Rapids, Bobby Lowe, tried to catch a half dozen of Ed Summers' "fingertip balls" and failed to catch any—with one of the floaters landing in the pit of the skipper's stomach when he failed to get any leather on the pitch at all.

An important distinction between Summers and his knuckling contemporaries is that he always held the ball with his fingertips, as opposed to Cicotte, who used his lower knuckles.

Following the tragic season of 1920 when Cleveland's Ray Chapman died as the result of being hit in the head with a pitched ball, the spitball and any other attempts to deface the baseball were outlawed. Although spitballing was no longer allowed for most pitchers, 17 hurlers received an exemption from the new rule and were allowed to finish their careers using the pitch, because it was their primary weapon. Those pitchers were: Burleigh Grimes, Doc Ayers, Ray Caldwell, Stan Coveleski, Bill Doak, Phil Douglas, Red Faber, Dana Fillingim, Ray Fisher, Marv Goodwin, Dutch Leonard, Clarence Mitchell, Jack Quinn, Dick Rudolph, Allen Russell, Urban Shocker, and Allen Sothoron. Grimes was the last pitcher to earn a major league victory throwing the legal spitball, with the Pittsburgh Pirates in 1934.

"By the time the spitball was banned, it was actually becoming viewed as an ineffective pitch," said author and historian Peter Morris. "Very few pitchers could control it. By and large, it had been a lethal pitch when it was conceived in 1904, but then it was viewed as not as effective a pitch anymore. As soon as hitters saw the pitch start to drop, they'd check their swing, and it would go out of the [strike] zone.

"Other pitches were coming along such as the scuff ball pitch and other illegal pitches. Eddie Cicotte had a whole repertoire of pitches that nobody could figure out. He would scuff the ball in ways that nobody could find out."

Just as not everyone could control the spitter enough to use it, not every pitcher had the ability to scuff or deface a ball to make it move against the laws of nature. So pitchers actually looked for legal ways to make a baseball do unnatural things, and the knuckleball was a great tool. However, it was not easy to throw, not easy to hit, and not easy to catch.

One of the best purveyors of the knuckleball was Eddie Rommel, who spent 13 seasons as a spot starter and reliever with the Philadelphia Athletics, ending in 1932. The right-hander turned into much more of a relief specialist late in his career. After his playing days ended, the knuckleball was seemingly in danger of extinction. At that point, the only knuckleball pitchers who remained in the majors were Jesse Haines and Fred Fitzsimmons, but many pitchers experimented with the pitch and would occasionally use it. And organizations often encouraged pitchers to learn the pitch. Branch Rickey of the Pittsburgh Pirates was one of them.

As the next decade unveiled itself, a new influx of knuckleball pitchers gained success with the pitch on the major league level. One of those pitchers was Dutch Leonard, whose transition from a starter to the bullpen is chronicled in chapter 3. But Leonard's influence in the game extended far beyond what he accomplished on the field. It seems that a high school student read an article about Leonard's knuckleball that convinced him to begin throwing the pitch. The high schooler was James Hoyt Wilhelm, who mastered the pitch to such a degree that he eventually became the first relief pitcher elected to the Baseball Hall of Fame. Unlike many pitchers, who only experiment with the pitch when they get older to make up for a loss of velocity, Wilhelm was on board with the knuckler early on.

"I realized when I was pitching high school ball that I wasn't fast enough to get by," Wilhelm said in a June 1959 *Time* magazine article titled "Knuckles Up." "I had read about Dutch Leonard and the kind of junk he was throwing for the Senators, and I set out to see if I could throw some too."

A hero in World War II, Wilhelm earned the Purple Heart for heroism during the Battle of the Bulge. Following his service, Wilhelm resumed his baseball career and spent six seasons in the minor leagues. Finally in 1952, at the ripe old age of 29, Wilhelm made it to The Show with the New York Giants. Seventy-one relief appearances later, Wilhelm enjoyed a 15–3 season with 11 saves and a 2.43 ERA.

Wilhelm was not much of a hitter, but you would not have known that judging by his two career at-bats. In his first trip to the plate, he hit a home run against Boston Braves hurler Dick Hoover. When his career ended, 21 years later, he still had one home run. Interestingly, Wilhelm and Earl Averill are the only members of the Hall of Fame who homered in their first major league plate appearance.

But hitting was not what Hoyt Wilhelm was about. Hoyt Wilhelm was all about throwing his knuckleball. He won 124 games out of the bullpen, which is still a major league record. He was the first pitcher to amass 200 career saves. Additionally, he was the first pitcher to appear in 1,000 games and was one of the oldest players to play the game, with his final major league appearance just days before his 50th birthday. He finished his career with a 143–122 record with 227 saves.

"In the 1950s and 1960s Wilhelm used to close," said Pat Gillick, a successful general manager with Seattle, Toronto, Baltimore, and Philadelphia, who was a teammate of Wilhelm's during his own pitching career. "I went to spring training in '62 with him. He didn't do any physical work at all. He just threw in the bullpen and sat in the training room and got treatment on his shoulder. Over a time frame of 40 years or so the myth builds up. But I think he had one of the best knuckleballs I ever saw. Wilber Wood had a good one and so did Charlie Hough and Eddie Fisher. But Hoyt had three or four different ones, and he could throw them for strikes."

Wilhelm pitched for nine teams during his career and was elected to the Hall of Fame in 1985, 13 years after his retirement from the game.

An interesting case, during the first six years of his big-league career, Wilhelm pitched in 361 games, all in relief. But he then was used as a spot starter in 1958 and 1959. On September 20, 1958, while pitching for

Baltimore, Wilhelm made history by pitching a no-hitter against the powerful New York Yankees. Coincidentally, the New York pitcher who opposed Wilhelm that day was none other than Don Larsen, who threw the lone no-hitter in the history of the World Series two years earlier.

Much is made about the difficulties involved in controlling the knuckleball. But at the end of Wilhelm's career, he had thrown 2,254 innings and walked 778 hitters while striking out 1,610. As baseball analysts would say, he had an outstanding strikeout/walk ratio.

"I don't even try to fool anybody," he said in a 1969 interview. "I just throw the knuckleball 85 to 90 percent of the time. You don't need variations because the damn ball jumps around so crazily. It's like having a hundred pitches."

Slugger Dick Allen just tried to take the knuckleball in stride and not change his hitting style at the plate. "I never worry about it," he said. "I just take my three swings and go sit on the bench. I'm afraid if I ever think about hitting it, I'll mess up my swing for life."

While the occasional starting pitcher such as Wilber Wood, Ken Johnson, Phil Niekro, and Joe Niekro featured the knuckler, for the most part pitchers who specialized in it, such as Wilhelm and Eddie Fisher, came in out of the bullpen. At the same time that the knuckleball became part of the game, another pitch came into prominence that made another relief pitcher a well-known name in the annals of baseball history.

Elroy Face was not a large man. Standing 5'8" and tipping the scales at 155 pounds, the right-hander had good enough regular stuff, as well as a fastball and curve, to make it to the majors with Pittsburgh in 1953. As a starter coming up through the Pirates' minor league system, Face sported a 69–27 mark, including 14–2 in 1949, 18–5 in 1950, and an outstanding 23–9 in 1951.

Face was a spot starter in 1953 and 1955 with the Pirates, going 11–15. But prior to the start of the 1955 campaign at spring training, his career took what would be an astonishing turn. He started less and relieved more. And he learned a new pitch that would become his trademark.

The Pirates' Elroy Face began his career as a starter but transformed into one of baseball's top relief pitchers after he mastered the forkball. In 1959 he compiled an outstanding 18–1 record, all earned in a relief role.

"I had a good career in the minor leagues as a starter, but I enjoyed the challenge of getting a couple guys out with guys on base and the game on the line," Face said from his home in McKeesport, Pennsylvania. "I enjoyed the challenge. I'd rather go in with guys on base than two outs and nobody on.

"In 1952 I was at Fort Worth, Texas, and Bobby Bragan was the manager there. Then he became the manager in Pittsburgh in 1955. I had started for him in the minors and relieved between starts. He knew I had an arm that could bounce back, and he had me relieving more than starting. Then, when Danny Murtaugh took over as manager of the Pirates, he put me in the bullpen.

"Up until my first year in the big leagues, I threw a fastball and curveball. But in the spring of 1955 Joe Page was trying to make a comeback with the Pirates and I saw him throwing the forkball, and I started working on it. Everything I did I taught myself. I never had a pitching coach or anyone to say to me to do this or do that.

"It made the fastball more effective, and they would be way out in front of the forkball."

The forkball has its origins early in the 20th century. According to John Thorn and John Holway in *The Pitcher*, an outfielder named Mike Lynch was experimenting with the pitch in 1905 in Chattanooga and found that he could make the ball have astonishing breaks. Three years later, he taught the pitch to Bert Hall of the Tacoma Tigers, who learned to control the pitch. In September 1908, he pitched a four-hit shutout against Seattle. How he threw his new pitch was described as putting the ball between his first two fingers and letting it fly.

The relationship between the forkball and the split-finger fastball, or splitter, has been debated for years. Is a forkball just a slower version of the split? Although some forkballs were thrown at different speeds, the split is always thrown at the approximate speed of the fastball. Regardless of its speed, the forkball would normally come toward the plate and then dive straight down, as if the ball fell off the table.

Then in 1920, pitcher Joe Bush was credited by some with inventing the forkball as well. When he first came up with the Philadelphia Athletics, Bush could get by with speed alone. But 10 years later, he needed another weapon in the arsenal. He discovered the pitch and then did some positive public relations in 1929 when he told the following to the *Saturday Evening Post.*

"Probably one of the most bewildering balls ever pitched was my own invention—the forkball, which I discovered in 1920 when I was essaying my comeback with the Boston Red Sox after I had hurt my arm several years before and was forced to stop throwing curveballs.

"It was while experimenting on different deliveries that I placed the ball between my index and middle fingers, resting the bottom of the sphere on my thumb, and threw it. I discovered that the ball took a funny hop. I tried it again, moving my thumb to the inside of the ball. It took another peculiar hop as it passed over the plate. I repeated the same thing a number of times, moving my thumb in different positions under the ball, and noticed that it broke over the pan in all sorts of strange ways.

"After developing and perfecting this delivery I gave it the name of *forkball.* When I first used it in the league I was almost unhittable. This one pitch had everything to do with my comeback."

Although it seems fair to surmise that Bush was not the first to throw the pitch and thus not the originator of it, he certainly was the first to jump on his own bandwagon citing the development and naming of the forkball.

No matter who discovered it, Elroy Face saw his career move into high gear once he incorporated the forkball into his repertoire on the pitcher's mound. As is the case with any other pitcher, Face had his own variation on the grip of the pitch. Even though he was a slightly built man, he was blessed with large hands and fingers. He placed the ball between his index and middle finger, cushioning the ball into the palm of his hand. The pitch that opposing hitters called a "freak ball" was an off-speed pitch that fell off the proverbial table as it neared home plate. Hitters would either flat out miss the pitch or hit ground balls.

Not only was Face anxious to go up against hitters in clutch situations, but he was a complete ballplayer who did other things to help his team win that don't always show up in the box score. Face had one of the best pickoff moves in baseball, to second base as well as first base. If a hitter got on base against the Pittsburgh ace known as "the Baron," he'd better be an attentive base runner.

"One time in a game in Cincinnati, I came in with guys on first and second and picked them both off before I even threw a pitch," Face said. "In 1960, they put Curt Simmons in at second base to run, and I picked him off. I had a decent move. That's another thing I tell young pitchers. Get a good move to first base because you can pick guys off. I picked guys off before I threw a pitch to the batter. But a lot of pitchers today don't pay attention to base runners, and they get a running start. I threw over to first base once with Orlando Cepeda at first, and I threw over there six straight times. He never thought I'd throw over there a seventh time, and I did and picked him off. You can't get into a routine that people expect. You have to do things differently so the runner can't pick up things."

Face authored one of the most remarkable years in the history of relief pitching in 1959, when he went 18–1 with 10 saves and a 2.70 ERA. During his record-breaking season—with the highest winning percentage in the big leagues ever of .947—he used to park his car at a gas station close to Forbes Field for a dollar. After his first few wins, the owner of the gas station told Face that he could park for free as long as he kept on winning. Suffice it to say that he saved lots of money on parking that season.

"Hoyt Wilhelm had a knuckleball, which was supposedly one of the better ones," said Face. "He started the '59 season with Baltimore 9–0 when I was 13–0 with the Pirates. We were on a magazine cover together.

"Nobody can walk out there and say you won't give up any runs. I was actually accused in 1959, when I had that 17-game winning streak, of letting them tie the game up so I could get wins. Hell, if I could do that I would have won a lot more games than I did. I would have been the greatest pitcher in baseball. That was ridiculous."

In his 16-year major league career Elroy Face had a 104–95 record with 193 saves. He led the league in winning percentage once, in appearances twice, in saves three times, and in games finished four times. In the 1960 World Series against the New York Yankees, he saved three of the four wins by the world champion Pirates. He had a fantastic out pitch in the forkball, but he was the epitome of a thinking man's pitcher. He used all of his pitches when the hitter didn't expect them.

As he told Danny Peary in *We Played the Game,* "Because I had good control, I threw all pitches on all counts. I'd throw harder stuff to a breaking-ball hitter and more breaking stuff to a fastball hitter. I didn't have a real pattern. If a guy had me timed on the fastball, I might throw my slider at the same speed and the little bit of movement took the ball to the end of the bat instead of the sweet part. If my forkball was working, I might throw in 70 percent of the time. Even if my forkball didn't work, I throw it around 30 percent of the time to keep the batters honest. There was no such thing as a good forkball hitter. Some batters would swing a foot over it. I was hurt by hanging curves and sliders but not with the forkball, if it broke properly."

Face still watches the game and said he feels that he has the knowledge and ability to be successful in today's game, much like he was in his era. His road map to success on the pitcher's mound transcends baseball generations.

"I think I'd fare quite well if I pitched in today's game," he said. "I'd throw strikes and let them hit the ball. Pitchers get in there now and try to get cute and nibble on the corners, get behind, and then they have to come in. You get ahead of the batter and you have an advantage over him. I always challenged the hitter. Hank Aaron got one home run off me and that was the last time I faced him. Without me, Aaron would only have 755 homers."

When Elroy Face was throwing breaking balls on a fastball count and vice versa, he was doing what is known today as "pitching backward." Throw what they're not expecting. There is a pitch that has confounded hitters since early in the game of baseball that seems to be a backward pitch: the screwball. Formerly known as the "fadeaway," the screwball goes in the opposite direction of a curveball. When a right-hander throws a curveball, it breaks down and away from a right-handed hitter. But when a righty throws a screwball, it actually curves down and inside to a right-handed hitter, sort of like a reverse slider, or "slurve." It has caused many a hitter to have a severe case of foot-in-the-bucket disease.

As far as the origin of the pitch is concerned, finding the first screwball pitcher is a little like naming the first forkball pitcher. Although Joe Bush happily shared his view that it was he who founded the pitch, when it comes to the screwball, pitcher Mickey Welch, who threw for New York throughout the 1880s, accepts responsibility for that pitch.

"I had a fadeaway, although I didn't call it that," Welch said in the *New York Sun*, reprinted in *The Sporting News* on March 2, 1933. "I didn't call it anything. It was just a slow curveball that broke down and in on a right-handed hitter, and I got a lot of good results with it in the 10 years I pitched for the Giants. Not until Matty [Christy Mathewson] came along and they began to write about his fadeaway did I realize that I had pitched it for years. Why, I learned it within a couple of years after I started to play ball, and I had no copyright on it. There were several other old pitchers who used it."

Mathewson was by far the most famous of the pitchers who first adopted what became called the "incurve" and later, the screwball. Another one of Matty's Hall of Fame brothers, Carl Hubbell, won 253 big-league games as a starter using the pitch. The southpaw used the screwball so much that his left arm had turned around to mimic the throwing motion.

A left-handed screwball (seems a bit redundant, does it not?) artist named Luis Arroyo broke in with a bang with the New York Yankees in 1961. After an impressive rookie campaign with St. Louis in 1955 when he went 11–8 primarily as a starter, Arroyo's career seemed to be on the downside until he was acquired by New York in 1960, following stops in Pittsburgh and Cincinnati.

The southpaw had a good fastball until he suffered an arm injury during the 1951 season with Rochester. He learned the screwball in 1956 from his manager at Puerto Rico, Al Hollingsworth, and it turned his career around. That pitch, along with the occasional knuckleball added to his arsenal of weaponry and a good idea of how to pitch, made Luis Arroyo a formidable adversary.

"Naturally, the hitter is expecting the screwball," he said in *Baseball Monthly* in June 1962. "They know that's my bread-and-butter pitch. He knows what's coming, and I have to stop him, even so. But I have two speeds on the screwball—and once in a while I can throw a fastball past a hitter."

Arroyo went 5–1 with the Yankees in 1960, appearing in 29 games out of the bullpen and earning seven saves with a 2.88 ERA. But the following year, in 1961, he led the league in appearances with 65 and saves with 29 en route to a 15–5 record with a miniscule 2.19 ERA.

"When I was a kid, relief pitchers were starting pitchers with bad arms," said veteran sports writer and author Maury Allen. "In the '50s and '60s, they became more important to teams with their own identification as relief pitchers. One of the things I've often said of players in the '20s and '30s was that they didn't have to be a pitcher who could throw 100 mph in the last innings of the game. Nobody was trained to come in as a relief pitcher in those days. There were guys like Johnny Murphy and then Firpo Mayberry, but there weren't too many trained as relief pitchers in that time.

"In the '60s they really began getting their own identification. The Yankees in '61 had a great left-handed relief pitcher, Luis Arroyo, who threw a screwball and an occasional knuckleball. He was as important to the team as the starters Whitey Ford and Ralph Terry."

Following his outstanding 1961 season, Arroyo injured his arm the next spring and saw his effectiveness wane. He appeared in just 27 games in 1962, sporting a 1–3 record with seven saves and a 4.81 ERA. Arroyo was out of baseball following six appearances in 1963. But he made his mark on the game as an outstanding left-handed relief specialist who threw trick pitches. He was also the first Puerto Rican to play for the Yankees.

In the early 1960s, Jack Baldschun came on to the scene in Philadelphia and was a bellwether of the bullpen. Manager Gene Mauch

In the early 1960s, Jack Baldschun of the Phillies was one of baseball's dominant relief pitchers thanks to his screwball, which broke like a reverse curve. *Photo courtesy of Getty Images*

would bring the right-hander into games, and more often than not No. 27 would get the job done. He had a 48–41 record with 60 saves from 1961 to 1970 with the Phillies as well as Cincinnati and San Diego. Baldschun's out pitch was the screwball.

He broke in with the Phillies in 1961, leading the league with 65 appearances and sporting a 5–3 record with three saves. Over the next two seasons out of the Philadelphia bullpen, Baldschun was a combined 23–14 with 29 saves. He was also part of the 1964 Phillies team that imploded and blew a seemingly safe lead in the last two weeks of the season. He went 6–9 on that star-crossed team, making 71 appearances and saving 21 games.

But Baldschun, along with some of his specialty-pitch contemporaries of the 1960s, helped revolutionize the game of baseball.

"Before guys like Elroy Face and I came into existence, relief pitchers weren't even known," said Baldschun. "Face was one of the first, and I was there at the same time. The starting pitcher would go as far as he could, and then they'd throw a starter, who usually couldn't go more than a few innings, into the game as a reliever. But a starter usually threw a fastball, curve, slider, and change-up. Hitters saw the same pitches from them as they did the starter. There were no specialists. But when Face and I came along, it changed things because we came up with pitches that made them hit the ball on the ground. I took over Turk Farrell's place with the Phillies. He was a high-fastball pitcher at the time. But high-fastball pitchers would get a lot of fly-ball outs so a guy on third would score.

"The forkball and the screwball came along, and it changed things to where the relief pitcher was the stopper who was more useful. Gene Mauch used to tell me after I asked him to let me start, that I could probably win 15 games as a starter. But he said that I was more valuable as a reliever. He said he could go out on the street and pick someone who could start. But when he wanted the game held or saved, that he wanted me in there.

49

"I was happy with my position in the game. If we didn't come along with these different pitches, they'd be stuck with starters in the bullpen who threw no oddball pitches. It was at that time that baseball pitching changed, thanks to our influence. It changed from guys being nobody in the bullpen to being a specialist in the bullpen."

One of the reasons for Baldschun's success was not simply that he threw a screwball. But Baldschun's "screwgie" had a more defined break than that of others who threw the pitch. While most screwballs resemble a backward slider, his was more like a reverse curveball. Had it not been for that pitch, he never would have been given the opportunity to be such a force in the major leagues.

"I couldn't throw that hard," he admitted. "I was no fastball pitcher. I just threw it to surprise somebody. But I had a fluid motion with the arm and had a strong forearm. I first learned the screwball in the minor leagues in Nashville, just about to be shipped down to Savannah. Dick Kennedy was catching me, and I was throwing it, and Dick told me to put it in my pocket because my fastball was sinking more. So I really broke one off backhanded, and he couldn't catch it. He asked me what in the world that was. I came up with the pitch, and it should not really be called a screwball.

"Most screwballs break like a slider but in the opposite direction. Mine broke more like a backward curve. This was a breaking pitch that I'd throw the opposite of a curve. I'd break it off backhanded and let it roll off my middle finger. I could make it go down and get really on top of it. I worked on it, and nobody could hit it because it looked like a fastball. Nobody could pick up the spin.

"It gets to where the hitter thinks he can hit it, and the bottom falls out. The speed of the pitch decided how much break you could have."

Following the devastating collapse of the '64 Phillies team, Baldschun slumped slightly the next season and was dealt to Baltimore and then Cincinnati prior to the start of the 1966 season. He went 1–5 with the Reds with a high ERA partly because his two catchers, Johnny Edwards and Jim Coker, never called for the screwball. Even though it was his most effective offering, they apparently chose not to endure the sometimes difficult task of catching the pitch, unlike Clay Dalrymple of Philadelphia, who caught the pitch with little difficulty.

Baldschun actually returned to the minor leagues in 1968 before resurfacing with San Diego in 1969 and 1970, appearing in 61 games in '69 with a 7–2 record for the Padres.

In addition to the trick pitches already mentioned, there were others. As early as 1867, pitchers were known to throw the "eephus" pitch. In 1869, Brooklyn Atlantics pitcher Jack Chapman used the pitch. The eephus pitch is admirable in its simplicity. It is tossed high in the air and slowly, almost like a dad throwing his son pop-ups to practice defensive skills. The pitch arcs down toward the plate, often confounding the hitter.

A century later, Pittsburgh's Rip Sewell brought back the pitch, enjoying success by lobbing high, slow balls up to the plate. The pitch, which he called the "dew-drop" ball, worked quite well for him with one notable exception. That being the 1946 All-Star Game when Ted Williams knocked one of Sewell's eephus pitches out of the park for a home run. Some more modern pitchers who also experimented with the pitch include Steve Hamilton, Bill "Spaceman" Lee, and Dave LaRoche, who called his eephus pitch "La Lob."

Another specialty pitch is the "palm ball," which is very similar to the circle change. Although the circle change came into prominence in the 1990s, the palm ball may have had its roots in the Negro Leagues, with a pitcher named Joe Bullet Rogan. Fellow Negro League star Chet Brewer discussed Rogan, who threw a fastball, drop curve, palm ball, spitball, forkball, slider, and side-arm curve.

"Rogan could throw a curveball faster than most pitchers could throw a fastball," Brewer told John Holway in his book *Blackball Stars: Negro League Pioneers*. "And he was the inventor of the palm ball. He had such a terrific fastball, then he'd palm the ball and just walk it up there. Hitters were well off stride. I saw him one winter just make Al Simmons crawl trying to hit that ball."

The palm ball is held in the palm by the thumb and the little finger, with the other fingers just staying out of the way. Jim Konstanty used the pitch often with Philadelphia and the Yankees. Dave Giusti and Eddie Guardado also used the pitch effectively, as did Joe Boever.

Another derivation of the palm ball was the slip pitch. But for the most part these were not signature pitches for those who threw them, unlike the knuckleball, forkball, and screwball. Rather, pitches such as the palm ball and the slip pitch were used in place of a change-up. The other better-known specialty pitches were knee-bucklers that hitters could not hit even when they knew what was coming.

It is also important to remember that, although defacing the baseball had been illegal since 1921, a number of pitchers continued to throw spitballs, shine balls, and grease balls. Some were caught, but most continued to use an outlawed out pitch because it was incredibly difficult for umpires to catch those who broke the rules. Gaylord Perry is in the Baseball Hall of Fame and has admitted to doctoring the baseball. Yankee great Whitey Ford reportedly had his catchers scuff the baseball, and he had been known to do so with his wedding band. One of the most dynamic relievers of the 1960s was Phil Regan, a former starting pitcher who switched to the bullpen and is alleged to have added a grease ball to his repertoire, which is believed to have broken more than 15 inches.

After being acquired by the Los Angeles Dodgers in 1966, Regan went 14–1 in 65 appearances and had a league-leading 21 saves. He also sported a 1.62 ERA in 116 innings, good enough to earn Comeback Player of the Year and *The Sporting News* Fireman of the Year awards.

He continued to pitch well and once again earned Fireman of the Year honors in 1968 with 12 wins and 25 saves with the Chicago Cubs.

Other pitches, such as the split finger, the slider, and flat-out heat, will also be discussed later. But these pitches and pitchers began to set the table for the future. A pitcher who came in out of the bullpen with something different to attack hitters with became a viable alternative to a starting pitcher used for an inning or two between starts.

It is this time frame in baseball where relief pitching grew in respect and acceptance in leaps and bounds. The pitchers mentioned in this chapter represent the tip of the iceberg as far as hurlers who brought relief pitching into the spotlight.

While relievers came into more prominence, a gradual change was occurring with starting pitching. Have no doubt that teams still had horses in their rotations who completed countless games, never wanting to come out of a contest. But the confidence and trust that managers and organizations started to have in relievers made the bullpen a destination for pitchers as opposed to a life sentence in baseball's Siberia. And one of the major contributing factors to this increased sense of confidence was the onslaught of specialty pitches that made those who threw them so successful.

CHAPTER 5

Starting with the Starters

The game starts with the starters. A baseball game cannot begin until the starting pitcher for the home team throws a pitch to the leadoff hitter for the visiting team. It is they who begin the contest and control the tempo of the game. Although the role of the reliever has changed appreciably during the long history of the game, so too has the role of the starting pitcher. To truly understand the changes that have affected pitching out of the bullpen, it seems prudent to examine the changes that have affected starting pitching in recent decades. After all, one leads to the other, and it all starts with the starters.

During the earliest decades of the game, pitchers were expected to let batters hit the ball, with the location of the upcoming pitch dictated by the batsman. As years wore on and pitchers were allowed to actually try to trick the batters, their importance to the game and position in the game increased exponentially. But even as they became a more important cog in a team's defense, they still did not get much respect, as most teams had only one or two pitchers on staff who would be responsible for pitching all of the games—and the entire game. There was no specialization on the pitching staff because hurlers were not considered particularly special.

With the advent of legal substitutions, teams gradually expanded the number of pitchers on the staff. But there was a class system, or caste system, that was part of every pitching staff. The starting pitchers were the ones who garnered most of the respect and money. The relievers were the redheaded stepchildren of the team. Although being a relief pitcher in the early years of baseball certainly beat working a regular job all summer long, there was not a lot of celebrity attached to the job.

"When teams started using two or three starters, it was considered bad strategy to rotate pitchers," said author Peter Morris. "That affected how relief pitchers were used. In the early days a reliever was not as good as a starter. Relievers were still in that mode in the 1920s. John McGraw had a few that he used that were pretty good pitchers, who he used as relievers. He had this weird idea of experimenting with different starters. But until the '20s, the starters were the best pitchers, and the relievers were not."

There was so little respect for the relief pitcher that managers would often rather have starting pitchers throw an inning or two between starts, rather than use relievers. But from early on in the history of America's Game, even after relief pitchers became more respected members of the team, the complete game was considered the goal of every starting pitcher. That feeling held true for decades. If you were a starting pitcher, the manly thing to do was to pitch complete games, or at the very least, pitch very deep into games.

Starting pitchers thought nothing of completing 80 percent of their starts, sometimes pitching as many as 14 or 15 innings. You were the starter, one of the bellwethers of the staff, and it was your job to finish what you started. In addition, just about everybody wanted to be a starter. So you had starters, starter wannabes, and some guys who were just happy to be in the big leagues, even if they got into only a couple of games a month.

"The premier position on a pitching staff is to be one of the starters in the rotation," said former pitcher Carl Erskine. "Normally it was the starters who represented a prestige thing. Kind of a pecking order thing. If you were a starting pitcher, there was more prestige in that. You were

Carl Eskine was both a starter and reliever during his outstanding career with the Dodgers. He readily admits that during his playing days (1948–1959) it was much more prestigious to be a starter—and that's what most pitchers aspired to be.

not exactly looked down on if you were a reliever. Just maybe not considered quite ready.

"My own mind-set as a pitcher in my era was that starting was more prestigious and sought after than being a relief pitcher. You were a relief pitcher with the ultimate goal of becoming a starter. The manager during a long season would rotate guys. If a starter was having problems, he'd put a different guy out there in the rotation and put him in the bullpen. The ultimate goal was to be a starter. That relates to the era when a complete game was important. It was also a plus to say I had 12 complete games the previous season at contract time. That has virtually no meaning anymore. I was always proud to pitch a complete game. The win was the big thing."

Consider that from 1893 to 1899 records indicate that starting pitchers completed nearly 84 percent of the games they started. From 1900 to 1909, the figure was not much lower at 79 percent. There was a considerable drop-off in the decade starting with 1910 as starters completed 56.8 percent of the games they started. It was during this time that managers regularly used starting pitchers between starts for an inning or two out of the bullpen.

Complete games still occurred more than 40 percent of the time through the 1940s. But from 1950 to 1959, the number dwindled to 33.5 percent and all the way down to 25 percent in the '60s and '70s. The trend has continued all the way to the new millennium, and the numbers are startling. In the 2008 Major League Baseball season, a whopping 6 percent of games were completed by the starting pitcher; 94 percent of the time the bullpen was used.

With the decline of the complete game, naturally there also has been a decline in innings pitched by starters. Back in the 1890s, the major league leader in innings pitched averaged 421 innings. That number declined to 401 during the first decade of the 20th century and down to 370 innings in the teens. Although the major league leader in innings pitched for each year steadily declined, the number always stayed above

311 innings from 1910 until 1980, when it dropped to 281 innings. In the new millennium, the figure is around 250 innings pitched.

Starting pitchers are completing far fewer games than ever and are pitching significantly fewer innings than ever before. The role of the workhorse—who would go out there every fourth day and give his team however many innings it needed to win—is gone.

"The role of the starting pitcher when I played in the '60s and '70s was to get into the late innings," said Hall of Fame pitcher Ferguson Jenkins, former member of the Philadelphia Phillies, Chicago Cubs, Texas Rangers, and Boston Red Sox and author of *Fergie: My Life from the Cubs to Cooperstown.* "There were no pitch counts in those days. The ability to get into the later part of the game was stamina. We built stamina by doing lots of running and a lot of throwing. The first or second time you pitched in spring training, you went for as long as you could to build up the stamina. We used to break camp with nine pitchers.

"The pitch count started in the late '80s, and it was adapted because a lot of these young men couldn't complete a ballgame and throw more than 100 pitches. The feeling was to get into the sixth or seventh inning and then turn to the good men in the bullpen. It hasn't hurt baseball, and guys have actually lengthened their careers as a result. Guys were throwing 300-plus innings as starters when I played; now they throw 160 innings or so.

"The game has changed a little bit because there is more strategy in the bullpen and less around the starter. I like the era I played in during the '60s and '70s. What you see now is that they have adapted a new theory as to how the game has been played. Strategy is all around the end of the game now. There are less regular reserve players and more pitchers. Some teams actually carry 14 pitchers and only 11 position players. As a result, a manager quite often has only one or two moves he can make during a game."

The idea of pitch counts and a starter being expected only to give his team a quality start, six innings pitched with three or fewer earned runs,

Fergie Jenkins was both a reliever and starter, but he became a Hall of Famer thanks to being a starter who rarely needed a reliever. "The role of the starting pitcher when I played in the '60s and '70s was to get into the late innings," he explained.

has changed the approach of starting pitchers. Stamina has gone the way of bell-bottomed pants and leisure suits. Just one generation ago the mind-set of a starting pitcher was completely different than it is today.

A pitcher would go through the lineup a few times facing hitters more during the course of a game than is typical today. How a starter pitched a certain hitter in the first inning helped set up how he pitched him in the third, sixth, and possibly the eighth or ninth.

"As a starter, you knew you'd have to go through the lineup at least three times," said Hall of Fame pitcher Dennis Eckersley. "When you would start a game, you knew it was yours to lose, for the most part. They would not go to the bullpen if you got in trouble in the third or fourth inning. Your mind-set as a starter was to go nine. Nowadays, if you pitch six innings you did a great job. That's the difference. Before, if you pitched you would throw 125 pitches come hell or high water. That actually started to change for me during my career. The last couple of years I started, I was with the Cubs, and it had already begun to change. All of a sudden, if you pitched six innings you did a good job. Plus, we had a bullpen with Lee Smith out there. Everybody followed suit."

But the widespread acceptance of relief pitching has morphed into a universal dependence on relievers. We've seen a shift in the strategy of the game. Whereas in the past, strategy often concentrated on the starting pitcher and the type of lineup he would oppose, now most of the strategy of the game is at the back end of the contest, where managers have bloated pitching staffs with which to attack key late-game matchups where, more often than not, the hitting team has very few options off the bench. That's because they are forced to carry more pitchers on their rosters than ever before and as a result have less position players, which means that managers can't always get the offensive matchups they want, sending up a particular hitter against a specialty reliever.

Teams are protecting their investments and limiting the number of pitches their starters throw. *Pitch count:* that's the term that has changed the core of baseball pitching. As soon as a starting pitcher throws 100 pitches, it's time to take him out. Doesn't matter if he's tired or not or pitching well or not. Ninety percent of the time, a starter who eclipses the 100-pitch mark is on his way to the showers shortly thereafter.

"With pitch counts, I guess the limit is 100 pitches these days," said Elroy Face. "Vernon Law went 17 innings one night in Pittsburgh. I wonder how many pitches he threw that night? They took him out for a pinch hitter. It was a 2–2 game. Bob Friend came in to pitch the eighteenth inning, got them out, and we got a run in the bottom of the inning and won it for Friend. Law pitched 17 innings and got nothing. Friend pitched one inning and got a win. Harvey Haddix went 12 perfect innings. How many pitches did he throw? Now they don't throw enough to strengthen their arms."

The idea of the pitch count can raise the ire of many former and some current ballplayers. For every baseball man who feels that pitch counts save a pitcher's arm, there is another who insists that pitch counts weaken a pitcher's arm. It is one of those endless baseball debates.

"Pitch counts are the biggest farce in the game," said former pitcher Gene Garber. "It only tells a guy when he should be getting tired. If I have thrown 90 pitches, then I must be getting tired. Not true. If you learn to pitch properly and get into a good rhythm, you can throw 200 pitches, which won't tax your arm as much as throwing 40 pitches out of sync. A lot of baseball is run by people who haven't played the game. You don't have many Nolan Ryans around now. He is expecting things out of his pitchers that no one else expects, and he will get what he expects. He has raised the bar.

"You are telling a guy when he should be getting tired and giving him an excuse to come out of a game. When you don't expect things out of your kids, you are not going to get the behavior you want. But when you expect certain behavior, you will get it. It's the same with pitching. If you expect seven or eight innings of shutout ball, you will get a better pitching performance.

"I never heard of pitch counts when I played. I pitched a 14-inning game in Toledo one night. I was with Charleston and threw batting practice the next day. I must have thrown 160 pitches the night before. But I had excellent mechanics and good rhythm. When your mechanics are good it doesn't take something out of your arm. Today, we have pitchers with injury after injury. A lot were caused by the split-finger fastball. And that pitch is becoming a pitch of the past because of it. But the majority of injuries to pitchers are more caused by disuse rather than overuse.

"People don't get their arms in really good shape. The majority of my career, I pitched batting practice and took infield practice every day, making throws in the infield. That was my pregame route that got me physically and mentally ready to play.

"You can't make more than 100 pitches these days. Goodness, I can't understand that. I would not be able to be a starter under conditions today. I can't imagine going out and taking Steve Carlton or Phil Niekro or Gaylord Perry out of a game because you have 100 pitches right now. It didn't hurt their arms."

Just knowing what the pitch count is can affect a pitcher. You can be fresh as can be, throwing well and with plenty of gas left in the tank. But when the giant-sized scoreboards show that you've thrown more than 100 pitches, well, you most certainly must be getting tired. After all, with a pitch count of 95, it's time to start thinking about heading to the shower.

"Pitch counts are an unsubstantiated, artificial limit that conditions pitchers to feel fatigued, based on a predetermined barrier established by others," Hall of Fame pitcher Don Sutton told Jerry Crasnick of ESPN.com. "We're teaching it in Class A ball. We're telling kids we're not going to let them pitch, we're not going to extend them, and we're not going to see what they're capable of. We're encouraging mediocrity and being very successful at it."

One of the things that pitch counts don't take into account is that there are times when a starter is throwing well and has a big lead. When his pitch count reaches the century mark, odds are it has been an easy, stress-free outing that he would easily be able to continue in. Other times, a pitcher can throw 75 pitches in constant trouble, putting much more strain on his arm. But he might still be allowed to trudge out to the mound for more innings.

The game has evolved to the point where starting pitchers are still royalty, but they are limited in each outing. And the old credo of the relief pitcher being taboo has gone the way of starters pitching deep into games. Starters actually come out of the game for no apparent reason except the new curse words among pitchers—*pitch counts*. And relievers have become stars in their own right, earning big-figure salaries and the fame and adulation that goes with it.

"When I broke in you didn't want to be in the bullpen," said Goose Gossage. "It was like you were part of an old junk pile. There has been a total evolution to where it is today from a place you didn't want to be.

"Pitch counts are the reason I'm not a pitching coach. Pitch counts give you an idea of where a guy is. But I don't need a pitch count to see if a guy is getting tired. The first thing to go is your control, and you start to get the ball up in the zone. Another reason I don't believe in pitch counts is that some days you can walk out there and throw 200 pitches, and it feels like you threw 20. Other times you'll throw 20, and you feel like you threw 200. You can't go by pitch counts. Statistics have become so important that you can get people off the streets to manage as long as they go by the numbers. That's what they rely on now. But the numbers only tell you part of the story. I'm not a real fan of the game today. I'd like to be a starter today. You see guys go five, and they are looking over their shoulder for help. I would buy pitch counts and protecting pitchers if pitch counts resulted in less injuries. But they are actually more injury prone now.

"We used to throw, throw, throw, and throw to build up arm strength. These guys are babies today. It's management's fault."

The way that the game has evolved, it seems that the magic number for starting pitchers is 100, as in pitches. It doesn't seem to matter the difficulty of the game or the name of the pitcher. Teams are built to use a whole series of one-inning guys to get you to the ultimate one-inning guy, the closer.

"I think the pitch count is a ridiculous thing," said former shortstop and manager Jim Fregosi. "How can you place a number on any pitcher unless you judge the effort he has made throwing pitches? They have this number now of 100, and every team seems to stick to it now. If a guy throws 120 pitches, then that's all the newspapermen write about. How will this affect his career? Hell, Gaylord Perry threw 230 pitches in a game, and he pitched forever.

"Every pitcher is different. Some guys can throw 150 pitches, and it doesn't bother them. It all depends on effort. Some guys run out of gas at 80 or 90 pitches. But if you look back at the history of the game, the guys who always pitched for an extended period of time and won a lot of games were all guys who threw a lot of pitches in games. Athletes are trained differently today. Pitchers are never forced to be able to use their legs in their delivery. They don't know how to pitch when they get a little tired or lose a little hop on their fastball. That's when you use your legs more in your delivery, bend your back more.

"I think that the conditioning aspect of the game has been taken out of the hands of baseball people. That hurts the conditioning of pitchers and the longevity of pitchers and how many innings they pitch during a season. Now they do more weight work than baseball skill work. I think that's why we have a lot more breakdowns. Most injuries in baseball usually happen when it's a day game after a night game, where the muscles in the body don't have a chance to recuperate. Players pull more hamstring muscles now than ever before because they don't run all the time. You'll see a pitcher get hurt covering first base because of the quickness of movement. The muscles are not used to it.

"Another thing that is happening now is that guys are not using the full windup. They use an abbreviated windup now. The guys who pitched for a long time in the game had a full windup."

There are those in the game who want to go against the tide of the pitch count. In fairness, pitch counts can certainly be a valuable tool in deciding whether or not a particular pitcher may have exceeded his comfort zone. Some guys are big, strong horses who might have a lot left in their tank. Other pitchers may not have the makeup to pitch deep into games and throw a lot of pitches. But the thing that upsets many baseball purists is their belief that although pitch counts are important to consider, they should not be the only factor in the decision as to how far your starting pitcher will go.

"I tried in Philadelphia to talk about innings and to forget about pitch counts," said former Phillies GM Pat Gillick. "Let's try a six- or seven-inning mind-set. Not 100 or 110 pitches. I think the mind-set of pitch counts alone has contributed to the situation we have at the moment. We have guys pitch in the sixth inning, then other guys in the seventh, and others in the eighth. It all depends on the individual. The manager and the pitching coach know their players well enough. Let them be the judge of when they are losing it out there. Robin Roberts pitched in Houston at the tail end of his career. Robin had to have thrown at least 120 pitches in a game. I'm not in favor of pitch counts. I think they are carried to the extreme. Give me seven good innings and forget about pitch counts. The only place I might be an advocate of them is in the lower levels. The bottom line is that if you do your long toss between starts, there is no reason you can't pitch seven innings."

Sometimes pitch counts can be a self-fulfilling prophecy. Lord knows there is not a big-league park in North America that does not show pitch counts, strikes, balls, the type of pitch, and pitch speed of every pitch a pitcher makes. You might feel great having pitched five relatively easy innings. But then you look up at the scoreboard and see that you're up to 95 pitches.

You could be throwing well, setting up hitters, and hitting your spots. But the scoreboard is there for everyone to see. It acts as your résumé for that particular game. But much like the game of baseball, pitch counts don't always give the true story of the effort of a particular game.

"You sort of knew you were getting there once you start hearing about pitch counts," said Dennis Eckersley. "I never thought that if I had to throw 30 pitches in the first inning that I might not make it deep into the game. Today, it's in everybody's head. If you have a hard time getting through five, you convince yourself you're at the end. They monitor you, and you only go 100 pitches, and you're at the end of the road.

"To me, starting isn't as tough as it was years ago. But it's tougher to win 20 games than it is to save 50. You aren't around in the game long enough, often enough to win 20."

But from the other side of the fence, agents want to protect their clients. Organizations have millions of dollars invested in the future of pitchers on their rosters. It is an accepted baseball practice to limit the wear and tear on a pitcher's arm by instituting pitch counts, from the time they throw their first minor league pitch until they heave their final major league pitch. Not many of the baseball purists like it. But it has been a gradual process that has evolved to where the game is today.

"I think back to the Dodger pitchers during my time as general manager," said Fred Claire. "Guys like Orel Herscheiser and Fernando Valenzuela considered it a personal insult to come out of a game. Fernando's competitive nature was such that he always wanted to stay in. That change has really been dramatic as far as complete games are concerned. It has something to do with the evolution of relief pitching, but not directly to the closer.

"If you look at the evolution of it, you saw when it became more focused, after the time of Joe Page and Jim Konstanty. You had a guy like Ellis Kinder who became a closer, or even Johnny Sain, who saved a ton of games for the Yankees one year. There is no question that the closer and his role has become so specialized. The respect and value of the closer is extremely high. The value of the eighth-inning guy is high.

There is so much of an expectation and a definition of how the game will be played out. You're not expecting complete games anymore. That becomes a rarity. The staff needs to be handled as far as who is going to close tonight and who we can use to get to the closer. That scenario is on the mind of every manager, pitching coach, and general manager in the game. If you get a complete game, you get a bonus.

"Even in the years when you had great Dodger pitching staffs with Don Drysdale and Sandy Koufax, you had Ron Perronoski. Clem Labine, who was a friend, established himself in closing games for the Dodgers. Phil Regan, who was known as 'the Vulture,' made a mark. But that has changed. What has happened is not just the role of the closer, but the specialization in the bullpens."

It hasn't happened overnight. But there has been a steady, startling change in the game that makes a starting pitcher's job just to last to the sixth or seventh inning. Baseball may be the greatest game ever invented, but it is also a business. Clubs spend millions of dollars every year bringing young pitchers along in their minor league systems. Many are high draft picks who got enormous signing bonuses, thanks to the influx of agents. And it costs money to teach them their craft. Complete games used to be the standard for starting pitchers. In this brave new baseball world, protecting a team's investment in a young pitcher is much more important.

"When you are throwing more complete games, obviously you have a greater number of pitches you throw during a game and a season," said Fred Claire. "But now there is more awareness of the number of pitches thrown, and clubs try to protect young pitchers. Another part of what has changed is that the starting staff used to be four men. Now it's five or even five plus. I think also you have the changes that have taken place in high school and college with metal bats. As a result, young pitchers don't pitch inside as much. Pitchers not challenging hitters I'm sure has something to do with smaller ballparks. A whole number of issues have changed pitching as it once existed.

"You have to be conscious of what is taking place. You have tremendous investments in signing pitchers out of high school and college. You have a history of pitchers, in every organization, who have encountered arm problems. There is not an organization out there that does not have an awareness of and stresses the importance of pitch counts. In years past that debate was more of an old-school versus new-school philosophy. But time has moved, and clubs are trying to protect their pitchers and their investments. That's very much at the forefront of what is happening. It is also why pitchers pitch longer in their careers than in years past. You have to listen not only to your baseball staff, but also your medical staff."

The business aspect of baseball cannot be minimized. Not only do teams have huge investments to protect, but every player has an agent who is looking out for his client's long-term benefit. So in this respect, baseball organizations, as well as players and their agents, are on the same page.

"Every athlete, from their time in the minor leagues, has an agent," said pitcher Fergie Jenkins. "A lot of these young pitchers are protected in the minors and are protected in the big leagues. Managers don't want to overwork them. The front office says that they don't want a franchise player worn out. I would not say that they are coddled, but protected a little more than we were when I played. In the bullpen, when the game is on the line, a closer is making a salary to close and finish games. That's what they are called upon to do. Just pitch to one batter sometimes or one inning."

The impact of agents cannot be ignored. The era of a pitcher throwing through pain is gone. Although taking better care of players and taking their long-term health into consideration is absolutely not a negative thing, it has revolutionized the game of baseball. But it's sad that it was the almighty dollar that started the revolution.

Jim Fregosi was a six-time All-Star during his 17-year big-league career as a shortstop with the Los Angeles/California Angels, Pittsburgh Pirates, New York Mets, and Texas Rangers. He was also a manager in

The Show for 15 seasons with the Angels, Chicago White Sox, Philadelphia Phillies, and the Toronto Blue Jays, amassing a 1,028–1,095 won-lost record. He has earned the reputation during his managerial career as a baseball man who truly understands pitching and pitchers. He is also a baseball man who is willing to share his opinions about the game that has been his life.

"Pitch counts really are a joke," he said. "They don't count an intentional walk as pitches. You don't look at warm-up pitches before the game or before each inning as pitches. They make such a thing about pitch counts, and a lot of managers are afraid to go over that magic number of 100. I don't know how that came in, but I have a great suspicion that it came in from agents who want to ensure longevity for their pitcher so they can make a lot of money."

For a variety of reasons, pitchers are getting a lot more special attention and cautious handling than in the past. Agents care about their pitcher/clients because of the future commissions they can earn with the next big deal they sign. (To be fair, agents can also develop a father-like relationship with their players in which they really do try to protect the players' welfare. But there are certainly some out there who don't seem to fulfill this role.) And organizations care about protecting their pitchers because of the tremendous amount of money they have invested in their talent.

"It is because of the advent of long-term contracts as well as the advent of agents that teams are now so wary of injuries," Chris Wheeler said of the mind-set that has led to the concept of pitch counts. "It starts in the minor leagues with the big contracts. Look at the cost involved in bringing young pitchers along. It used to be a guy kept pitching if his arm hurt. Now you get a little twinge, and he gets shut down. I'm not saying that's wrong, because it's probably better for their health. Teams are protecting their investment. It has all evolved into this caution-first, pitch-count mentality. You become so cautious because you have a huge investment in these people.

"Before, if a guy got hurt, his career was over. There was no Tommy John surgery or MRIs. There was no caution-first mentality of shutting somebody down the minute a problem occurred. There were no rehab starts before. That is what evolved into the shorter amount of time guys pitch in a game. A guy can't throw more than 100 pitches anymore. You shut a guy down so fast now, and as a result somebody else has to pitch those innings. This has all evolved into the specialty staff."

Hitters deserve some credit as well. Sure, there will always be free swingers who lunge at a pitch a foot out of the strike zone. But it seems that the successful teams have a lineup that works opposing pitchers. They are taught to make a pitcher throw a strike, work the count, and settle on a good pitch to hit in their zone. Just like pitchers can nibble, so can hitters. That too has changed the dynamic of the game and led to fewer complete games.

"Pitch counts are a result of a combination of things," said author Peter Morris. "Teams have become more sensitive to it. The other team realizes that if we can run up a pitch count on the starter, that they can get this guy out of the game. Teams, I think, stress batters being more selective. Teams also emphasize power a lot more than they used to. It used to be a team would have two or three power hitters in their lineup and the rest would be singles hitters. An intelligent pitcher would let guys put the ball in play because they couldn't hit the ball out of the park. Get the guy out by giving him something to hit. If he hits a single, it's the same as a walk. Now pitchers need to bear down on most of the hitters since most guys in the lineup can hit home runs. A lot more guys hit 10 homers a season these days. If you hang a curveball or throw them a batting-practice fastball, they have the ability to hit it out of the ballpark. Pitchers are throwing their best stuff all the time and wearing themselves out. Guys who throw 100 pitches now are working harder than guys who threw 120 pitches a generation ago.

"Teams have a five-man rotation now. It used to be a four-man rotation until the '70s. Up until World War II, the rotation itself wasn't even considered good strategy because they would plug in a starter between starts. There's a big difference now.

"These days you've done pretty well by going six or seven innings as opposed to going nine, and that has fundamentally changed pitching. A pitching coach will talk about the pitches they use. They are encouraged to use three good pitches now. It used to be guys would throw four or five pitches."

There are even those who feel that the instant access that millions of fans have to baseball games thanks to ESPN, the MLB Network, and other cable outlets has changed the game. Because any minute managerial moves are sure to be questioned by announcers, former players, color analysts, and studio personnel every night across the country, that adds to the baggage a pitching coach and manager must deal with.

A generation ago it was bad enough to have the local scribes writing that you were an idiot. Now your every move is scrutinized in front of a nationwide audience by baseball experts who have the advantage of being Monday morning quarterbacks. The terminology has all changed. Expectations have all changed. That affects managers, coaches, and of course, the pitchers.

"A quality start is a 4.50 ERA, which is absurd," said Gene Garber. "I remember when I played for Don Hoak in Triple A. I lost a game 1–0, and he heard a teammate tell me helluva job. His comment to me was helluva job, my ass. You lost 1–0. That was back when if your team didn't score any runs you did a good job only if you gave up none. If you gave up five and your team got six, you did okay. When they lowered expectations, this is what they got."

Another interesting observation about the changes in the role of modern-era pitchers deals with coaching. We've established that in the early decades of the game pitchers were not the most respected players on the team. There was a mind-set that because they played only every four or five days that they weren't really ballplayers. Sort of like the way football players often look at kickers. They're nice little guys, but they're not one of us.

The lack of respect afforded to pitchers extended to coaching staffs as well. In the new millennium, a look at just about every big-league coaching staff will show the pitching coach to be a former pitcher, with the notable exception being former catcher Dave Duncan, a longtime member of any Tony La Russa coaching staff. Although there is a long line of former pitchers who mentor hurlers dating back to Bobby Mathews, who became the first paid coach in 1888, there are also numerous catchers who have held that position.

These generals of the baseball field certainly understand the strategy involved in pitching, such as desired matchups, pitch sequences, and what you want your pitcher to do. But because they were never out there on the pitcher's mound, the actual interpersonal help that they could offer pitchers was negligible, at least as far as having a shared experience. They were never out there and really don't know what is going through the mind of the pitcher (many position players have often questioned whether or not anything goes through the mind of the pitcher, but that's a different subject altogether). Their ability to help a pitcher with mechanics or to develop a feel for a pitch may not be as evident as it might be with a former pitcher.

During his playing career, Carl Erskine never had a former pitcher as a pitching coach. It was always a former catcher. He theorizes about how a change in this way of thinking may have helped lead to the specialization of the pitching staff today.

"The handling of pitching is one of the biggest changes from my era to this one," he said. "If you look back at old rosters up until the early '50s, you almost never see ex-pitchers on the coaching staffs. It was always a catcher. I had four pitching coaches in my career, and they were all former catchers. The mind-set in those days was that pitchers weren't really ballplayers. They didn't play every day, so they weren't real ballplayers. It was that old macho idea.

"In the minors my pitching coach was Paul Chervinko; next was Bobby Bragan, a former major league catcher. My third was Clyde Sukeforth, and the fourth was Joe Becker, who served under Walt Alston. He was the pitching coach in L.A. for Don Drysdale, Sandy Koufax, and Johnny Podres. But it wasn't until Jim Turner of the Yankees was the first former pitcher to get a lot of credit. He helped guys like Bob Turley and Don Larsen, both hard-throwing wild pitchers, to develop the no-windup delivery. He was a pitcher who knew how to talk to pitchers about how to pitch and how to pitch to hitters. The pitching coach as a catcher couldn't help you very much. He would warm you up and knew what pitches were working. But he could not help you with mechanics.

"The theory is that the catcher can tell what the guy is doing, how his stuff is, and evaluate how the guy is throwing. But he can't help a pitcher to alter his delivery or work on his psyche. Bases loaded and 3–2 on the hitter, and a former catcher has no idea what's going through the pitcher's head. But a pitching coach who was a pitcher knows exactly how the guy is feeling and can give him some clue and help.

"This change to former pitchers is what I believe led to more specialization in pitching. A former pitcher can evaluate a pitcher better. They know if a guy can pitch deep into games or not. Or if a guy has the stuff and the makeup to be a closer. The pitching coach has really changed the mind-set of how pitching staffs are used.

"These days you get six or seven innings out of a starter, and it's a quality start. Man, I had a lot of quality starts then. In my day, a quality start was a complete game. The manager would hug you after a complete game because you saved the staff. The manager was delighted because you gave everybody a day's rest."

These days, it's very seldom that most relievers on a big-league pitching staff get a day's rest. We live in a fast-paced society with the need and desire for instant gratification. You can make the argument that the same ideas are true in baseball.

"If you're a fan of a certain team, you always wanted to see your guys pitch a complete game," said Erskine. "The culture of the era is reflected in baseball. Technology in the broader world affects baseball. Lights, drugs, air travel are not just in sports but all over society. Baseball reflects society. I think in fact that it's a more permissive society.

"People in my era wanted the players to be reprimanded severely for breaking the rules. Younger people are much more permissive now and don't want to see guys get suspended. That's another example of how baseball reflects society.... Today, the players association has an influence; the owner who has big money invested in players doesn't want to see multimillion guys suspended. The culture on the streets reflects in baseball."

Certainly, while starting pitchers are not being given the opportunity to pitch deeply into games, the hitters aren't making their lives any easier either. And the strike zone always has been, is now, and always will be a subject of contention in baseball.

"You hear people talking about hitters working the count," said Gene Garber. "When I played I sure hoped they'd try to work the count against me, because if they did they were down 0 and 2. If pitchers could throw strikes and get ahead of hitters, things would be different. But pitchers don't have the command to stay ahead of hitters. So hitters can be patient and sit back and wait for a pitch.

"Small strike zones and the fact that the plate does not have an inside corner anymore make it more difficult for a pitcher. Plus umps now reward mediocrity by calling hanging breaking balls that are inside strikes. You can't pitch fastballs inside anymore, and you never get a called strike with a fastball inside. But if you work the outside, they'll call that. It eliminated controversy, but the umps rewarding mediocre pitches by calling them strikes is beyond me. Umpires that are willing to call strikes who are what are called 'pitcher's umpires' do not hurt the offense. It might even encourage and quicken the game because hitters will realize that they can't work the count, and they need to swing at good pitches.

"But you are not as a pitcher allowed to take control of the inside part of the plate."

Nolan Ryan was one of the great pitchers in history who controlled the entire plate. He began his Hall of Fame career out of the bullpen of the New York Mets. But after being included in a trade with the Angels, in exchange for the aforementioned Jim Fregosi, he became as dominating a pitcher as the game of baseball has ever seen. In his 27-year big-league career, Ryan had a 324–292 record with a 3.19 ERA. But he was a dominating pitcher who possessed one of the best fastballs in the game, accentuated by loud grunts he would utter with each pitch, as well as a 12-to-6 curveball that could buckle the knees of the most fearless hitter.

Ryan, elected to the Baseball Hall of Fame in 1999, holds several records that may never be broken, such as seven no-hitters, striking out 5,714 batters in 5,386 innings, and also walking 2,795 batters. Now president of the Texas Rangers, one wonders how many pitches Ryan threw in 27 seasons that saw him become the all-time leader in both walks and strikeouts. It has been calculated by pitch-count estimator Tom Tango that in 1973 when Ryan set the modern record for strikeouts in a season (with 383) and also walked 162 batters, that he averaged 134 pitches per start.

Compare that stat, obviously at the top of the charts, with the average workload of a starting pitcher in today's game. Midway through the 2009 season, 1,543 starters (who went a minimum of five innings in a game) had an average pitch count of 99.2. In 2008 there were only 71 times in the entire season that a starting pitcher was allowed to throw 120 pitches.

Many baseball purists scoff in frustration at the idea of pitch counts and the domino effect that they have had on pitching staffs for the last 20 years. But unlike many critcs who simply throw their hands up in the air, Nolan Ryan is doing something about it.

Sports commentator Gary Thorne called Ryan's plan "back to the future on the mound," and it is a very apt description. As president of the

Texas Rangers, Ryan has dictated that his organization stop using pitch counts as the deciding factor in how long pitchers remain in games. Although they will monitor and be aware of how many pitches their hurlers throw, managers and pitching coaches in the Texas organization will no longer automatically ring for a reliever at the 100-pitch mark.

Ryan spoke of his own experience as a pitcher who needed to develop stamina, because his intent was to pitch a lot of innings. Ranger pitchers are expected to pitch deeper in games. The organization isn't just throwing them out there for dozens of extra pitches right off. Since spring training of the 2009 season, their pitchers have been throwing more, including live batting practice, to strengthen their arms.

Ryan told the *Dallas Morning News* in spring 2009 what he was looking for from his starting pitchers. "The dedication and work ethic that it takes to pitch an entire season as a starting pitcher and the discipline to continue to maintain his routine all year," he said. "And he wants the ball every fifth day, and he's going to go out there with the intent of pitching late into games and not complaining."

Flocks of baseball executives all across the game will be watching this experiment closely over the next couple of seasons to see if Texas pitchers do pitch more deeply into the game and if they break down physically more than they do now. Should Ryan succeed, it could result in rolling back the tremendous specialization we see in baseball, with fewer pitchers throwing more innings.

"I know what Nolan is trying to do, and I commend him for it," said Pat Gillick. "You have to approach it the way we educate kids about drug addiction. Do it from down below with the kids in the farm system. When you get into pro ball you need to get a mind-set that is carried through the entire organization.

"I don't know if they throw enough today. They need to throw a lot. The only way to strengthen your arm is to throw and then long toss between starts. Good pitching is very difficult to come by, and I think there is a tendency to baby them a little."

The tail wagging the dog theory is hard at work here. Did quality starts and pitch counts lead to the specialized game of today, or did the specialized game of today lead to quality starts and pitch counts? Those questions will be pondered and discussed for years to come. Has the advent of the pitch count led to fewer sore-armed starters or to more brittle pitchers who don't have the arm strength to pitch deep into games?

Baseball has evolved to this point where starters rarely throw many more than 100 pitches in a game, and the bullpen is filled with role players with specific jobs that are a bridge to the closer. It will be interesting to see if Nolan Ryan's grand experiment with the Texas Rangers is successful. As much as any other business or sport, baseball will copy success and knock off whatever technique, idea, or strategy works. Who knows? We might even see a resurgence in the lost art of the complete game in baseball.

Perhaps baseball will eventually go back to the future.

CHAPTER 6

R-E-S-P-E-C-T: Firemen of the 1970s and 1980s

One of the most popular songs of the late 1960s was Aretha Franklin's version of the song "Respect," written and originally recorded by Otis Redding, which propelled her to superstardom in 1967. At the time it became a rallying song for the feminist movement. But in baseball, a new era of relief pitchers saw a formerly scoffed-at group of hurlers gain in respect *and* salary.

A year after Franklin's "Respect" was playing on radios all across the nation, an interesting thing happened in baseball. In 1968, Bob Gibson of the St. Louis Cardinals went 22–9 with an ERA of 1.12. He threw a league-leading 13 shutouts, striking out 268 batters, also a league best. That was also the year in the American League that Denny McLain, previously an above-average pitcher for the Detroit Tigers, stunned the baseball world with a 31–6 record, completing a league-best 28 games and pitching 336 innings.

Good pitching usually stops good hitting, and good pitching and good fielding usually win championships. But good pitching and good fielding rarely fills the stadium with fans. As a result, the Lords of Baseball deemed such dominance contrary to the offensive style of baseball that generates a spike in attendance. Although a baseball purist loves a 1–0 or 2–1 game, the average fans like hitting and home runs. So baseball's rulemakers lowered the pitching mound from 15 inches to 10 inches and narrowed the strike zone in an effort to get baseball's hitters on a more even playing field. Prior to the strike zone changes, the zone was from the batter's knees to his armpits. But after the "Year of the Pitcher," a strike was now from the hitter's knees to his belt.

But while baseball legislated against pitchers following the 1968 season, relief pitching continued to become a more important part of the game. The trend that had begun in the previous decade grew with each season. Relievers gained more respect, and short relievers, or closers, gained prominence in the game. Successful teams had strong starting pitching, but they also needed a strong stable of relievers to be successful. Although top-of-the-rotation pitchers still completed more games than they didn't, more often than not winning teams dipped into their bullpens.

"Throughout the 1960s, you saw pitchers like Elroy Face of the Pirates who won 18 games, 17 in a row," said Maury Allen. "That really changed the status of relief pitching. In 1969, the Mets had a great staff of starters with Tom Seaver, Jerry Koosman, and Gary Gentry. But they also had a great relief staff with Ron Taylor, Tug McGraw, and Cal Koonce. Relief pitching really developed in the late '60s. In the '70s, all teams had a serious closer.

"In those days they [relievers] were not treated well. In baseball and life, it's all about money. The relief pitchers were not paid what the starting pitchers were paid. As a result, they were second-class citizens. There was a lot of resentment from these pitchers, who could pitch in 60 games and get paid half of what Bob Friend or Vernon Law would be paid. In the '70s they became more important, especially with free agency.

"Baseball was in a financial crisis, and they encouraged home runs. That fabulous pitching year of 1968 when Bob Gibson had a 1.12 ERA caused some changes. They changed the height of the mound, and the umpires were instructed to call more balls than strikes to give the batter more of a chance to hit a home run. The way the teams combated the increase in hitting was to come up with these specialists late in the game to close out. Part of it was also the attention these guys were getting."

Another new wrinkle was the divisional playoffs, which debuted in 1969. Not only did the new playoff system open up the game to a more wide-open postseason with additional teams vying to get into the Fall Classic, but the new system also made it possible for fans to see a greater number of outstanding players perform on the national level. Some of those performers were relievers.

The year 1969 was also when the New York Mets shocked the baseball world by winning the World Series. The game was different, and pitching was certainly different. One of the greatest pitchers in the history of the game, a young Nolan Ryan, pitched out of the bullpen for the Mets, gaining notoriety for his flaming fastball. He was not ultimately to be a reliever, but he was a dominant starting pitcher with multiple no-hitters and was the all-time strikeout leader.

The 1970s saw some outstanding individual statistics from relievers, who not only included closers but also set-up men and teams of relievers who had specific jobs on every successful staff. While relievers saw increasing specialization of the roles they were expected to fill, it was still quite commonplace for the closer on the staff to pitch two or three innings to notch a save and complete a ballgame for his club.

Not all of these new-wave relievers had an unhittable trick pitch or serious cheese that the hitter just couldn't catch up to. But they had a more specialized role that bred success, and success led to more fame, and more fame led to more money. There was still a caste system, and relievers were not exactly equals to the starting pitchers on staff, but their importance on a pitching staff was now undeniable. They were beginning to make their mark, and many of them did it on a national spotlight during the playoffs and World Series.

Darold Knowles

One of the pitchers who made a name for himself out of the bullpen in the 1970s was diminutive left-hander Darold Knowles. Traded in consecutive seasons from Baltimore to Philadelphia to Washington, the solid

81

southpaw was a sought-after entity. His manager with the Phillies in 1966, Gene Mauch, said that he had the courage of a daylight burglar. Pretty good praise from a spunky manager who was not known for giving faint praise to ballplayers, particularly pitchers.

Knowles credits his lone year in Philadelphia as being an enormous help to him later in his career. Those were the days when veteran players took young players under their wing to teach them the way of the game.

"The year I played with the Phillies was my rookie year, so a lot of really important things happened," Knowles said. "Richie Allen was on that team, and when he came up to the plate, everything stopped because everybody wanted to watch him. I played with some great players that year, like Jim Bunning, Dick Groat, Larry Jackson, Bill White, and Chris Short. That was a helluva team for a rookie to break in with, and they all took me under their wing and took care of me.

"Playing with so many great veterans probably helped me a lot later in my career. I was a brash, cocky little guy, which was why I became a closer. These guys helped you know what to do in certain situations and more importantly, what not to do. If I messed up, there were eight guys there to let me know."

Pitching for the lowly Senators after being acquired from Philadelphia, Knowles continued to do a credible job out of the pen. In 1970 he had one of the most fascinating seasons a reliever has ever had. Appearing in 71 games for Washington, he saved 27 games and had a sparkling 2.04 ERA. But his record was 2–14!

Things got better for Knowles following a trade to the Oakland A's. In 1972, his first full season in green, white, and gold, he appeared in 54 games with a 5–1 record, 11 saves, and an incredible 1.37 ERA. He only got better in the World Series the following season when he became the only pitcher to ever appear in all seven games of the Fall Classic, saving two of the A's four wins over the Mets while not allowing an earned run.

Knowles also pitched for the Cubs, Rangers, Expos, and Cardinals during his 16-year career, sporting a 66–74 record with 143 saves and an ERA of 3.12.

Dave Giusti

Right-hander Dave Giusti became a successful starting pitcher with the Houston Astros in the 1960s. He had his best season in 1966 with a 15–14 record and a 4.20 ERA. He followed that with back-to-back 11-win seasons prior to a trade to St. Louis, where he slumped to a 3–7 mark. Traded to Pittsburgh prior to the 1970 season, Giusti became a reliever, and his career was reborn. Sporting a fastball, slider, curve, and palm ball, he went 9–3 in 66 games with 26 saves and a 3.06 ERA.

In 1971 Giusti went 5–6 in 58 games but had a league-leading 30 saves with a 2.93 ERA—good enough to earn him *The Sporting News* National League Fireman of the Year honors. His excellence continued in the League Championship Series against the San Francisco Giants, when he became the first National League hurler to appear in every game of a four-game LCS and saved all three of the Pirates' victories. In the Fall Classic that year, Giusti did not give up a run and earned a save as Pittsburgh upset defending champion Baltimore in seven games.

Giusti finished his 15-year career, which also included stops in Oakland and with the Cubs, with a total of 145 saves.

Mike Marshall

One of the more interesting pitchers of the era was right-hander Mike Marshall, who pitched for Detroit, Seattle, Houston, Montreal, the Dodgers, Atlanta, Minnesota, and the Mets during his 14-year career. He featured a fastball, slider, and an outstanding screwball that made him a very successful pitcher. To say the least, Marshall was a workhorse. He holds the single-season major league record for appearances, with 106 in 1974. But he also had the fifth-busiest season ever in 1973 with 92 outings and the seventh-busiest with 90 games in 1979.

Marshall graduated from Michigan State University with a trio of degrees, including one in kinesiology, the study of the principles of mechanics and anatomy in relation to human movement. As successful as Marshall was on the pitcher's mound, he was equally controversial in the dugout and clubhouse. He was very unpopular with some of his team-mates, who considered him an egomaniacal know-it-all. Or as genial Tim McCarver wrote in his book, *Oh Baby, I Love It,* in 1987, "Pitching in relief for us was Mike Marshall, who specialized in kinesiology and being an asshole."

Asshole or not, Mike Marshall's knowledge of kinesiology allowed him to develop his own training regimen, which enabled him to pitch more often than anyone else in the game. He believed that training certain muscles properly would allow pitchers to go out there just about every day. And he proved his theories correct.

Playing under Gene Mauch in Montreal, Marshall thrived. In 1971 he appeared in 66 games, winning five and saving 23. The following season he pitched in a league-leading 65 games, sporting a 14–8 record with 18 saves. It got only better in 1973 when he earned *The Sporting News* Fireman of the Year honors by once again leading the league with 92 appearances, going 14–11 with 31 saves. But after three straight 65-plus appearance seasons, Mike Marshall had the year of all years in 1974.

Dealt to the Los Angeles Dodgers in exchange for speedy outfielder Willie Davis, Marshall set the all-time record with 106 appearances. He sported a 15–12 record with 21 saves and 208 innings pitched. He won the Fireman of the Year Award as well as the Cy Young Award following the 1974 season.

Injuries affected Marshall over the next few years until he was reunited with the "Little General," Mauch, in Minnesota in 1978. He responded with a 10–12 mark, with 21 saves in 54 games. Then, in 1979, Marshall once again led the league with 90 appearances and 32 saves en route to a 10–15 season. He finished his career with a 97–112 record over 14 seasons with 188 saves.

Rollie Fingers

During the 1970s, when the powerful Oakland A's won five division titles and three World Series, one of the mainstays of that team was reliever Rollie Fingers. Known for his handlebar mustache, which made him resemble a 19th-century player, Fingers was a stalwart of the bullpen who was well on his way to a Hall of Fame career. Not only did Fingers receive that hallowed award, he was also named to the team of baseball's 100 greatest players of the 20th century by *The Sporting News.*

After struggling as a spot starter and reliever for parts of two seasons, Fingers became a full-time reliever during the 1971 season, appearing in 48 games for the A's, all but eight in relief. He responded with a 4–6 record with 17 saves and a 2.99 ERA. He threw a sinking fastball, a slider, and a hard forkball, which resembled today's split-finger fastball.

Rollie Fingers may be best remembered for his handlebar mustache, but the Hall of Famer was the A's bullpen ace during their run of three World Championships (starting in 1972). Late in his career he was the closer on the Brewers' 1982 World Series team.

Come 1972, Rollie Fingers was a steady performer out of the Oakland bullpen, appearing in 65 games with an 11–9 record, 21 saves, and an ERA of 2.51. Unlike the typical closer of today's game, he averaged nearly two innings per appearance. This season also marked the first of three consecutive world championships for the powerful A's of owner Charlie O. Finley. The likes of Fingers, Catfish Hunter, Ken Holtzman, Sal Bando, Joe Rudi, Bert Campaneris, and others were simply too talented for most other teams.

Fingers led the league in appearances in 1974 and 1975, with a combined 19–11 record with 42 saves. In his final season with Oakland in 1976, he won 13 games while saving an additional 20 and maintaining his average of just under two innings pitched per appearance. Taking advantage of the Christmas gift given to the players in December of that year, Fingers became a free agent, signed a deal with the San Diego Padres, and promptly led the National League in appearances with a career-high 78 and saves with 35. The following season he slumped to a 6–13 record but still led the league with a career-high 37 saves and had a fine ERA of 2.52.

Fingers finished his career in 1985 after four seasons with the Milwaukee Brewers. His final record was 114–118 with 341 saves and a lifetime 2.90 ERA in 17 seasons. Fingers was elected to the Baseball Hall of Fame in 1992.

Gene Garber

Gene Garber came up through the Pittsburgh Pirates' farm system and thought of himself as a starting pitcher. But the right-hander with the Luis Tiant-esque corkscrew delivery, in which he turned toward second base before slinging the ball toward the plate, excelled in the role of the reliever. After a few up and down seasons with the Pirates and Kansas City Royals, Garber was dealt to the Phillies in the midseason of 1974.

Prior to his success in Philadelphia, Garber had designs on a spot in the starting rotation of a big-league staff. But that never quite worked out,

Gene Garber's distinctive twisting windup helped make him one of the top closers of the '70s and '80s; he amassed 218 saves in 19 seasons. Many fans remember him as the pitcher who in 1978 ended Pete Rose's 44-game hitting streak with a strikeout.

and he made the best of the situation. It's hard to believe that Gene Garber would have been any more effective as a starting pitcher, because he became one of the best out of the pen.

"I enjoyed both starting and relieving," Garber said. "When I got to the big leagues I considered myself a starter. I only did a little relieving in the minors. When I got to the big leagues, I got put in the bullpen with the Pirates, and that didn't work out so good. I wasn't prepared mentally or physically.

"When I went to Philly—I got sold there in July of '74—Danny Ozark was the manager, and Eddie Watt, who had been a great reliever when the Orioles had all those 20-game winners, was the short reliever. He was in Philly that year and was having problems, and they were looking for some-body else. That August and September, Ozark ran the bullpen different than most managers. Mac Scarce was the left-hander, and I was the right-hander. We were both short relievers. But we might come into the game in the fifth inning. Danny said he had a good offensive club and didn't want to give up the lead in the fifth inning of a game. He wanted to stop the other team's momentum right then, feeling that the fifth inning was as important as the ninth inning. Mac and I worked early as well as late. That's when I really started enjoying short-relief pitching. Short relief back then was the seventh, eighth, and ninth innings. Once I pitched in that role I had no desire to be a starter anymore. I really enjoyed pitch-ing in game situations every day."

Garber was in game situations every day, as he appeared in 34 games with the Phillies during the last half of the 1974 campaign and had a 4–0 record with four saves and a miserly 2.06 ERA. Firmly ensconced in the Phillies' bullpen, the following season saw him partner with newly acquired Tug McGraw to form a great righty-lefty combo. Garber appeared in a league-high and career-high 71 games, in which he won 10 games and saved 14 more while McGraw won 9 and also saved 14.

During his five seasons in Philadelphia, Garber won 33 games and saved 51 more. But one game in particular will be forever etched into the minds of baseball fans in Philadelphia. In Game 3 of the National League Championship Series against the Dodgers on October 7, 1977, he came into the game in the seventh inning to hold the lead. Garber retired the first eight batters he faced and had two outs and two strikes in the ninth inning when Vic Davalillo laid down a perfect bunt for a hit.

Unlike what he had done during most of the regular season, Phils skipper Danny Ozark failed to replace left fielder Greg Luzinski with slick-fielding Jerry Martin. Pinch-hitter Manny Mota then hit a fly ball that bounced off of Luzinski's glove at the wall. The Dodgers eventually won the game. Phillies fans still refer to October 7, 1977, as Black Friday.

"That was one of the strangest games I've ever been in," Garber said. "It was the most memorable game I've ever been in. It was the most fun I've ever had pitching and then the most nightmarish. I got eight hitters out in a row in the seventh, eighth, and ninth, and then, with two strikes, Davalillo laid down a perfect bunt for a hit. People ask me about Mota's hit, but when he hit it I knew the game was over. The ball kept drifting and Bull [Luzinski] went with it, and it hit his glove, but he didn't catch it. That was the only time I ever saw him not catch a ball that hit his glove."

Philadelphia was desperate for more starting pitching in 1978 and dealt Garber to Atlanta for Dick Ruthven. With McGraw, Ron Reed, and Warren Brusstar in the pen, the Phillies rolled the dice. In Atlanta, Garber pitched for parts of 10 seasons, becoming the Braves' leader in career saves with 141, and his 557 games rank him third in team history after Warren Spahn and Phil Niekro.

While with the Braves, Garber was involved in another of the most memorable moments in baseball history, when on August 1, 1978, he ended Pete Rose's 44-game hitting streak. Immediately after the game, Rose complained that Garber pitched him tough, striking him out on a change-up, his best pitch, to end the game and the hitting streak. Baseball's all-time hits leader said that Garber pitched to him like it was the seventh game of the World Series.

"When the Reds came to town, I hoped for an opportunity to stop him," Garber said. "I'd be less than professional if I didn't want to end the streak. Phil Niekro once told me to make every pitch like it was the last pitch I was ever going to make. That really stuck with me, and that's how I pitched Rose. I think any criticism he might have had about my pitching him the way I did may have had something to do with the fact that it was also the final out of the game, and he didn't have much time to compose himself before the postgame interviews began."

Garber retired in 1988 after 19 seasons in the majors with a 96–113 record and 218 saves. He also averaged about an inning and a half per outing, which is at odds with today's game.

Sparky Lyle

One of the most influential pitchers in the 1970s was Al "Sparky" Lyle, who came into prominence after being dealt from the Boston Red Sox to the New York Yankees in exchange for infielder Danny Cater in spring training of 1972. In five seasons with the Bosox, Lyle had a 22–17 record with 69 saves. This trade may not be as bad as the sale of Babe Ruth to the Yankees, but the ramifications of the deal were almost as widely felt. While Ruth revolutionized and quite possibly saved the game of baseball following his sale to New York, Lyle would be a pivotal figure in the way relief pitchers came to be used and viewed. A left-hander in the truest sense of the concept, the clubhouse prankster possessed a good fastball and an outstanding sweeping slider. With his flowing hair, long mustache, and tobacco chew, he went after hitters with a confidence that enabled him to be one of the best ever.

Upon his trade to the Yankees, Lyle, who never made a big-league start, immediately began to pay dividends for the Pinstripes. In 1972 he went 9–5 with a league-leading 35 saves and an ERA of 1.92. Following the trend of the times, Lyle was no one-inning wonder, averaging nearly two innings pitched per appearance. He maintained his mastery in 1973, nabbing 27 saves with an ERA of 2.51.

Lyle continued to pitch well but had a breakout season in 1977 that set him in a league of his own. He appeared in a league- and career-high 72 games and had a 13–5 record, 26 saves, and a 2.26 ERA, pitching 137 innings. He also pitched extremely well in the playoffs and World Series, helping the Yankees defeat the Dodgers in the Fall Classic and becoming the first relief pitcher in the American League to win the Cy Young Award. Although Mike Marshall had won the National League Cy Young Award three years earlier, he was still considered an outcast in many ways. Lyle, on the other hand, was pitching in New York, amid a frenzied media.

"To me, the game really changed dramatically in the middle '70s when they started to really emphasize the one-inning relief pitcher," said Maury Allen. "When Sparky Lyle won the Cy Young Award in 1977, that really changed the game. In 1973 the designated hitter changed the lineup. But that did not change the game, just the lineup. The DH kept guys in the game who could no longer run or play on the field. But the closer role in the '70s with Sparky Lyle, through manager Billy Martin, really did change the game....

"Lyle had a great slider, and in the '70s you saw guys who could throw one unhittable pitch. It could be a blazing 100-mph fastball, a forkball, or a screwball like Tug McGraw had. [Any] kind of an 'out' pitch like that, they made guys into the relievers who came in to get the last outs. Gossage's argument was the relievers used to come into the game in the sixth and seventh inning and finished the game. The big change was that the closer became more important. And they also got the big salaries. Suddenly, guys pitching 80 innings were making as much as guys pitching 250 innings."

But not long after the conclusion of the World Series, the Yankees repaid Lyle for his phenomenal season by signing relievers Rich "Goose" Gossage and Rawley Eastwick. While Eastwick struggled and was eventually shipped off to Philadelphia that June, Gossage fought through some tough times and won over his teammates and the New York fans as the new closer, saving 27 games. Lyle's workload and attitude suffered. He pitched in 59 games and went 9–3 but had just nine saves in 11 attempts.

Lyle was then traded to Texas and also spent parts of three seasons with the Phillies, helping them reach the postseason in their world championship year of 1980, before finishing up with the White Sox in 1982.

Upon his being part of the megadeal that sent him to the Rangers, his former Yankee teammate Craig Nettles told Lyle, "You went from Cy Young to sayonara."

Tug McGraw

Described by some as a flake with a screwball, Frank Edwin "Tug" McGraw is one of the most memorable characters in the history of baseball. The loveable lefty pitched for only two teams during his 19-year career: the New York Mets and the Philadelphia Phillies, and he was fortunate enough to help lead both teams to World Series championships.

McGraw came up with the Mets in 1965 and spent the next few seasons struggling as a starter. But Ralph Terry taught him how to throw a screwball following the 1966 season, and by the time McGraw switched to a relief role in 1969, he had one of the best screwballs in the game. The pitch helped him post a 9–3 record and 12 saves in the team's first championship season, and he became a fan favorite in the Big Apple. He won 11 games in 1971 and then saved 27 the following year and 25 in 1973, when the Mets rallied behind McGraw's "You Gotta Believe" slogan that swept them into the World Series, where they lost to Oakland in seven games.

In his book, *Screwball*, McGraw explained his pitching technique and just how much he used his out pitch.

"Since we're talking about trade secrets, you throw the 'screwjie' maybe a third of the time—at least I do. Mostly I'll throw fastballs. To put it in percentages, maybe 60 percent fastballs, 30 percent screwballs, and 10 percent curveballs. Nowadays I'm trying to break in the curveball more all the time so that I don't actually have to throw the screwball so

Tug McGraw's career numbers aren't as lofty as other elite closers, but few can match his impact on baseball. Colorful, emotional, and a natural leader, he keyed two teams (the Mets and Phillies) to World Series titles during his 19-year career.

much, and save the wear and tear on my arm. What the hell, it's just as effective if they look for the screwball, and I throw the fastball."

Following a subpar campaign in 1974, the Mets made a blockbuster deal that sent McGraw and his screwball to Philadelphia. He became an instant fan favorite and the epitome of a clubhouse prankster. His best season in the City of Brotherly Love was no doubt 1980, when he went 5–4 in 57 games with 20 saves and a fantastic ERA of 1.46. He was the key man out of the Philadelphia bullpen in the World Series against Kansas City, eventually striking out Willie Wilson to bring the title home.

McGraw pitched four more years for the Phillies before retiring in 1984 with a career record of 96–92 with 180 saves.

"Tug was one of my favorite guys I ever spent time with," said his teammate Gene Garber. "He was a lot more squared away than people gave him credit for. He had created this image as a screwball, and he had to live up to the image.

"I don't know of one teammate who didn't like Tug. He was always in a good mood and had lots of confidence. Of course, he also had doubts, like the rest of us. But what a great guy."

After his career ended, McGraw remained a man about town in Philadelphia working for a local television station. Gene Garber was not alone in his feelings about his former teammate.

"He was a wonderful friend," said another former teammate on the 1980 Phillies, pitcher Larry Christenson. "Tug told me that I was his best friend. He was always so friendly, bouncy, and fun. Even if he felt down or upset, he kept it inside. He had such a big heart. My locker was between his and Steve Carlton's. Tug would walk into the locker room on a day he knew I was pitching and would say loud enough for everyone to hear, 'Hey, L.C., are you pitching tonight?' I'd say 'yes' and then he would say, 'Then so am I.'

"He was so good to people, always friendly. He was crazy but a good and charitable person. He was a pitcher who loved competing. He loved to fool the hitters. He was very good. It was all about trickery."

McGraw, the father of country music star Tim McGraw, lost his long struggle with cancer and passed away on January 5, 2004.

Goose Gossage

While Tug McGraw featured the screwball and Sparky Lyle had a big, breaking slider, Rich "Goose" Gossage just reared back and threw the ball through a wall. Unlike tricksters who did everything they could do to fake and outguess the hitter, Gossage threw 100-mph heat and had a snarl to match the velocity. He was as dominating a closer as the game has ever seen, leading the American League in saves on three separate occasions and was second two other times. When he broke into the major leagues in 1972 with the Chicago White Sox, there was little doubt of his ability, but the magnitude of his career was honored in 2008 by his election to the Baseball Hall of Fame.

Goose Gossage was one of the first elite relief pitchers to succeed with sheer power and intimidation, staring down batters and barraging them with his pinpoint fastballs. Unlike today's one-inning closers, he usually pitched the final two or three innings of the game.

After three years with Chicago, Gossage was an average pitcher with an 11–11 record, three saves, and a high earned-run average. Using his blazing fastball, Gossage had a breakout season in 1975 when he went 9–8 for the White Sox, with a league-leading 26 saves and a miserly 1.84 ERA. Converted to primarily a starting role in 1976, Gossage went 9–17. But after the season, he and Terry Forster were traded to Pittsburgh in a move that would forever end Gossage's career as a starter and ultimately lead to his election to Cooperstown.

In 1977 he won 11 and saved 26 games for the Pirates but signed a free-agent deal with the New York Yankees in another career move that gave Gossage the opportunity to perform on the big stage—and there has rarely been a stage larger than the Bronx Zoo. He responded with a 10–11 record with a league-leading 27 saves and a 2.01 ERA, supplanting Sparky Lyle as the Yankees' closer. Goose was also one of those closers who could throw more than a single inning, as his 134 innings in 63 appearances proves.

"It was very different on me to go over to the Yankees," Gossage said. "I came to the Yankees to be part of the best right-handed and left-handed combination of relievers ever. With Sparky having won the Cy Young Award, I envisioned us being the best righty-lefty combo ever. But then they gave me his job on a silver platter, and I stunk the place up for a couple of months and dug us into a hole. We repeated as world champions, but I lost a ballgame in every conceivable way. It was the roughest time I had in the big leagues. I put so much pressure on myself. It didn't work out the way I had planned.

"I enjoyed every team I played on. Putting on the pinstripes was something special because I grew up a Yankee fan out here in Colorado, and I just put too much pressure on myself."

Gossage won a game and saved one in the ALCS and then won a World Series game against the Dodgers, not even surrendering an earned run in six innings pitched. He obviously survived his difficult start and the uncomfortable situation of his predecessor Lyle being banished to the set-up role.

Gossage was one of the most dominant pitchers in the era before the one-inning close. He was not a closer or a specialty guy. He was a relief pitcher. Make no mistake, he takes pride in the role he filled with Hall of Fame competence.

"I'm not a closer; I'm a relief pitcher," he said. "I came in the game in the seventh inning with the bases loaded, got out of the jam, and would pitch the eighth and the ninth. You always have the fear of failure, but you can't be afraid to go out there and fail. You walk that fine line. That one-inning deal is not really it. These guys pitching just one inning have to be durable, but you don't really have to be durable pitching just one inning. It's another example of them being protected.

"I was a ferocious competitor. I had a great fastball. I came into many, many tough situations where you couldn't allow the ball to be put into play. I'd have to get two strikeouts and a pop out and then come out and pitch the eighth and ninth innings. I loved being a workhorse. I loved the innings. It was grueling because every pitch was maximum effort with pressure on every pitch for three innings. I got stronger as the season went on.

"I really take exception when guys talk to me about how guys today are so dominant in one-inning roles. You can't compare us. It's apples and oranges. When you go out there for an inning and then sit back for an [half] inning and then have to go out there and crank it up again, it's a different ballgame than they have today. Don't compare me to these one-inning guys. I take exception to people saying that Mariano [Rivera] is the greatest closer of all time. Don't tell me he's the best relief pitcher of all time until he can do the same job I did. Let him do what I did. He may be the best modern closer, but you have to compare apples with apples. Do what we did."

Gossage obviously has not lost his competitive nature. He was surely one of the best of not just his era but any era in the history of the game. What was it that made him a successful relief pitcher?

"It was a focus I had that you were not going to beat me," he said. "The team had worked hard for six innings, and I was not going to come in and screw up this game. I was not going to blow it. I'm gonna get you out, and we're gonna win this ballgame. I scared myself out there. I would not want to be facing me. What you saw was what you got. It's what happened. The transformation I had from the bullpen into the game was amazing. Bring it on and let's go. I didn't put a lot of thought into who was up. It was my power against theirs. The better you were, the better I was. You have to want that challenge.

"I had tremendous control as a power pitcher. I could throw a ball just about as hard as I wanted to anywhere I wanted to throw it. My ball moved, and people were intimidated by me because I was mean. I kept guys loose. I only drilled three or four guys intentionally in my career. They really deserved it. I had a lot of things going for me out there."

The big right-hander pitched for the Yankees for six seasons, amassing a 41–37 record with 160 saves, including a league-leading 33 in 1980. In his final year with New York in 1983, Gossage went 13–5 with 22 saves and a 2.27 ERA. But he also blew 13 save opportunities, and as his contract with the Yankees expired, he opted to sign a new free-agent deal with the San Diego Padres, where he enjoyed similar success, including his first year on the West Coast in 1984, when he anchored the bullpen with a 10–6 mark with 25 saves and a 2.90 ERA, helping San Diego to its first World Series appearance against the Detroit Tigers.

Gossage finished his 22-year career with 124 wins, 107 losses, 310 saves, and a fine ERA of 3.01. He averaged nearly a strikeout per inning and nearly two innings per appearance. The nine-time All-Star finished his career second in saves to Rollie Fingers (Gossage is currently fourth), ranks third in games pitched with 1,002, third in relief wins with 115 and innings pitched with 1,556⅔, and second in relief strikeouts behind Hoyt Wilhelm with 1,502. He is also the career leader in blown saves with 112, three more than Fingers. But you have to be a great relief pitcher to blow that many saves. Clearly, he saved many, many more than he did not save.

Goose Gossage also pitched in some historical games in his illustrious career. Certainly all baseball fans who followed the game at the time remember the famous (and infamous in Boston) one-game playoff pitting the Yankees against the Boston Red Sox on October 2, 1978. A generation later Yankees shortstop Bucky Dent is still referred to as "Bucky Fucking Dent" in Beantown and Red Sox Nation for his seventh-inning home run against Red Sox starter Mike Torrez. But it was Gossage who came in to protect a 4–2 lead with one out in the last of the seventh inning. Although he allowed two runs in the eighth inning, Gossage held on to preserve the 5–4 victory. The final out of the game came when Gossage induced legendary Red Sox star Carl Yastrzemski to pop out to Graig Nettles with two outs and two runners on base.

On the flip side, Gossage surrendered a three-run homer to George Brett to spark the Royals' sweep of the Yankees in the 1980 ALCS, and it was he who surrendered Brett's controversial two-run homer in the 1983 Pine Tar Game. He played on one World Series winner in 1978 and was also the AL Rolaids Relief Man of the Year that season.

Gossage was elected to the Baseball Hall of Fame in 2008, garnering 86 percent of the votes. The only other relievers in baseball's hallowed hall are Hoyt Wilhelm, Bruce Sutter, Rollie Fingers, and Dennis Eckersley.

"My God, when I got word about being elected to the Hall of Fame I almost passed out," Gossage said. "I waited for nine years. The longer you wait for something, the sweeter it is. To this day, I can't comprehend it. When it came around to the voting, I got a lot of support from a lot of great writers, just not enough for a number of years. I think part of the holdup was that Mariano Rivera and Trevor Hoffman are so dominant now. That really left us in the dust. People have forgotten about what we used to do and how different our jobs were. There is no comparison in terms of what we used to do. Today is easy compared to what we did, but it's still not easy. The times I did a one-inning save, I felt guilty about it. It's like it was too easy. These guys today don't know the difference."

Bruce Sutter

Flamethrowers like Gossage are the exception rather than the rule. Proof of that statement could be the career of another Hall of Fame pitcher, Bruce Sutter. A minor league pitcher with a sore arm, he was taught the split-finger fastball by Cubs pitching instructor Fred Martin in 1973. This was the first time since Elroy Face mastered the forkball in the 1950s and '60s that such a pitch was thrown with such frequency and so much success.

Former pitcher, pitching coach, and manager Roger Craig is usually credited with being the father of the split finger. Although Craig certainly deserves credit for teaching the pitch, Sutter has an interesting angle on the evolution of the pitch. He appreciates what Craig accomplished, but he feels that the real credit lies elsewhere.

"I keep hearing Roger Craig's name associated with the pitch," Sutter told Ron Fimrite in his *Sports Illustrated* article on September 19, 1979, titled "This Pitch in Time Saves Nine." "He has become the guru of the pitch, but I'll tell you what pisses me off about that. I taught Roger Craig the split finger. That still doesn't sit right with me. I understand that he's teaching it, and he's doing a good job with it. Some of the guys he's taught have been very successful. I don't think that just because Fred Martin and I started throwing it that we should have a patent on it or that anybody that wants to learn has got to come to me. Roger is a very qualified coach, but here's how Roger Craig learned the split-finger fastball. He was the pitching coach of the San Diego Padres. In fact, this happened one of those times when the Cubs had Fred up in the major leagues working with me. We were in San Diego playing, and Roger called us over by the batting cage and wanted to know all about the split-finger fastball, how to hold the ball and that crap. So now, when the split finger is mentioned, all you ever hear is Roger Craig.

"When people start talking about the split finger, Fred Martin should get the credit. Roger is doing a good job, and he deserves everything he can get as a major league coach and manager, that's his job. But as far as being the guru of the split finger, that doesn't sit right with me."

Bruce Sutter led the National League in saves for five out of six seasons starting in 1979. The key to his success was the split-finger fastball. He was the first pitcher to effectively use the now-common pitch, and it took him all the way to the Hall of Fame.

No matter who deserves most of the credit for the popularity of the pitch, two facts remain: Sutter brought the pitch into the mainstream of baseball, and he was taught the pitch by Fred Martin. The difference between his split finger and the forkball of prior generations was that the pitch was so difficult for batters to adjust to. He threw the ball with the forkball grip but snapped his wrist as if he were throwing a fastball. As a result, his split finger broke in the same manner that a breaking ball or screwball would.

"Think of the split-finger fastball," wrote Tim McCarver in *Oh, Baby, I Love It!* "The reason it's so effective is that it gives the illusion of a strike. Bruce Sutter almost never threw it for a strike."

After spending parts of five seasons in the Chicago minor league system, Sutter got the call to Wrigley Field in 1976 and responded with a 6–3 season, 10 saves, and a 2.70 ERA. He had the first of his All-Star seasons in 1977, earning 31 saves and going 7–3 with a stunning 1.34 ERA in 62 games. After saving 27 games the following season, Sutter led the league in saves with 37 in 1979 and 28 in 1980. In fact, he won the National League Cy Young Award for his efforts in 1979. In addition to 37 saves, he went 6–6 with a 2.22 ERA in 60 games.

Following the 1980 season, Sutter was traded to the St. Louis Cardinals, who sent Leon Durham, Ken Reitz, and Tye Waller to the Cubs. He didn't miss a beat with the Cards, leading the league in saves in 1981 with 25 and 1982 with 36. He was a member of the world champion Cardinals team that went all the way in '82. Sutter won one World Series game and saved two others.

"He was the Sandy Koufax of relievers," said former St. Louis manager Whitey Herzog.

Sutter played for two more seasons in St. Louis, again leading the league in saves in 1984 with 45 and earning a stellar ERA of 1.54. Coming off such an overpowering season, he was primed to test the free-agent market. He was, for a moment in time, the highest-paid player in baseball when he signed with the Atlanta Braves on December 7, 1984, but opted to have his contract dictate that he was paid $750,000 for six years with the rest going into an insurance fund that would pay him $1 million for 30 years.

Injuries slowed Sutter, who had one good season with the Braves—1985, winning seven games and saving another 23. But in his final two years, he went 3–4 with 17 saves combined. When he retired, Sutter had a career record of 68–71 with 300 saves and a 2.83 ERA in 661 games. In addition to being a six-time All-Star and Cy Young Award winner, he was a four-time Rolaids Relief Man of the Year. He had his number, 42, retired by St. Louis.

In January 2006, Bruce Sutter was elected to the Hall of Fame, receiving 76.9 percent of the vote in his 13th year of eligibility. He was the first pitcher to be elected to Cooperstown who never started a big-league game.

Jeff Reardon

Jeff Reardon broke in with the New York Mets in 1979 and spent parts of three years in New York enjoying some success with a 10–9 record and 10 saves. But his big break came in May 1981 when he was involved in a trade to the Montreal Expos in exchange for heavy-hitting, strong-armed out-fielder Ellis Valentine. Montreal received a dozen red roses in that deal as Reardon became one of the most dominant closers in the game. He went 2–0 with the Expos with six saves following the trade. But in 1982, the bearded, hard-throwing right-hander began a string of 11 consecutive seasons in which he saved at least 20 games, including six seasons with 30-plus saves and three seasons with at least 40 saves.

In 1985 Reardon had a 2–8 record in 63 games but led the league with 41 saves while possessing a respectable ERA of 3.18. Established as one of the best closers in the game while pitching for the struggling Montreal team, Reardon caught the eye of other teams needing that one ingredient to seriously contend for postseason honors. One such team was the Minnesota Twins, a strong club in need of a dominant closer. On

In 1982 Jeff Reardon began an impressive string of 11 consecutive seasons in which he recorded at least 20 saves. After establishing his credentials in Montreal, he moved to the Twins and played a key role in Minnesota's 1987 title run.

February 3, 1987, Montreal traded Reardon and catcher Tom Nieto to the Twins in exchange for pitchers Neal Heaton, Yorkis Perez, and Al Cardwood and catcher Jeff Reed. Reardon proved to be the missing link in Minnesota as he starred for manager Tom Kelly's squad in 1987, appearing in 63 games with an 8–8 record and 31 saves, striking out 83 batters in 80 innings. But more important, Reardon helped the Twins get to the playoffs. In the American League Championship Series against Detroit, he won a game and saved two others. And in the World Series against the Cardinals, he helped Minnesota win its first Fall Classic since the franchise left Washington, with a save and a perfect 0.00 ERA.

Reardon continued to be a dominant closer with the Twins before moving on to Boston in 1990 and then called it quits in 1994 after stops in Atlanta, Cincinnati, and New York with the Yankees. In his 16-year career, Jeff "the Terminator" Reardon pitched in 880 games, all in relief, and sported a 73–77 record with 367 saves and a 3.16 ERA.

John Franco

One of the most dominant closers in the history of the game was lefty John Franco. Breaking in with Cincinnati in 1984, he began his 21-year big-league career by appearing in 54 games, setting up closer Ted Power. The following season, he went 12–3 with 12 saves and used his screwball to keep opposing hitters off balance. The epitome of a competitor, Franco moved into the closer's role in 1986 and won six games, saving 29 more. He led the league with 39 saves in 1988 but struggled the following season, going 4–8 with 32 saves, but he still had a fine 3.12 ERA.

Following the season, a lifetime dream was fulfilled when the Reds traded Franco, a Brooklyn native, to the New York Mets in exchange for another top-flight reliever, Randy Myers. But it was the opportunity to return to his roots that Franco embraced. He had attended Lafayette High School, the same school as the great Sandy Koufax and New York Mets president Fred Wilpon.

Embraced by the fans, Franco certainly got off on the right foot with the Mets in 1990, going 5–3 in 55 games with a league-leading 33 saves and a strong 2.53 ERA. After saving 148 games with the Reds, he continued to dominate with New York. In his stellar career, Franco saved at least 30 games eight times and at least 20 eleven times. He finished his career with a 90–87 record and 424 saves.

When the popular Franco entered a game in New York, it was to the music of the old Chuck Berry song "Johnny B. Goode." More often than not, he was very good. He saved 63 games in his first two seasons in New York. Unlike the many cool competitors who hide their desire to win, Franco wore his heart on his sleeve, showing fierce competitiveness, and was a vocal leader on the team. He talked the talk, but he also walked the walk.

Randy Myers

While the Mets were willing to give him up to get John Franco, Randy Myers was no slouch either. After moving into the closer's role in 1988, Myers was 14–7 with 50 saves over two years.

After two strong seasons closing in New York, Myers was sent to the Reds along with Kip Gross in exchange for Franco and Don Brown.

Upon his arrival in Cincinnati, Myers stepped up in 1990, appearing in 66 games with a 4–6 record and 31 saves with an outstanding 2.08 ERA. Myers joined fellow relievers Rob Dibble and Norm Charlton and collectively became known as "the Nasty Boys," a descriptive nickname for their demeanor. The trio helped Cincinnati to a World Series victory against Oakland. Myers saved one of the Reds' four victories in the Fall Classic, pitching three innings.

For some reason manager Lou Piniella inserted Myers as a spot starter in 1991, but the lefty slumped badly, going 6–13 with six saves and a 3.55 ERA. Myers was traded that off-season to San Diego in exchange for Bip Roberts and Craig Pueschner. (Randy Myers may be the only player in history to have been traded with a Kip and for a Bip.)

He had a good season as a Padre in 1992 with a 3–6 record with 38 saves and a 4.29 ERA, good enough to earn him a free-agent contract with the Cubs. In three years in Chicago, he led the league in saves in 1993 (53) and 1995 (38). Another free-agent signing sent him to Baltimore, where he saved 31 games in 1996 and again led the league in 1997 with 45. Myers pitched for 14 seasons with a 44–63 record but with 347 saves and a 3.19 ERA.

Willie Hernandez

Sometimes a pitcher is almost like a shooting star that appears in the sky, shines brightly, and then sort of fades away. One such player was Guillermo "Willie" Hernandez. Not that Hernandez exactly came out of nowhere. He pitched for the Chicago Cubs for the better part of six seasons. In his first two seasons in Chicago, Hernandez was a combined 16–9 with seven saves in 121 games. But he struggled in 1979, causing the team to attempt to change him to a starting pitcher in 1980. He went 1–9 with a high ERA, and his career was seemingly at an impasse. In fact, he returned to the minor leagues for most of the 1981 season.

He rebounded nicely in 1982, going 4–6 with 10 saves in 75 appearances. After going 1–0 in 11 appearances the following spring, he was traded to Philadelphia. Sixty-three appearances later, Willie Hernandez went 8–4 with the Phillies with seven saves and a fine ERA of 3.29. He then caught the eye of the Detroit Tigers, who needed a left-handed relief specialist. So in March 1984 the Phillies dealt him, along with infielder Dave Bergman, in exchange for outfielder Glenn Wilson and catcher John Wockenfuss.

In Detroit, Hernandez went from being a serviceable relief pitcher to the best in the game. Suddenly his screwball became a lethal weapon that opposing hitters couldn't pick up. He went 9–3 with 32 saves and a miserly 1.92 ERA. Appearing in 80 games, he pitched 140 innings and fanned 112 hitters. In 1984 he copped the American League Most Valuable Player Award, the American League Cy Young Award, and the American League *TSN* Pitcher of the Year.

Led by Hernandez, starters such as Jack Morris, Dan Petry, and Milt Wilcox, and position players that included Kirk Gibson, Lou Whitaker, Alan Trammel, Larry Herndon, and Lance Parrish, the Tigers got off to a blistering start and never looked back—finishing 104–58. They swept the Kansas City Royals in the American League Championship Series and then beat San Diego in the Fall Classic 4–1. Hernandez had two saves in the World Series.

Cy Young and MVP seasons that result in a world championship are difficult acts to follow. Although the Tigers did not have the same success in 1985, Hernandez had another solid season. He went 8–10 with 31 saves in 74 appearances. But unlike 1984, when he blew just one save during the season, 1985 saw him blow nine saves.

He had one more strong season in 1986 with an 8–7 record and 24 saves in 64 games. Hernandez pitched for three more seasons in Detroit before being released in August 1989. In his 13 big-league seasons, Hernandez had a 70–63 record with 147 saves and an ERA of 3.38 in 744 games.

Lee Smith

While Willie Hernandez threw an assortment of pitches to complement his screwball and fool batters, big Lee Smith took a completely different approach—intimidation. He menaced batters before he even threw a pitch. Standing 6'6" and weighing 250 pounds, often grimacing and sweating profusely on the mound, Lee Smith gave not an inch in the battle between pitcher and hitter. He was an intimidating figure on the pitcher's mound, almost seeming to be leaning over the hitter. He played for eight teams during his long career but is probably best remembered for his eight years in Chicago with the Cubs. He sported a 95-mph fastball, slider, cut fastball, and an occasional forkball, which he used as a change-up. But more often than not, Smith was throwing cheese.

Lee Smith held the major league record for career saves from 1993 until 2006, when San Diego's Trevor Hoffman broke his record of 478. But Smith was not a pitcher who was groomed for the bullpen during the early stages of his career. In fact, he was a starter through most of his minor league career, and he had little interest in becoming a reliever. The big right-hander was pitching for the Cubs' Double A team in Midland when his manager, former Cubs catcher Randy Hundley, suggested he move to the bullpen.

"At first it was like a smack in the face to be in the game as a reliever," Smith said. "It's like you weren't good enough to start. I was a starter all through my career. Randy Hundley was my Double A manager and was the first guy to talk to me about being a relief pitcher. I felt like…they thought I wasn't good enough to start, so they had to find a place for me. It was like being a utility player, waiting to play every other week or something.

"When the Cubbies told me that I'd be a reliever, I packed my bags and went home, where I had a basketball scholarship. So many guys jumped on the bandwagon to get me to relieve. But it was Hundley and Bill Williams who talked me into it. I really didn't want to be a reliever. But Billy Williams came to my home and talked to me about coming back. He told me to try this thing. He told me, 'Boy, you ain't done shit. Hell, I got sent back to D ball. Why don't you just give it a try?'

"Once I got into the role, I realized that I had an opportunity to play every day. I had like six starts in the big leagues. If you did do good, then you had to wait. I really enjoyed the role of coming to the ballpark knowing I had a chance to play every day. So the Cubbies sent me a contract, and I went to try relief pitching."

In 1980 at Triple A Wichita, Smith pitched in 50 games with four wins and 15 saves, good enough to earn him a trip to the major leagues for the balance of the season. He appeared in 18 games in Chicago with a 2–0 record.

It took Smith a couple of seasons to get his feet wet with the Cubs, as he was 5–6 with one save combined for 1980 and '81. The following season, Fergie Jenkins returned to Chicago and developed a friendship with Smith that has lasted to today. Jenkins helped Smith with his delivery and arsenal of pitches as well as the art of pitching and setting up hitters.

"I learned a lot from Fergie Jenkins," Smith said. "The only thing in life that he needs to learn is the word *no*. He wears himself out for people. But I wanted to be like Fergie Jenkins. He even got me to wear cowboy boots. Fergie taught me so much about how to handle myself and how to act on and off the field."

Even though he started five games for the Cubs in 1982, Smith relieved in 67 others and saved 17 games while blowing just one save opportunity. He was the Cubs' closer, and that was not about to change anytime soon. The role may not have been what he had planned for in his career, but he was not about to fail. His competitive nature would just not allow that to happen.

In 1983 Smith had a 4–10 record, but he had a league-leading 29 saves and an impressive 1.65 ERA in 66 games. The Cubs made it to the postseason the following year, and Smith continued to dominate National League hitters. He went 9–7 with 33 saves in 69 games. From 1983 through 1987, Smith went 33–40 with 162 saves for Chicago.

"After my 1983 season, I led the league in saves with 29, and I liked the idea of making the All-Star team and all," Smith said. "I liked the idea of more recognition. But I don't have any of the baseballs from my first 50 career saves at least, because I still didn't want to be a relief pitcher. I'd just throw the ball to a kid in the stands after the game ended. I think I really started to get recognition around 1987. I ended up pitching three innings in the All-Star Game and was the winning pitcher. I was the [next to last] dude in and got the win."

Even though his 180 saves as a Cub were a club record, discussion about his weight affecting his knees fueled a trade. In December 1987, the Cubs dealt Smith to the Boston Red Sox in exchange for pitchers Al Nipper and Calvin Schiraldi.

Over the next two seasons in Boston, Smith was a combined 10–6 with 54 saves and a good earned-run average. In May 1990 Smith was sent to St. Louis for outfielder Tom Brunansky. He went 3–4 with 27 saves over the rest of that season before leading the National League in saves in both of the next two seasons with 47 and 43.

After a brief stint with the Yankees at the end of the 1993 season, Smith signed with the Baltimore Orioles where he again led the league in saves, with 33 the following year. The hard-throwing right-hander, who could still bring the ball up to the plate in the upper 90s, saved 37 games for the California Angels in 1995. After that, two brief stints, in Cincinnati and Montreal, saw his illustrious career come to an end.

He wasn't just a guy who went out and tried to throw the ball past hitters. Although he certainly had the ability to do that, he also was a pitcher who used other pitches and his outstanding control to succeed. Smith was a student of the game.

"I'd watch the umpires and see how their strike zone would change," he said. "If you were a pitcher who had good control, you could control the strike zone and hit the paint. When you had control and threw hard, you could expand the strike zone a little. I like to think of myself as a pretty smart pitcher."

Not only was Smith a smart pitcher, but he was an incredible competitor. He was well-versed in the game and knew exactly what he wanted to accomplish. He felt the excitement of the crowd but always tried to stay within himself. It is interesting to learn from Smith the makeup of a prototypical closer.

"I didn't like to lose at anything," he said. "Even when you play with your kids, it's tough to even let your kids win. But that competitiveness in you makes it tough. I try winning at everything I do. I just don't like to lose at anything. As a reliever, you have nine guys against the hitter. My chances of winning were good. You think about hitting. If I face you 100 times, you will make 70 outs if you were really good. I figured if I made good pitches with nine on one, my chances were pretty good. A lot of guys give the hitter too much credit. But I respected them. If I made good pitches, only a micro few were good enough to hit it where guys can't catch it."

One of the great pitching debates in the history of the game is whether a pitcher should pitch to his strength or to the hitter's weakness. So if a particular batter can't hit the curveball a lick and you are a fastball pitcher, what should you throw? Much like his friend Goose Gossage, that was an easy question for Lee Smith to answer.

"I would pitch to my strength," he said. "They'll tell you that guys were good fastball hitters. Well, who wasn't? But you couldn't hit my fastball if I made the pitch where I wanted to make it. Plus I had nine guys on one.

"I'll tell you, the toughest thing for me was pitching at home when you had two strikes on the last hitter. You try to stay within yourself and not overthrow. But you've got the fans cheering and yelling your name, and it's hard not to overthrow. That's why I took a lot of time between pitches. I wanted to get it right the first time. Just make sure that you don't throw a pitch without a purpose. You hear people talk about wasting a pitch. I don't do that. Every pitch had a purpose, and I stayed within myself. I had to do it right the first time. Even if a guy got a hit, as long as it was a pitch I wanted to make, okay. I never wanted to underestimate the hitter. But I didn't give him a whole lot of credit either."

In 18 seasons, Smith went 71–92 with 478 saves and an ERA of 3.03 in 1,022 games with 1,251 strikeouts. While Bruce Sutter, Goose Gossage, and Rollie Fingers have all been elected to the Hall of Fame, Lee Smith still sits on the outside looking in. It is a fact that confounds most baseball experts who saw Lee Smith pitch. If there were ever a relief pitcher, a closer, who deserves to be in the Hall of Fame, it's Lee Arthur Smith.

Dennis Eckersley

Entrance into the Hall of Fame was not a problem for Dennis Eckersley. But the right-handed, side-armed slingshot artist got there not just because of what he accomplished during his career as a reliever. Before making the switch to the bullpen for Tony La Russa's Oakland A's in 1987, Eckersley was an accomplished starter who had a 151–128 record during his 12-year tenure as a starter, including a no-hitter against the California Angels in 1977.

Eckersley became the first of only two pitchers in the history of the game to have both a 20-win season and a 50-save season during his career. Atlanta's John Smoltz is the other.

Blessed with Hollywood good looks, long stylish hair, and a bushy mustache, Eckersley also had a unique delivery that made him recognizable to most baseball fans.

"With a whip-like delivery, he lives on the black, willing to pitch inside but going away when he needs an out," *Bill Mazeroski's Baseball* (1993) says. "Eckersley uses his fastball on right-handed hitters and goes after lefties with his slider. His reputation and quick work give him marginal calls, making batters swing at pitches just off the plate."

Eckersley broke into the major leagues with Cleveland in 1975 after leading the Texas League in wins (with 14) and strikeouts (with 163) in 167 innings. But he had to earn his way into the Indians' starting rotation.

"I made the club in '75 as a reliever," Eckersley said. "Luckily, our manager, Frank Robinson, said that he wanted to bring me up and get my feet wet and see what happens. I had gone only one inning or two, max. Then they made a trade, and I got to pitch against the A's and go nine innings and shut them out. That's crazy. I go from throwing 30 pitches to throwing 100-something. I could have broken my arm, and nobody thought anything of it."

After he became a starter, there was no turning back. He started 24 games and ended the season with a 13–7 mark and a 2.60 ERA, good enough to nab the American League Rookie Pitcher of the Year Award. He again won 13 games the following year and had a 14–13 mark in 1977, including his no-hitter.

Prior to the start of the 1978 season, the Indians dealt Eckersley and catcher Fred Kendall to the Boston Red Sox in exchange for Rick Wise, Mike Paxton, Bo Diaz, and Ted Cox. The side-wheeling righty responded with a 20–8 season for the Bosox, with 16 complete games and three shutouts.

He won 17 games, then 12, 9, and 13 games over the next four seasons and then went 9–13 in 1983. He wasn't quite the overpowering pitcher he had been earlier in his career, and after getting off to a difficult start in 1984, 4–4 with an ERA of 5.01, he was dealt to the Chicago

Cubs in May along with Mike Brumley in exchange for Bill Buckner. Eckersley pitched well with the Cubs, going 10–8 with a 3.03 ERA. He followed that up with an 11–7 season in 1985. But he slumped badly the following season to 6–11 and was traded in April 1987 to Oakland in exchange for outfielder Dave Wilder.

Having lost something off his fastball and having struggled the previous year, A's manager La Russa had a surprise in store for Eckersley. For the first time in his career, he was to be used as a full-time reliever, as a set-up man or long reliever. To say the least, Eckersley was not thrilled with the prospect. But he accepted his new role and was determined to make the most of the opportunity.

"Hey, it was a demotion," he admitted. "I think a lot of it had to do with my accepting it, which helped me be successful. I had to go out there and make something happen and prove myself again. If I was fighting it, I'd be in trouble. The second I had a bad outing, I'd be saying, 'Why are they doing this to me?' Not only was my arm not as strong, but when I started they would stock left-hitting lineups against me, sometimes eight out of nine being left-handed hitters. It was crazy. I had such difficulty with left-handed hitters throwing sidearm, and it became a problem. My velocity was down, and I had to paint [to throw a pitch at the edge of the strike zone, or on the black edge of the plate]. It was tough.

"I just ran out of gas as a starter. If it wasn't for relieving, I don't know what would have happened. I relieved in a game in '87 and pitched six perfect innings out of the bullpen. Then Jay Howell got hurt, and then I went into closing games."

His improved slider and competitive nature, along with the opportunity to move into the closer's role with the injury to Howell, made Eckersley the right man at the right time. He went 6–8 with the A's in 1987 with 16 saves and an ERA of 3.03. One of the most consistent parts of Eckersley's game was his command, the way he could control the baseball. In 115⅔ innings that year, he issued just 17 walks while fanning 113 hitters.

In 1988 he got only better, pitching in 60 games with a 4–2 record, a league-leading 45 saves, and a 2.35 ERA, good enough to earn an All-Star berth as well as the American League Relief Man of the Year. He saved all four of the wins in the American League Championship Series against the Red Sox, and he also saved two of the victorious A's wins in the World Series in the 1989 Fall Classic, which was delayed by an earthquake.

He was a perfect 4–0 the following season in 51 appearances, saving 33 games with a 1.56 ERA, surrendering just three walks in 57⅔ innings. In addition to posting some incredible numbers out of the bullpen, Eckersley became the poster child for the reliever of today. Basically he was just coming into the game for one inning, to get the save in the ninth. While Danny Murtaugh is given credit for creating the closer role with Elroy Face back in the 1960s with Pittsburgh, Eck was the ninth-inning man who would finish out the game for Oakland. Although pitchers such as Lee Smith and Bruce Sutter also closed, it was Eckersley who made it a one-inning art.

"When I came up in '75, there was no such thing as a closer," Eckersley said. "It didn't develop until the mid-'80s, halfway through my career. Early on there was a 10- or 11-man pitching staff. Sometimes guys didn't pitch for two weeks at a time. It was all about complete games. It was a totally different game.

"But it made sense; it's pretty simple. Now you just have to bolster your bullpen. Now you can go out there and dip out there three or four times a week. I could pitch five times in a week just going one inning. At the same time, if you go 2⅔ with your closer, he needs a couple days off. For a guy like Goose Gossage to air it out for three innings, it's tough to recover."

As the new king of the one-inning save, Eckersley needed little time to recover, and so he made a new career for himself out of the bullpen. In 1990, he had an astounding season, going 4–2 with 48 saves and an ERA of 0.61. That's right, 0.61! He walked just four batters in 73 innings. But the most amazing statistic of his season was that he became the only relief pitcher in the history of the game to have more saves (48) than base runners allowed (41 hits and four walks).

He had yet another fantastic campaign in 1992, which earned him the American League Cy Young Award, the American League Most Valuable Player Award, the American League Rolaids Relief Man of the Year Award, and his sixth All-Star berth. In 69 games he sported a 7–1 record with a league-leading 51 saves and an ERA of 1.91.

Eckersley continued to thrive with Oakland through 1995, although his ERA did climb over 4.00. In 1996 he was reunited with his former manager, La Russa, with the St. Louis Cardinals. Although not the same overpowering closer, he was still effective while going a combined 1–11 over two seasons and saving 66 games. He then completed his illustrious career by going 4–1 with Boston in 1998.

He finished his 24-year career with a 197–171 record, 390 saves, a 3.50 ERA, and just 738 walks in nearly 3,300 innings pitched. Dennis Eckersley was elected to the Baseball Hall of Fame in 2004, his first year of eligibility.

Mitch Williams

In the movie *Major League*, Tom Berringer and a ragtag team of misfits bring a season of unexpected success to the Cleveland Indians. One of the most popular players on the team is pitcher Ricky Vaughn, played by Charlie Sheen. An ex-convict, Vaughn is a hard-throwing right-hander who eventually gets Ryne Duren glasses, which helps him to finally see the strike zone. But his early inability to come anywhere near the strike zone earns him the nickname "Wild Thing." Whenever he comes into a ball-game in the movie, that old song plays, and fans serenade their young star by singing the words, "Wild thing, you make my heart sing."

The fictitious right-handed pitcher had a real-life example in a left-handed pitcher who really was the Wild Thing. Mitch Williams spent 11 years in the major leagues and had some ups and downs. He finished with a 45–58 record but also had 192 saves. In 691 innings he fanned 660 hitters. But in true Wild Thing fashion, he also walked 544.

Not blessed with a blazing fastball, he did have a very deceptive motion in which he hid the ball well and was able to fool hitters. But he also regularly had difficulty throwing strikes, which often made his saves a high-wire act. But make no mistake, Mitch Williams had the heart of a champion.

He broke in with the Texas Rangers in 1986, appearing in a league-leading 80 games with an 8–6 record and eight saves. After two more seasons in Texas, Williams was involved in a blockbuster of a trade that sent him, Paul Kilgus, Steve Wilson, Curtis Wilkerson, Luis Benetiz, and Pablo Delgado to the Chicago Cubs in exchange for Rafael Palmeiro, Jamie Moyer, and Drew Hall on December 5, 1988.

In 1989 the Wild Thing appeared in a league-leading 76 games, going 4–4 with 36 saves and a 2.76 ERA. But he stumbled in 1990, going 1–8 with just 16 saves, which was the precursor to another trade that sent him to the Philadelphia Phillies in exchange for Bob Scanlon and Chuck McElroy.

Williams had three outstanding seasons with the Phillies with a combined 20–20 record (including 12–5 in 1991) and 102 saves, including 43 in 1993. His fine season in 1993 helped the Phillies advance to the playoffs against the heavily favored Atlanta Braves. He pitched 5⅓ innings in the National League Championship Series, earning two victories and two saves to help Philadelphia advance to the World Series against Toronto.

That Fall Classic was not kind to Williams or the Phillies. Although he was completely spent following his workhorse regular season and playoffs, he continued to take the ball whenever manager Jim Fregosi called on him. Compounding the issue was ace starter Curt Schilling's unprofessional behavior—showing Williams up when he was in the game by putting a towel over his face.

But what was a very entertaining, back-and-forth series had the Phillies rally and score five runs in the seventh inning to take a 6–5 lead into the last of the ninth inning in Game 6. A Phillies win would have forced a seventh and deciding game. But with one out in the home half of the ninth inning, with two runners on base and a 2–2 count on Joe Carter, Williams surrendered a dramatic World Series–winning, walk-off home run over the left-field wall. Just like that, the Phillies' season was over, and Toronto had won its second consecutive Fall Classic.

"I'm not going to go home and commit suicide," Williams said. "I wish I hadn't thrown it down and in to Carter. I was trying to keep the ball away from him. It was a mistake. It ain't coming back. I can't replay it and win it. I can't change this one, much as I'd like to, if only because my teammates busted their butts. I let them down. But don't expect me to curl up and hide from people because I gave up a home run in the World Series. Life's a bitch. I could be digging ditches. I'm not."

It did seem cruel that, following Mitch Williams' best season and post-season, he and his 1993 season will be judged by the gopher ball he served up to Carter.

Williams was dealt to the Houston Astros that winter and was out of baseball following stints with the Angels and Kansas City after that. Fregosi had nothing but praise for the star-crossed reliever who did everything his manager asked.

"Mitch always wanted the ball," Fregosi said. "He never turned the ball down, and he was always healthy enough to give you everything he had. Mitch is very much a stand-up guy. If he screwed the game up, he said it was his fault. Even after that World Series game. If you look at the game film, he always used a big motion, even with runners on base, and would never slidestep. But he slidestepped on that pitch, trying to keep the runners from getting a big lead.

"We were in a situation where all of our guys had pitched more than they ever did in their lives. Mitch got us there. He was used in save situations. All year long he had got it done for us. He was a good guy. He handled things much better than some of the fans of the Phillies did.

"You very seldom ever see a guy go through the year that [Brad] Lidge did, or [Eric] Gagné did. You just don't see them. There is going to be failure. How you handle the failure makes you a good pitcher or not a good pitcher."

Had there been a game the next night, Williams would have asked for the ball in a save situation or whenever his manager needed him. He handled what must have been a heartbreaking and devastating event: surrendering a walk-off, World Series–winning home run. But he was available to reporters afterward and took the blame for what happened. He made no excuses. And that is what earned him the respect of his teammates and his manager.

"The way I looked at it, I was never going to be a hero," Williams said in a *Baseball Digest* interview in February 2001. "You have no chance to be a hero when you're a closer. If you come into somebody else's game with the bases loaded and nobody out, you only get one chance. If I'd got three outs in that game, there would be no mention of me pitching in the World Series."

Dave Smith

The best relief pitcher in the history of the Houston Astros franchise was right-hander Dave Smith. A real battler with a great forkball to augment his other pitches, Smith was a member of the Astros from 1980 to 1990. When he first joined the team in 1980, he teamed with lefty Joe Sambito and Frank LaCorte to form one of the most consistent bullpens in baseball. In one six-year stretch, from 1985 through 1990, he never saved fewer than 23 games, and he had a career-high 33 in 1986.

Smith pitched his last two seasons with the Chicago Cubs in 1991 and 1992. But he remains Houston's career leader in games (562), saves (199), relief wins (53), relief innings (760), and games finished (400). He concluded his 13-year career with a 53–53 record, 216 saves, and a 2.67 ERA. One of the most popular players in the Houston franchise, who was known for his generosity and friendly nature, Dave Smith passed away of a heart attack at the age of 53 on December 17, 2008.

Tom Henke

After spending parts of three seasons trying to get an opportunity to pitch with the Texas Rangers, going 3–1 with three saves, Tom Henke was acquired by the Toronto Blue Jays as compensation for having lost slugger Cliff Johnson to free agency. He started the 1985 season with the Blue Jays' Triple A team in Syracuse but was recalled after making 39 minor league appearances. The big, bespectacled right-hander made quite a splash north of the border, going 3–3 in 28 games with 13 saves and a 2.02 ERA. At 6'5", Henke was an imposing figure on the mound. He became even more so when a hitter took into consideration his 95-mph fastball and outstanding forkball. In fact, he struck out nearly 10 batters for every nine innings pitched.

Henke appeared in 63 games in 1986, posting a 9–5 record and what was a team record of 27 saves and an ERA of 3.35. Although the 1987 season saw his record dip to 0–6, he led the league with 34 saves and a fine 2.49 ERA. Known as "the Terminator," Tom Henke accumulated 247 saves during his eight seasons in Toronto, helping the Blue Jays win the World Series in 1992.

After returning to Texas in 1993, he won five and saved 40 more games for the Rangers. Following another year with the Rangers, Henke pitched one season in the Senior Circuit in 1995 with St. Louis, going 1–1 with 36 saves and a stellar 1.82 ERA, good enough to earn him the National League Rolaids Relief Man of the Year Award.

Surprisingly, Henke retired from the game after that season, although, at 38, he may have had lots of good baseball left in him. He had a 41–42 record in his 14-year career with 311 saves and a 2.67 ERA.

Rick Aguilera

One of the better pitchers of his era was right-hander Rick Aguilera. While he wasn't blessed with a blazing fastball, he had good enough stuff and a dipping forkball, or splitter, to fool hitters for 16 seasons. Originally a starter when he first came up with the New York Mets in 1985, he had consecutive 10–7 seasons followed by an 11–3 record in 1987. His ability to learn new pitches really helped him become an outstanding pitcher.

"Rick Aguilera's fastball is light and in the strike zone, and batters teed off on it when it was his only pitch," wrote Tim McCarver in his book *Baseball for Brain Surgeons and Other Fans*. "He became a great reliever when he added the splitter to the fastball. His splitter is so good he gets away with a so-so fastball."

Following a trade to the Minnesota Twins in July 1989, he became a full-time reliever in 1990. The results were pretty dramatic, as Aguilera responded with a 5–3 record in 56 games with 32 saves and a 2.76 ERA. The following season, 1991, he went 4–5 with 42 saves to help the Twins get into the playoffs, where he saved five more games to help manager Tom Kelly lead Minnesota to a World Series championship. Not only did he win one game and save two others in the Series against the Atlanta Braves, he became the first pitcher since Don Drysdale of the Los Angeles Dodgers to be used as a pinch-hitter in the World Series.

"He might not knock your eyes out, but he has three above-average pitches [fastball, slider, forkball] and can use any of them to finish off a batter," the *Scouting Report* wrote about Aguilera in 1990.

Aguilera never led the league in games, wins, or saves, but his consistency was uncanny. In nine years with the Twins he accumulated 254 saves, including 42 in 1991, 41 in 1992, 34 in 1993, and 38 in 1998.

Rick Aguilera pitched for 16 seasons in the major leagues, compiling an 86–81 record with 318 saves and an ERA of 3.57.

* * *

A change was taking place that was reshaping baseball. More and more interest, impact, and strategy was now focused on the bullpen. Although starting pitchers had been the key members of the pitching staff in the late 1970s and early '80s, the bullpen became the most important—and interesting—strategic part of the game. Even in the American League, with the designated hitter, the bullpen became a focal point thanks to the increased prevalence of pitch counts and the increasing number of really good relievers.

"The prominence of relief pitchers is arguably the biggest change in pitching since 1872, when the rulesmakers decided that pitchers would be allowed to snap their wrists," wrote George F. Will in his book, *Bunts*. "Real pitching began then, and the profession of pitching did not change all that much until after the Second World War, then relief pitching became a recognized job description. Before that, although complete games were much more common than they are now, many pitchers—often starting pitchers—appeared in relief. And a few were relief specialists. Today relief pitching includes two kinds of specialists: 'set-up' men who are bridges between starting pitchers and closers, and 'closers' who usually come into games in the ninth inning in 'save' situations."

It's a different game from just a generation ago. Relief pitchers have gone from the outhouse to the penthouse, getting glory, All-Star berths, specialized roles, and big-time salaries. Managing relief pitching is probably the most strategic part of the game. It took relievers a long time to gain respect, but substantiating their value, determining whether or not they were doing a good job, was not something that just wins and losses and ERA could prove. Something was missing. A new statistic was needed to show the value of these late-inning guardians.

CHAPTER 7

The Save: Giving Value to the Role

Seemingly countless times in the previous six chapters, the statistic of the save has been mentioned. As America's Game moved forward, and as the value of relief pitching increased, there needed to be a measure to rate those who replaced starting pitchers and protected leads. Although Elroy Face did win 18 games, the chance of a reliever winning 20 games is remote. No reliever will pitch 250 innings, throw a shutout, or lead the league in strikeouts.

The idea of the save seems to represent simplistic logic at its best. Give a pitcher credit for saving a win if he has protected the lead when the game ends. There have been different save rules throughout the years, but an interesting realization is that even though pitchers have been given credit for saves, the statistic never even existed until 1960, and it did not become an official baseball stat until 1969. So any saves that pitchers have on their records prior to 1969 were awarded retroactively and, in most cases, posthumously.

The idea of the save came into being in 1960 after the World Series performance of Los Angeles Dodgers closer Larry Sherry in the '59 Fall Classic. The big right-hander finished all four Dodger wins. He won two of the games himself and "saved" the other two.

A writer for *The Sporting News*, *Chicago Sun-Times*, and *Chicago Tribune*, the late Jerome Holtzman, came up with a new way to ultimately measure the quality of the work of the relief pitcher closing the game: the save.

"I invented the first formula for saves in 1960, in my fourth season as a baseball beat writer," Holtzman wrote in the May 2002 edition of *Baseball Digest*, in an article titled, "Where Did the Save Rule Come From? Baseball Historian Recalls How He Developed Statistic That Measures Relievers' Effectiveness." "At that time there were only two stats to measure the effectiveness of a reliever: earned-run average and the win-loss record. Neither was an appropriate measure of a reliever's effectiveness.

"The ERA wasn't a good index because many of the runs scored off a reliever are charged to the previous pitcher; the reliever's ERA should be at least one run less than a starter. The W-L record was equally meaningless; the reliever, particularly the closer, is supposed to protect a lead, not win the game.

"Initially, to earn a save the reliever had to come in with the tying or winning run on base or at the plate and finish the game with the lead. The following season, the degree of difficulty lessened; a two-run lead was sufficient.

"It was baseball's first new major statistic since the run batted in was added in 1920. I knew it was a significant advance but never realized it would escalate to the current proportions. Also, it didn't occur to me that the managers would twist the rule and summon only their best reliever in save situations."

The term *save* is used to indicate the successful maintenance of a lead by a relief pitcher, who is normally the closer, until the end of the game. According to Rule 10.19 of the *Rules of Baseball*, a pitcher earns a save when all four of the following conditions are met: First, he is the finishing pitcher in a game won by his team. Second, he is not the winning pitcher. Third, he is credited with at least a third of an inning pitched. And lastly, he must also satisfy one of the following conditions: a) he enters the game with a lead of no more than three runs and pitches for at least one inning; b) he enters the game, regardless of the count on the hitter, with the potential tying run either on base, at bat, or on deck; or c) he pitches for at least three innings.

Although Holtzman is credited with being the inventor or father of the save, he was nevertheless willing to share some of the honor. In an interview conducted by Bill Deane, Holtzman credits three other people who were tracking saves before he came along: Irving Kaze at Pittsburgh, Jim Toomey at St. Louis, and Allan Roth at Brooklyn. Those three gentlemen suggested that all a pitcher needed to do to earn a save was to finish a winning game. But Holtzman refined the idea and created the basics of the formula to earn a save that was taken from the *Rules of Baseball* mentioned earlier.

When *The Sporting News'* publisher, J.G. Taylor, hired Holtzman to keep track of relievers and saves, the result was that publication awarding the Fireman of the Year Award to the pitcher with the highest combined total of wins and saves in each league. Much like the save rule itself, which has endured some changes since its inception, the Fireman Award has changed as well. The award is now decided by a consensus of *The Sporting News'* editors.

Although saves have been tracked since the 1960 season, they became a formal major league statistic in 1969. Ironically, the first official save was credited to a pitcher who was much better known as a starter, Bill Singer, of the Los Angeles Dodgers. On Opening Day, April 7, 1969, Singer replaced starter Don Drysdale in the seventh inning of a contest that the Dodgers led over Cincinnati 3–2. All Singer did was shut down the Reds over the final three innings, pitching hitless ball and allowing just one walk. Singer won 118 games during his career. He saved two games in his 14 years in the major leagues. Who would have thought that he would be the pitcher to earn the very first official save in major league history?

Some of the great relief pitchers mentioned previously were credited for saves after their careers ended. But this new statistic gave relief pitchers something to point to that spoke to their performance on the job at pressure-filled moments. The relief pitcher had grown in stature from a guy who wasn't good enough to start. Today, a reliever in general, and a closer in particular, had a real sense of value to a team.

Over time the definition of a save has changed. At one point, a relief pitcher could earn a save by simply finishing a game that his team won. But when Ron Taylor of the New York Mets earned a save in a 20–6 win over the Atlanta Braves, it was obvious that the qualifications to earn a save needed to be adjusted.

"The original save rule was deemed too soft," said Bill Deane, "and it was revised accordingly in 1973. The revised rule was then judged too demanding and changed again in 1975. The current rule credits a save to a pitcher who finishes another's victory, meeting one of three criteria: pitching effectively for at least three innings, holding a lead of no more than three runs for an inning or more, or entering a game with the potential tying run either on base, at bat, or on deck."

It was after saves were awarded in such instances as the Ron Taylor save that the baseball establishment augmented the rule about the tying or winning run being on base, at bat, or on deck came into play. It took a while to refine to its current state, but today baseball has a statistic that seems to adequately gauge the effectiveness of a closer. Because the saves that were awarded retroactively used less stringent qualifications, the number of saves "earned" by pitchers in bygone eras might not qualify under today's rules. But the idea of giving more credit to hurlers coming in out of the bullpen had gained momentum enough to cause baseball to make the save an official statistic and to give closers of generations past a wide berth in accumulating saves. In the words of the television commercial of the 1970s, "You've come a long way, baby!"

"Several years ago, when Johnny Oates was managing the Baltimore Orioles, he discovered I had originated the save," Holtzman wrote in *Baseball Digest*. "'You changed the game,' Oates said. 'You created the ninth-inning pitcher.'

"I told him it was the managers who did it, not me. Instead of bringing in their best reliever when the game was on the line, in the seventh or eighth inning, which had been the practice in the past, they saved him for the ninth. The late Dick Howser and Tony La Russa were mostly responsible for this change in strategy."

Certainly, the perfect Brad Lidge season of 2008, when he converted 41 of 41 save opportunities during the season and an additional seven more in the playoffs and World Series, is an aberration. Closers simply don't have perfect seasons like that. But they do save a high percentage of their opportunities, because if they don't they'll be replaced by a new closer, and they'll become the team's mop-up pitcher. So as a result, another important statistic to consider when grading a closer is the BS (blown save). A blown save is charged to a reliever who comes into a game in a save situation with the opportunity to earn a save but instead allows the tying run to score.

When it comes to saves, there is little room for error. If the tying run is scored by a runner who got on base when a previous pitcher was in the game, the new pitcher is charged with a blown save, but the run that scored is not charged to his record because he didn't allow the runner to get on base. The previous pitcher who gave up the hit or walk is charged with the run because it was he who allowed the runner to reach base.

To take the scenario a step further, should a reliever blow the save and not only allow the other team to tie the score but to also go ahead and win the game, the pitcher is charged with both a blown save and the loss. The key to being the losing pitcher is that you have to have been the pitcher who allowed the eventual winning run to get on base.

Elroy Face explained earlier that some people actually accused him of the preposterous notion of giving up runs so he could then become the winning pitcher when his powerful Pirates teammates scored deciding runs late in games. When it comes to saving games, a pitcher can't create his own save situation. So if he comes into a game with more than a three-run advantage, he could not earn a save by giving up enough runs to get within that three-run save area. If it's not a save situation when a pitcher enters the game, he cannot earn a save by making the score closer.

However, if a pitcher comes into a game in a save situation, say with his team leading 7–4, if his teammates score five runs to make it a 12–4 game, he can still earn a save because he entered the game in a save situation. If it's 7–4, and he comes in and gets out of a bases-loaded jam in the eighth inning, it doesn't matter if his club scores five runs in the top of the ninth. Even though the game evolved into a nonsave score, the fact that the pitcher met the criteria to earn a save in the previous inning makes it a save. But if the score were 7–4, and the team scored five runs in the top of the ninth inning to make it 12–4, should a reliever come in to pitch the bottom of the ninth only, he would not earn a save.

In 2007 an interesting happening played itself out when Texas faced Baltimore on August 22. Texas reliever Wes Littleton came into the contest with his Rangers leading 14–3, well above the three-run maximum. But Littleton pitched the final three innings of the game to earn a save. Not only that, but while he was pitching, his Ranger teammates added 16 more runs. Even though the final score was 30–3, Littleton got credit for a save by the rules of the game because he pitched at least three innings and did not surrender the tying or winning run.

Although saves are one of the most important statistics in the game today and an official baseball stat, the blown save is not as yet part of any official record keeping. But you can rest assured that whenever the closer of your favorite team comes into a game in a save situation, that his save/blown save comparison (for instance, 12 of 14—only two blown saves) will be discussed by the game's announcers, written about by newspaper beat writers, and discussed around water coolers in offices all around the area.

"Relief pitching as a strategy has undergone a long evolutionary process, which continues to this day," said Bill Deane. "In 1882, the first year of two major leagues, pitchers recorded 1,080 complete games, as compared to just two saves—a ratio of 540 to 1. By 1900, there were just

78 complete games for every save. That number was down to 14 by 1910, 10 by 1920, and five by 1930. It was not until the 1980s that saves regularly outnumbered complete games. By 1995, there were nearly four saves per complete game. And keep in mind that there are twice as many opportunities [winning and losing] for complete games as saves."

For a statistic that has been part of the baseball landscape for a relatively short period of time, considering the long history of the game, the save has revolutionized the way that relief pitchers are graded. As the role of the relief pitcher and the short reliever (or in today's game, the closer), has grown, saves and blown saves have become a fair and equitable manner in which to gauge the effectiveness of these late-inning game enders.

CHAPTER 8

The One-Inning Save

Whether a starting pitcher relieving between starts, a spot starter coming in out of the pen, a former starter holding on as a reliever, or a new one-inning closer who has been trained for the role since high school, a pitcher who holds a lead in the ninth inning is a different animal. The first 24 outs are tough, the next two are tougher, but getting that elusive 27th and final out is the toughest one of the game. Many pitchers can start and give a team six strong innings. The set-up men have a vitally important job in today's game, and there are countless examples of hurlers who have carved out a career niche for themselves in that role. But having the ability to close, to get the final out of a ballgame—with your teammates living and dying with your success or failure in that role—takes a special breed.

An out is an out, but ending the game has separated the men from the boys for years in America's Game. Guys can come in out of the pen and look like world beaters in the seventh and eighth innings. They've got backup. But get them on the pitcher's mound in the ninth inning of a one-run game with everything on the line, and it's a whole new ballgame. They start to hear the crowd. They sweat a little more. They squeeze the baseball so hard they could seemingly alter its shape. Ninth-inning madness is a creature that only a select handful of hurlers can handle.

There is always pressure to perform. But that pressure is magnified in the final inning. A mistake in the first eight innings can be rectified. To use a hockey parallel, set-up men are like defensemen. If they make a mistake, they have backup—the goalie. But in the ninth inning, a pitcher is like a hockey goaltender—the last line of defense. The crowd seems a little louder, the hitters seem a little better, the strike zone seems a little smaller, and that lump in your throat is ready to choke you. If you blow it, a red light doesn't go on behind you like an NHL net minder, but everyone knows you blew it anyway. Especially you.

You have to want to be there, and you need to be able to handle whatever happens. Not everyone has that ability. And how you handle failure is a key ingredient in whether or not you have the right stuff to close.

"When everything about winning the game falls on their shoulders, it's a difficult thing," said Jim Fregosi. "As a closer, you need to have a certain makeup to handle the success and the failure. You have to have a very tough inside to be able to handle that role. They can put too much pressure on themselves. If they do the job, that's what they're supposed to do. If they blow a game, they feel like they alone blew it. You have to come back the next day in the same role and not let the newspaper interfere with your job. A closer needs to have a short memory."

Some position players pray that the ball will not be hit to them in a pressure-filled, game-on-the-line situation. But others want the ball hit to them because they know beyond a shadow of a doubt that they are capable of making the plays, pressure or not. They trust themselves to perform more than they trust the guy next to them. That is the same personality type as a closer. They don't want to read about a hurricane in the newspaper; they want to be in the eye of the storm.

"If you're going to be a closer, you have to want to be the guy who is called on in those situations," said pitcher Gene Garber. "You need to have the feeling that if your team wins or loses, it's because of you. You are the best man in that situation. I felt my team had the best opportunity to win if I was on the mound. Every short reliever has to have that feeling. If you don't have that feeling, you are not going to be successful."

Relief pitching isn't rocket science. You need to have the right frame of mind, but it also helps to be able to throw strikes. After all, the old baseball axiom holds true. The best pitch in baseball is strike one. Falling behind in the count in the earlier innings can be problematic, although you can get past it. But pitching back in the count and walking batters for a closer can be downright fatal.

"You need to throw strikes," said Elroy Face. "You need to have control and confidence. You have eight guys out there on the field to help you. The batter has no one to help him. Throw strikes and let him hit the ball.

"Everybody would say that they thought that I was cocky because of the way I went into the game. When I walked in I had confidence. I wasn't cocky. I just believed in myself. I used to sit in the bullpen during the game, and there would be situations where I'd hope a guy would get a hit so I could come in to the game. I loved the challenge. My career developed the closer's role."

No matter whom you talk to about what makes a relief pitcher great, with the ability to close games, they all seem to agree that it is the mental aspect of the game that is the most important. You make good pitches and you make bad pitches. Sometimes the hitter swings through the ball that slipped out of your hand. Other times you can make what you consider the perfect pitch, and the hitter gets a little dink single, or a Texas League hit. But at the end of the day, the closer needs to stay focused and stay confident, because that all eventually evens out. That's baseball.

The tough thing is that a closer can lose a game through no fault of his own. But he can also totally blow it all on his own. While his teammates have toiled for the better part of three hours to get him the lead he's been entrusted with, he can blow the team effort with one good, bad, or indifferent pitch. That can weigh on the mind.

"You hear more about the blown save now," said relief pitcher Lee Smith. "People don't understand how tough relief pitching is. You get more press if you give it up than if you succeed because you are supposed to get the save.

"It's a mental thing. Most of the guys when they get to the big leagues have the makeup stuff wise, or physically. But the mental thing is the next thing. You might give up a home run, but you have to want to be out there the next day. You want to be there. You can't second-guess yourself because it will only snowball. You can't be tentative. During my career I had pitching coaches who wanted to call my pitches for me. I felt the confidence in myself to make those decisions. If you call for a fastball, and I want to throw a slider, my heart really isn't in the fastball on that pitch. The main thing with me was that I knew that my arm could come back from day to day. A guy like Curt Schilling could not be a closer because he couldn't pitch day after day after day.

"You need to have a short memory. If you are out there and closing and you are a sensitive person, you won't last long. So many guys like the prestige of getting the save. But in order to get the save, you have to risk getting a blown save. I always think of the mental aspect. I prepared. People would say I was napping in the clubhouse before a game, but I was relaxing and watching the umpires. I'd sit on the bench during hitting and would watch the other team's batting practice. To learn you had to watch the new guys and the young guys who would come up to bat against you.

"The one thing that used to get me was that you were a better interview when you gave it up. That really drove me nuts. It's like, man, I got my ass kicked out there today. But I'll be back tomorrow. I had a short memory."

It's tough out there 60 feet, 6 inches from the batter. An athlete's psyche can be a delicate subject. So much is involved when trying to get the final outs of a game. The proper mind-set is paramount. The guys who go through it know the score. But the guys who get the pitchers to close games have to know the score as well. They are betting their careers on personnel decisions they make. Talk about Russian roulette. Executives, managers, and pitching coaches are risking their jobs on a pitcher's ability to get the last out. It's no wonder that teams do an incredible amount of due diligence before committing to a particular player or consummating a trade.

"It's all mental," said Pat Gillick of closers. "The mental approach when you go to the mound is what's most important. And basically, it's the ability to, no matter whatever stuff you've got, to locate the ball and throw it over the plate and let happen what happens. If it's positive, that's fine. If it's negative, that's fine too. Just forget about Saturday because you have to look forward to Sunday and Monday. Challenge the guys. Here is my best, and you try to hit it. If you locate the ball, you will be successful. If not, put a bad outing behind you."

No matter what your strength as a pitcher, be it great control, an unhittable out pitch, or flat-out heat, you have to be comfortable in your own skin and confident in your ability. You need to believe that, all things being equal, you will get the hitter out. If you sit in the bullpen and fret over the possibility of getting into a game situation, you are not long for the job. You need ability and confidence. You also need to have fun with it.

In the great baseball movie *Bull Durham*, Kevin Costner's character, Crash Davis, tells young hurler Nuke LaLoosh as he leaves for the major leagues that the secret to big-league success is to approach the game with "fear and arrogance." Not bad advice.

"You have to enjoy the situation," said Gene Garber. "I always felt like I was at my best when things were the toughest, when I had something to pitch for. I wasn't a real good pitcher with a five-run lead, but I did pretty well with a one- or two-run lead. These guys are pitching a very tough role in a tie game or a game where you have a one-run lead. If you can pitch successfully in those situations, you know you've only got one thing to do and that's not give up a run.

"I think it's different for every individual. Some guys are so tremendous from a command standpoint, like Mariano Rivera. The command that he has, let alone that he's throwing 96 mph, is incredible. A pitcher needs three things to succeed: the command, the control, and the movement. If it's not velocity as in speed, it could be velocity in a lack of speed. Guys who can throw 98 mph don't have to have the great command because velocity will take care of them. If you don't have great velocity, you need a lot better control, or movement, or a combination of both. You've gotta have one or two of those—a really hard thrower, or have a tremendous change-up or curveball, or exceptional command with a pitch that moves really well. One of the three must be outstanding."

The changes that occurred back in the late 1950s and early 1960s with pitchers such as Wilhelm, Face, Arroyo, and Baldschun are still a big part of every major league bullpen. These guys revolutionized the game by bringing nearly unhittable trick pitches into the equation that, quite frankly, were not there before. Unlike their predecessors, who were in many respects washed-up starters, they began a whole new generation of pitchers who brought something different to the dance. Hitters faced a talented starter for the first seven innings or so, and then they'd have to deal with a completely different animal. Before the reliever appeared in the modern game, players faced a new pitcher who threw pretty much the same stuff as the starter, only in many cases his repertoire wasn't as good as the starter's.

Although the various roles of the pitching staff are the rule rather than the exception now, a generation ago roles were not as clear. But that's not to say that relievers didn't know what was expected of them. Most of them pitched for more than one inning, but all of them knew what their job was. Whether they came in with ungodly heat, a specialty pitch, or just guile based on years of experience, they knew the challenge, and they answered the call.

"I played against guys like Rollie Fingers, Dennis Eckersley, Lee Smith, Tug McGraw, and 'the Mad Hungarian,' Al Hrabosky," said Fergie Jenkins. "I think that certain individuals know their roles better than

After more than a decade as a top-flight starter, Dennis Eckersley found himself banished to the bullpen with the A's. But he took advantage of the switch and transformed himself into one of the best one-inning closers of all time, recording 390 saves along the way.

others. They go out there and fulfill that role. I think it's a mind-set. Bruce Sutter, Smith, Goose Gossage, and Eck all had it. When you are out there you know the game is on the line, and it's your job to close off that part of the game. If you become a weak relief pitcher, you won't be out there too long.

"You have to have a short memory. You can't dwell on what happened before. Every game is different, every team is new, every series is different. I get paid to stop that ballclub that day. If you fail one day, you have tomorrow. This is what the team relies on you to do. You are the backbone of the team. You have to close the game off.

"A lot of guys I've seen have one dominant pitch. But you need a set-up pitch too. Eck had the hard slider. Lee Smith and Sutter all had one pitch. But what they really do more is have grit. Regardless of the situation, they go out there to get you out. That's what the game was all about. Now it's different. There is a new relief corps now."

There is a whole group of pitchers in the bullpen now, sometimes numbering as many as eight or even nine. But no matter how many pitchers are in the pen, the ones who have the ability to close a game have that something special that enables them to handle the pressure, step up, and succeed. They are all different, but in some ways they are all the same. No matter what they throw, the results aren't logical or predictable.

Some can break a radar gun, and others can just break a hitter's heart with pitches that dip, slurve, and hop over the plate while somehow avoiding the bat. They can totally fool a hitter and see him hit a Texas League blooper to bring in a pair of runs. No matter, they are out there again the next night. Or they can come into the game and strike out the side and look unbeatable. No matter, they are out there again the next night.

"The best closers are either overpowering or have a trick pitch," said Chris Wheeler. "The key for late-inning guys is strikeouts. To me, the best guys are the guys who strike people out. Not even so much ground balls anymore. That was especially true back with all the turf fields. The Kent Tekulves of the world, there weren't many of them. Guys need either trick pitches or heat. Some of the greats are strikeout guys like Gossage and Sutter. Nothing happens when they come in the game. All these great closers all have way over strikeouts per innings than innings pitched. Mariano Rivera? He's a freak. He gets his strikeouts, but the contact that is made, when it's made, is so weak because of the movement on his cutter. They just don't hit it hard. Even when he got beat in the World Series, he got beat with a blooper with the infield drawn in. He is just different. He's not a strikeout guy; he's a contact guy. But it's bad contact. It's a dud.

"He may be the greatest of all time, but he doesn't fit the bill in the typical way. Nothing happens when he comes in but for different reasons. That cutter he has learned to control. He can throw it for a strike, and it's in on your thumbs before you know it. Hitters will tell you that they can't see the spin on the ball.

"But no matter what, when save situations come up, they want to be in the game. If they are not used that way, I've heard of their agents calling the team and saying to 'get my guy in the game for saves. If you don't, how am I going to get him a long-term deal?' He might have to move to a different team."

While Mariano Rivera might arguably be the best in the game today, one of his predecessors may have been the best before him. Dennis Eckersley was elected to the Hall of Fame because he combined two careers. He was an outstanding starter who won 20 games and threw a no-hitter. Then he became the quintessential one-inning closer.

Make no mistake. He wanted to be out there with the game on the line.

"I loved the adrenaline," Eckersley said. "It was incredible. You have to calm down to get into it. As a reliever, you are sky high. That never changed. I loved it. But when I was doing it, it was frightening. It's like a drug, and you never know how it will affect you. It's hard to key down. I wasn't a 100-mph guy, but when you get so keyed up, you overthrow.

"So I'm trying to blow a guy away rather than paint. But when the combination worked, I could bring it and paint at the same time. Managing that adrenaline is the most difficult part of the job.

"It took a couple of years. When I first got to the bullpen, I thought you had to go as hard as you can. But I learned that's not the case. Ninety percent is better than 100 percent. I learned that you don't have to throw the ball as hard as you can. After that, I learned to spot the ball. I fought that my whole career because I was so into velocity. I was fixated with throwing the ball hard. It was all about the radar gun. You know, not all stadiums had them in those days, but at a place that did, you'd always look at the gun.

"Until the day I quit, I was velocity oriented. It was all about how hard I was throwing. My 92 mph from the side is a lot hotter than someone right over the top that you can see all the way. I think that gun is full of shit because everybody throws 95."

Eckersley also has the special perspective that so many pitchers from past generations enjoyed. He has experience as both a successful starter and a world-class closer.

"I think it's easier to relieve," he said. "You get matchups out of the pen. I'm gonna face, over the course of a season, 75 percent right-handed hitters as a reliever. I guarantee you it's in the majority. That's me. I'm gonna get right-handed hitters out. Period. The matchups are greater, much more in my favor. And it's not like you come into a one-run game every time. If I had to save 50 one-run games I am going to give it up sometimes. But if you give me a two- or three-run save, I might get them all."

Eckersley's view of his advantage as a reliever was widespread throughout the league. He was one of those incredibly talented individuals who had the ability to start and close. In his book, *3 Nights in August: Strategy, Heartbreak, and Joy Inside the Mind of a Manager*, written with Tony La Russa, Buzz Bissinger discussed Eck and his banishment to the bullpen in Oakland.

"Eckersley, for example, after a career of starting, chafed at being sent to the bullpen by Oakland in 1987 after his trade there," writes Bissinger. "He considered it banishment, purgatory for lesser pitchers, an absolute affront to his machismo. Until he realized the joy of being able to come into a game and throw whatever you wanted as hard as you wanted, just let it rip and not fret too terribly much over pitch selection. Along with his imperviousness to pressure, it gave Eckersley, a Hall of Fame reliever, the luxury of concentrating his stuff into 10 or 12 pitches."

Although Eckersley was not thrilled with the prospect of pitching out of the bullpen at first, he accepted the "demotion" and then got a break when closer Jay Howell broke down. He assumed the spot and never looked back. After creating with La Russa the one-inning save that is so prevalent in the game today, he enjoyed his time out of the bullpen.

Other pitchers may or may not have the right stuff to close. But after you've been a starter, it can be tough to make the transition. To a large degree, many pitchers prefer to have the ball in the first inning rather than the ninth. There is a lot less pressure.

"I think it's easier to start because you have more time in between appearances," said Fergie Jenkins. "Now, with a five-man rotation, you pitch once a week. In my day you'd get two starts a week. But when you sit on the bench and chart pitches, I think it's boring.

"With the time in between appearances, you can build up your stamina by throwing and running between starts. You should have good arm strength, and you also strengthen the core of your body to make sure you can go late into games."

What a pitcher needs to be a successful starter is similar to what it takes to be a successful closer. But the elements are different. The starter is out there to last as long as he can, up to around 100 pitches, and try to show consistency over a number of innings. But the closer comes in with the game on the line with no room for error. Good starting pitchers can sometimes be beaten in the early innings. If you beat a closer early, the game is over.

"I think that the characteristics of a great closer are focus, health, and relationships," said Jim Gott, who saved 91 games during a 14-year career in which he pitched for Toronto, San Francisco, Pittsburgh, and Los Angeles. "Focus helps you keep your confidence and concentration on the job at hand. You need to stay healthy and follow your routine that could include stretching, weight training, cardio programs, icing or

Over his 14-year career, Jim Gott learned a lot about what made for a great closer. His three keys to success: focus, health (including training and diet), and relationships—especially with pitching coaches and catchers. *Photo courtesy of Getty Images*

whirlpool, Bengay, rest, and the proper diet. Relationships are also important. You need to be able to communicate with your pitching coach. He is your protector who gets you rest when you need it, kicks you in the butt or pats you on the back, and is your emotional protector also.

"You also need to trust your catcher. I had some great catchers to work with, such as Mike LaValliere, Bob Brenly, Buck Martinez, and Mike Scioscia. Let your catcher lead, because a good catcher sees things that you don't. He sees the way hitters react to pitches, hitters' movement in the batter's box, and hitters' attitude at the plate.

"You also need to have the confidence to believe in yourself and your stuff and have the ability to control your emotions so that you have ice water in your veins. You can't get too high or too low. It also helps to know the home-plate umpire. They all have their own strike zone and personality and as a result, can either help or really hurt the outcome."

Closers not only do one of the most difficult jobs in all of sports, but they are well paid for their efforts. In decades past, relievers were treated with a lot less respect than they are today, and they were also paid a lot less than today. Now a top-notch closer can make the same kind of money as a starter. The financial considerations alone make it logical to use a closer often.

"I think it gets back to the money," said Maury Allen. "Salary is how ballplayers judge each other. A-Rod is the best player in the game and the highest-paid player in the game. That's what they all care about.

"If you are paying Rivera $15 million, you have to get him in 60 or 70 games. They will go quicker to a reliever in their minds than they did years ago. They tend to think in terms of 'give me six innings as a starter, then give me guys for the seventh and the eighth, and then I'll win it with my closer.' A lot of teams build a team from the back to the front. Start the team out with a good relief pitcher, and go from there."

The true value of a good relief pitcher has dramatically increased. Is it because of their actual value, or once again, do finances dictate policy? Baseball is a game of followers. If something works for one team, copycat teams will follow and try to imitate the same success formula. Teams started to platoon players, and pitchers were not far behind.

"It's kind of a circular process," said Peter Morris. "Once you have the relievers you should try to use them. The gap between the quality of a good starter and a good reliever lessened; it changed. The gap in the quality became less. Once you have the relievers sitting around getting paid, you might as well use them.

"A lot of times you can take a mediocre starter and turn him into a good reliever. I was not surprised when John Smoltz saved 40 games. But I don't think that Mariano Rivera would be a good starter. So it's easier for a starter to become a good reliever than it is for a reliever to become a good starter.

"Starting pitchers are still better than relievers, and I think that relievers are overrated. Pitching six good innings is still more valuable than pitching one inning. To me, if I had a starting pitcher with an ERA of 4.00, I would never trade him for a reliever with an ERA of 3.00."

That might be a particularly controversial opinion in the game of today. A starting pitcher doing his job and a reliever doing his job both have great value. The role of the bullpen has grown a great deal in recent years. But the role of the starter is equally important. Whether or not it's easier to pitch in relief or start, both roles are important. At the end of the day a team needs five major league starters and a minimum of six big-league-caliber relievers. As has been said previously, it seems easier to find someone who can start capably than uncover a pitcher with the guile and the stuff to close.

"To me the closer has to have stuff," said Chris Wheeler. "You have to have talent. If you don't have the talent to do it, it's not going to work. Then there's the whole makeup thing. I don't know what that is. A guy who can stand out there for one inning after his teammates have had three hours of playing and have it rest on his shoulders? There is tremendous psychology involved here. A closer needs to have talent and the psychology of being able to do it successfully. And just as important is to be able to go out there the next time after you screwed up the night before.

"A closer does not have the luxury a starter does. They say to get to a starter early. Hey, you get one or two off a closer, and it's over. It's a whole different mind-set. There is absolutely no margin for error. Even in a three-run game, it's a much more hitter-friendly game now with bats, balls, and smaller ballparks. I can understand the way the game has evolved. It's much more of an offensive game, and it's meant to be because they can sell a 9–8 game more than a 1–0 game. They appeal to what sells tickets, and that is high-scoring games. The irony of it all is that it's pitching and defense that wins championships, not offense.

"If they are not goofy when they start closing, they are when they finish. They have to be a little nuts and off center to be able to do that. If they aren't, that role will make them crazy. They'll tell you about the adrenaline rush and how their heart is pounding. No matter what some of them might say, they hear the crowd. They look cool and confident out there, but they are like that duck paddling like hell under the water. I've never had one reliever I've been around who is like ice water. Some just shut it out better than others."

That is an interesting point. So many pitchers will tell you that they never hear the crowd. That they never hear the cheers, and they never hear the jeers from the opposing dugout. Although some might be able to block out all the elements of the venue, it's a pretty safe bet that pretty much every one of them hears the noise. Again, those who are successful use whatever they can find to make them get the final out.

"The best thing for me was when I was getting booed on the road," said Lee Smith. "That really gave me goose bumps because it was a show of respect for me. If you can go and pitch in a major league ballpark in the ninth inning and get booed, that is a sign of respect because you are one of the best at what you do. They are trying to play a mind game with you. But it gives you more adrenaline.

"I had this knack for ignoring people. I had tunnel vision from home to the mound. I'd be warming up in the bullpen, and guys who knew me were calling out to me, and I never heard them. Leon Durham and I were best of friends, but when he was at first base he knew better than to come to the mound. He'd tell me that he wasn't coming to the mound because I was crazy. But I don't tell you how to play first base, so get the hell off my mound. Roger Clemens used to talk about a tunnel from him to the plate.

"When I'm out there with the game on the line, I love that situation. I was a low-key guy. But nothing came between me and that 27th out."

The differences of opinion on what makes a great closer could be as different as each closer in the game. They certainly need competitiveness, and they certainly need talent. But we've all seen closers who looked like the proverbial deer in the headlights under the bright lights of the ninth inning. When that happens, we don't see them for long.

Clearly, a closer has something within himself that differentiates him from the typical pitcher. And as the role of the closer has changed and gained importance, the persona of the closer has developed over time and with acceptance. Additionally, the pressure on the closer has grown exponentially.

"The closer is one of the most interesting parts of baseball," said Maury Allen. "Most of the closers are Lyle types. They come in and are very competitive. But no matter what happens, 20 minutes after it's over, the game is history. You cannot be a closer if you carry the burden of what you did yesterday. Ralph Branca says to this day he never carried any of that into the next season. What happened is that he got an injury and was never the same pitcher.

"With most relief pitchers I've known, they've had two things: incredible confidence in themselves and their ability. It's a commanding position as a closer. The game rides on his arm more than it does with the batter. The attention on the closer is the greatest attention that anybody has in baseball. He has to have tremendous confidence, and he has to have the confidence of his teammates, who need to feel that he can win the game because he is in the game."

One subject continues to surface in discussing the makeup of a successful closer. There is mind-set and ability, but there is also something that separates them from other pitchers. There is a sense that they are just different.

"In my mind, as a general manager, when I think about a closer or a great relief pitcher, there are several things that struck me," said Fred Claire. "First, with any successful closer, there is a mind-set and a makeup that is very different. We see this time and again. You can look at a guy's stuff and velocity all you want. But there are very few guys who can pitch the ninth inning. It's a remarkable thing. They can pitch great in the seventh and eighth innings but not the ninth. It takes something special as far as makeup is concerned.

"The big thing that I see as far as successful relief pitching is concerned is command. If you look at a guy like Eckersley, his command was uncanny. It was there when he was a starting pitcher too. He simply didn't walk anybody. To be successful as a closer, you have to have heart and command. The other ingredient we see time and again is that different, unhittable pitch. Elroy Face had that with the forkball. You think of the great breaking ball of Bruce Sutter. Mariano Rivera of the Yankees with the great command of the slider. Even now, the all-time save leader, Trevor Hoffman, has a great change-up. When you go through the list of great closers, you see that they are different in some ways.

"Heart, command, and an outstanding pitch, or the power to overpower guys like Lee Smith could do. There can't be any fear in those guys. None of the great ones are nibbling. Once you walk the first guy in the ninth inning, it's all but over. You see a dominant pitcher like Eric Gagné during his great years. I never saw anything else like it. He had a couple of years where when he came into the game, the game was over. But it takes a toll. When you look at successful closers, they have streaks when they are successful. But to be at the top of their game, even for the very best, it's usually a three- or four-year run at the most; then it's gone.

"But the mind-set of a closer is that you have to have a very short memory. You have to be able to erase last night's game almost immediately and get it behind you. You can't fake it. You have to have that confidence. If you blow a game you need the ability to come back the next night and mentally be there."

A wide variety of very knowledgeable people have spoken to the value of the closer's role and the special characteristics that they need to succeed. But when talking to one of the best in the history of the game, some of the ideas remain constant as far as stuff and confidence and consistency are concerned. Dennis Eckersley agrees with many of the ideas that have been discussed here. But there are differences. Eckersley does not necessarily agree with the concept of putting a bad game behind you.

Not in the least. Fear was a real motivating factor for him. The fear of failure.

"I dealt with failure not very well," Eckersley said. "Turning the page is a bunch of shit. The more difficult the blown save, the worse it was. Some are worse than others, depending on how it happened. Forgetting it? You never forget it. The fire is hotter the next time out because you don't want to do it again. I wasn't timid out there, which helped me a lot. I didn't forget it at all. The fear that motivated me just got worse.

"Not everything I did was the perfect reliever. You are not supposed to be as anxious as I am. Some people took offense to how I reacted, but it was real. It wasn't like I planned it and decided that I'm gonna punch this guy out and point to the sky or point to him. It just happened. For me it was absolute relief because of all the pressure. People think it's almost like an act on my part, but my reactions were real.

"Closing takes a mentality of aggressiveness. I didn't have a finesse pitch. You have to bring a presence out there, an aura, a body language of confidence to the mound. You want to bring a sense that the game is over to the mound. You can't be faking it, but I did that too. That's the mentality along with the presence. I just was aggressive because to me every game in the ninth inning was life or death. I took that to the mound later in my career as a closer. My motivation was fear. The fear of failing. A lot of guys can crumble with that. But it made me as good as I could be. 'This is life or death. I can't screw this up.' You have to bring out this feeling that the game is over and carry that confidence to the mound."

On his way to Cooperstown, Eckersley obviously had a mind-set that set him apart from most relievers. But he also used his attitude to get it done on the mound. He was not typical, but that is exactly what made him successful and the epitome of the prototypical closer of this era. For it was he, along with Oakland manager Tony La Russa, who created the role.

"More times than not, you have to be aggressive and throw strikes," he said. "My whole thing was bang, strike one. Bang, and we'll go from there. Strike one is the most important pitch because it sets everything else up. Lots of times you give them a first pitch breaking ball. You throw that for a strike, and they don't know what the hell is going on. Ultimately, it's all about throwing strikes. Now you have to be a guy who punches guys out. I was not overpowering, but I could get my strikeouts. I couldn't walk anybody because I couldn't hold anybody on because I was so slow to the plate. The slide step killed me."

Of course, in order to get on base a hitter has to get a hit, a walk, be hit by a pitch, or live on an error. And for just about his entire career out of the bullpen, against Dennis Eckersley, that rarely happened.

Eckersley embodied the typical mind frame, stuff, command, and guile of a successful closer. What young pitchers trying to find their place in the sun saw was a new role, a new way to live their American dream. Money, fame, and confidence. That's what it's all about. If you want money and fame, you need the confidence to go out there where few others can succeed.

"A lot of it depends on salary," said Maury Allen. "An organization can convince a guy that he'll make more money as a relief pitcher, like Eckersley and Smoltz did. Give a relief pitcher salary equal to that of a starter. That's what they want.

"Money and ego has a lot to do with it, but self-confidence is very important. The attention on them is enormous. All around baseball, they make a fuss over these closers. They have their own theme song, fans have banners for them, and they become much more important. A closer is never in a 10–1 game. He's in a 2–1 game or a tie. The tension, the fan involvement, and the involvement of your teammates is second to none."

Confidence and belief in your ability to close on the major league level. Sounds simple on paper, but on the mound with a stadium full of people shouting expectantly and your teammates hanging on every pitch, your future seems to be in the balance. Success in the closer's role is something that you as a pitcher either make happen or you're back in the set-up role.

There are those who feel that you can't really learn how to win until you've experienced defeat, such as right-hander Jim Gott, who had just arrived in Pittsburgh following a trade with the San Francisco Giants in 1987. His story exemplifies the tentative nature of the closer.

"When I was traded to Pittsburgh from San Francisco at the end of the '87 season, I established myself as the Pittsburgh closer for the next year," Gott said. "As 1988 began, we were hot, but so were the Mets. In June we had a home series with them, and there was a packed house at Three Rivers [Stadium]. I came in to close a one-run game and had two outs in the top of the ninth. The fans were standing in anticipation when Howard Johnson came to the plate.

"I quickly got a no balls–and–two strikes count and started to be more aware of the moment instead of my focus on pitching. I stepped off the mound, and Mike LaValliere came out to calm me down. After a few moments, we decided on a fastball, slider sequence. When he went back, I decided to do the opposite. With a slider grip, I shook him off, but he kept going back to the fastball signal. So instead of stepping off and regrouping again, I went into my stretch, changing my grip to a fastball, paused, and grooved a fastball for HoJo to silence the crowd with a game-tying home run.

"Boy, did it get quiet in a hurry. I finished the inning, we went on to lose in extra innings, and I was crushed. I drove around the Pittsburgh freeway system for a couple of hours before I went home. That one mistake was hashed over by everyone for the rest of the season. In fact, when I went back to play there for the Pirates in '95, I was still asked by reporters and fans why that happened."

Jim Gott was at a career moment. Brought over to the Pirates with the idea that he was going to be the closer, he had a blown save that could have ruined his season, not to mention his career.

"How do you shake off a game like that?" Gott asked. "Well, manager Jim Leyland and pitching coach Ray Miller played a huge role in that. Before and during the time leading up to my next appearance, those two great coaches taught me what it takes to be a big-leaguer. Just forget about bad outings. Be prepared for your next appearance and most of all, relax and enjoy being in the big leagues.

"Because of that home run, that was the greatest season of my career. I ended up breaking Kent Tekulve's single-season record that year with 34 saves. I expected to win every time out after that crucial moment."

To really appreciate success, in baseball and in life, you have to experience failure. Success and failure are the ultimate end of a closer's life every time he pitches. And it's how he handles succeeding or failing that often dictates his future in that role. Of course, it is the manager of the team who has to handle how his pitcher handles it.

CHAPTER 9

Managing the Staff

The many changes that have occurred at the back end of the bullpen in the last two decades have also had an enormous effect on the way the game is run from the dugout. The incredible level of specialization in the game has dictated that most pitchers have a specific role on a ballclub. The manager and his staff must plug in the correct pitchers to the various roles.

Most teams have five starters that form the rotation. It used to be four. In the past a starting pitcher would normally pitch two times per week, but now a starter gets in one game per week, depending on off days and the like. Suffice it to say that starters are starting fewer games, completing fewer games, and pitching fewer innings.

So major changes have influenced what teams want from their starting pitching. Rather than expecting your starting staff to pitch you deep into ballgames, going as long as they can, today's game has an artificial number that spells the end for most pitchers in most games—the 100 pitch count. Some pitchers are just getting loose at the century mark. No matter. After a starter gets close to 100 pitches in a game he is looked at with a doubting eye from the dugout. That's the time when bullpens start to get cranked up and relievers start to stretch, the precursor to warming up.

Baseball people will tell you that it's not the number of pitches that counts, it's the *difficulty* of the pitches that is more important. An easy game in which the pitcher is not in stressful situations could very well mean that the pitcher could throw a lot more than 100 pitches. Conversely, a guy who is struggling and scuffing on a particular night could be shot after 80 throws.

But baseball wisdom sometimes is not wise, and regardless of how many baseball people will bemoan the pitch count, it is, at this place and time, the rule of the game. And at that point the strategy of the game moves to the bullpen.

Out in the pen, most clubs carry a closer that owns the ninth inning, a set-up man who pitches the eighth, another hurler who can pitch in the seventh or eighth, a left-handed specialist, a guy who might come into a game in the sixth inning, a long man who can come in if the starter is knocked out early, and a swing man who can be versatile and fill a couple of roles. That's seven relievers to go along with five starters, totaling 12. At any given time during a game, there are eight position players. So 20 of the 25 roster spots are taken up.

Consider that teams rarely use their backup catcher in a game because, should the other backstop be injured, there would be no replacement available. So on many nights a manager has only four moves off his bench with regard to position players. That is especially challenging for National League skippers who might have to pinch hit for pitchers twice in a game, which could leave one other move plus the second-string catcher. Because of the need for so many pitchers on the staff, rather than the nine- or 10-man staffs of yesteryear, in an extra-inning game you can often see teams simply run out of position players. As a result, if a game reaches 13 or 14 innings, it's quite possible to see starting pitchers coming out to pinch hit.

The challenge in the dugout is not limited to having enough position players. Even with a 12- or 13-man pitching staff, a manager's hands are often tied by his pitchers' specialized roles. With some relievers unable to throw for more than one inning, managers sometimes run out of available pitchers and find themselves with a predicament on the mound. Thus, on a few occasions during a typical season, teams will be forced to have position players toe the rubber and pitch an inning or two. It could be said that, with specialized pitching staffs, more can be less.

"Carrying 13 pitchers is ludicrous," said Jim Fregosi. "When you go back not too long ago, guys had nine-man pitching staffs. Instead of letting a starting pitcher go as far as he can, after a certain amount of pitches they take him out. It's not like the pitcher doesn't want to pitch longer or can't pitch more. It can be a case of more of a protection for the manager.

"Inexperienced managers have to answer questions in a press conference after the game. The younger guys have a definite fear of being second-guessed. So when the ninth inning comes along, they will always

Jim Fregosi managed 15 seasons in the majors and led the Phillies to the 1993 World Series. He thinks pitching-heavy rosters are a crutch for inexperienced managers fearful of being second-guessed for leaving starters in the game too long.

use the closer. In the eighth inning, they'll use the set-up guy. The aspect of four pitchers going one, one, one, one, where each guy out of the bullpen pitches an inning each is how it's done now. But you can't do that. Their arms need time to recuperate. I always had a rule that if a guy got up to warm up three times during a game, I canceled him for that night.

"It doesn't affect the American League as much as it does the National League because of the DH. You've still got 13 pitchers and 12 players, which means you've got four bench players. You have a second catcher you can never use, so that brings it down to three bench players. If you make a double switch you only have two left."

The technology that brings postgame press conferences to a worldwide audience is no small factor in the way games are managed. A veteran skipper like a Fregosi will take what he thinks is the right path more so than a young manager trying to make his mark and keep his job.

"There is an awful lot of pressure on managers today," said former pitcher Gene Garber. "ESPN has changed the sport. Every game and every highlight are on TV. The manager has a pitching staff of five starters and seven or eight relief pitchers, and they all have their role. As long as the manager uses the pitcher he has for each role, you can't criticize him for bringing the wrong guy into the game. Somewhere along the line, managers and organizations decided that players couldn't pitch nine innings anymore. They are happy with a whole staff of Milt Pappases, guys who have no intention of going that long. What they've done is taken expectations away from the starting pitchers."

Pitch counts limit the starters, and what Fregosi's mention of the one, one, one, one nightly routine with relievers throwing a single inning usually means is that quite often a pitcher needs to be shut down for a game.

"Can you imagine Rollie Fingers being unavailable for one night?" asked Garber. "He might pitch four innings one night and two innings the next night. Did it hurt his arm and career? He's a Hall of Famer. I think the pressure of television magnifies every move the manager makes with regard to pitchers and hitters. The manager discovers that if he has 12 pitchers and each one has a job, if he brings one into the game who fails, it's not his fault. He made the right move. It's the pitcher's fault. As a result, managers don't get second-guessed for their use of pitchers anymore.

"You can have your short reliever pitch two innings a couple days in a row and then he's unavailable? I'm thinking that maybe he pitched three innings in three days. Big deal. I pitched eight innings in four days and thought nothing of it. When Larry Bowa was managing the Phillies a few years back, on the pregame show he said he had nobody in the bullpen. But he had 12 guys sitting down there.

"Agents and organizations have tremendous investments in these guys. I can understand that. You give a guy $50 million, and you are going to protect him. But it hurts the overall performance."

It's a sad commentary that in this day and age a manager can put his job in jeopardy simply by uttering eight fateful words: "Let's leave him in there for another inning."

If you don't buy that particular logic, two words might change your perception: Grady Little, who has a .559 winning percentage as a major league manager. He must be a successful, well-respected skipper. Well....

Little's Boston Red Sox were five outs away from earning a World Series berth in 2003. They were leading the New York Yankees in Game 7 of the American League Championship Series 5–2, with one out in the eighth inning. Boston's ace right-handed starter, Pedro Martinez, surrendered three consecutive hits and a run in that stanza. Out came Little to the mound, no doubt to replace his tiring future Hall of Fame starter with a fresh arm out of the Bosox bullpen to protect what was now a 5–3 lead.

But Little chose to ignore baseball's book and left Martinez in the game. One out later, Yanks backstop Jorge Posada tied the game with a two-run double. Worse yet, New York eventually won the game and the pennant in the eleventh inning. Grady Little was not brought back to manage the Red Sox in 2004. The job went to Terry Francona, who guided the Red Sox to the world championship in 2004 and used his bullpen and closer Keith Foulke by the book that Little ignored.

Regardless of a manager usually being a baseball lifer who has probably been around the game in any combination of player, scout, coach, instructor, and manager, you can't go against the grain. Because when baseball's new "book" dictates that starters leave the game at around the 100-pitch mark, and relievers normally just pitch an inning apiece, ignoring the book puts a manager squarely in the crosshairs. Particularly if a decision results in a pitcher being injured, in which case the decision will be on *SportsCenter* as it happens and printed and editorialized in most newspapers the next day, making the manager the object of ridicule and scorn and in danger of losing his job. If you go against the book, you'd better be right.

But that reality doesn't keep pitchers from yesteryear wondering what has happened to their game. But it's a different time, and the rules have changed.

"If a closer comes in two or three days in a row now, he needs a couple days off," said Elroy Face. "In 1956 I went in and pitched for nine straight days and pitched 16 total innings. I guess I was a little tired. There were times when I'd got to bed at night and my elbow would be throbbing. But you'd wake up in the morning, and it would be fine. Now, if you get a little tingle, you can't pitch for three or four days.

"And these guys who are getting saves now wouldn't have nearly that many saves if they went in from the seventh inning or like we had to do. With us, from the seventh inning on it was the closer. Set-up guy? You were your own set-up guy."

Relievers of that era pitched often, but they pitched more innings as well. Although there were specialized roles, they were not followed as strictly as they are today. More was expected of relief pitchers.

"In my day you had middle relievers and all, but sometimes you had to go three innings as the closer," said Jack Baldschun. "That was my limit as far as being able to pitch the next day well. As a short reliever who was pitching every day, you had to watch yourself and keep your muscle tension there. But it wasn't wearing out the arm. If you went three or four innings, you could not usually go the next day. But there is no reason why a pitcher today should not go three innings in relief."

But it's one inning per pitcher out of the bullpen these days, more often than not. Using the prior example of a starting hurler hitting the 100-pitch mark, the sixth-inning man can be succeeded by the seventh-inning pitcher, the set-up man, and the closer pitching in a tie game in the ninth inning. But come the tenth, it gets tricky. And come the fourteenth, the last reliever standing might have to take one for the ballclub and pitch more innings than he might normally feel comfortable with.

In the American League, the added roster spots are not as difficult to deal with because there is the designated hitter in the Junior Circuit. The effect of the DH is that no pinch-hitter is ever needed for the pitcher because he never bats. So the chance that a manager in the AL will run out of position players is much less apparent. But even in that league, if a manager isn't careful, an extra-inning tilt can see a team sacrifice a pitcher for too many innings or bring a spare position player in to pitch—if he has one left.

Those who have played the game find it difficult to believe that a team could run out of pitchers with a 12- or 13-man staff. But the reality is that teams are handcuffed by the roles that pitchers fill.

"I can't buy into today's strategy in regards to relief pitching," said Gene Garber, who pitched for Pittsburgh, Kansas City, Philadelphia, and Atlanta during his 19-year career (in which he was the Braves' all-time leader in saves). "I know why it's done. I know why you have 12 pitchers on every major league staff and sometimes 13. It's a tremendous misuse of pitching or a waste of pitching. You have five starters, and all you want out of them is six innings. If you are ahead, you have three guys to use for the seventh, eighth, and ninth. If you're behind, you have three separate guys, so that's six relief pitchers at your disposal. Then you have another long reliever in case your starter gets knocked out, or the game goes into extra innings.

"But now, games get into the tenth or eleventh inning and quite often they have no one left in the bullpen. I can't fathom that. The emphasis is on throwing hard, so much so that a lot of relievers don't know how to pitch. It's just 'throw as hard as you can and we'll get somebody else.'"

Not only do pitch counts and the specialization in baseball's bullpens cause problems with the management of pitchers, but sometimes a starting pitcher will be left in a game in which he has nothing. There have been examples of long men who are available to come into a ballgame in the early stages and give their team some innings. On some nights a starting pitcher just doesn't have his best stuff.

But there are times in the game today when the starter will get his 100-pitch quota whether he is pitching a competitive game or losing by a touchdown. That does not sit well with all baseball people.

"It's inconceivable to me how you can let a starting pitcher in to let up seven runs in a game when you have seven pitchers in the bullpen," said Garber. "Why as a manager are you just throwing the game away? Are you afraid you're going to deplete your pitching staff?

"A couple of times a year you might need a sacrificial lamb. I saw Paul Lindblad with Oakland come in and give up 10 or 11 runs because they had an eight-man pitching staff. They had no choice, because they just had to get innings. But there's no excuse in this day and age when you have seven pitchers in the pen to let a starter give up seven runs and get your team down."

The roster challenge extends to general managers and other front-office personnel who are responsible for acquiring the players to fill out big-league rosters. They need to make sure that the mix of pitchers on the staff will work in baseball's brave new world.

Relief pitchers certainly have gained respect, acceptance, and millions of dollars as a result of how their role has evolved. The huge investments that teams make with starting pitchers have a lot to do with pitch counts, and the equally large investments they make in the bullpen also dictate pitcher usage. Early in the history of the game, finances played a large part in the competition. That has been a constant in America's Game. The only thing that has changed is the dollar figures.

"The big thing is that when you look at guys who are playing the game now, a good bullpen pitcher is making $6 million or $7 million," said Fergie Jenkins. "Good starters are making $12 million. That's what Ted Lilly makes. Ryan Dempster makes $13 million. Randy Johnson is in his mid-40s and makes $8 million. If you can still do your job, you can make good money. Jamie Moyer is making $8 to $10 million, and he is 46. The game has evolved around what your capabilities are and what you can do, and clubs will pay for that.

"A lot of times, guys who were demoted to the bullpen were guys who couldn't start. They became quality relief pitchers. But now they are groomed in the minor leagues for the bullpen. They work at it and perfect it. The specialized part of the game is now around the bullpen."

When organizations pay big money for a player in a particular role, it is the manager's duty to get that guy in a situation to succeed and earn the big bucks he is getting from the organization. That means keeping him in the role envisioned for him when he was signed. But sometimes he may not be the best man for the job.

"The Catch-22 as a manager now is that you have your organization paying a guy $13 million a year to pitch the ninth inning," said Chris Wheeler. "If you don't use that guy in that role, then what the hell did you sign him for? They pay a guy big money to pitch the ninth inning, so let's go.

"When save situations come up, they want to be in the game. If they are not used that way, I've heard of their agents actually calling the team. So there is pressure on the manager to use these guys."

There is much more involved for today's managers than simply filling out the lineup card and letting the game proceed along its natural path.

Managing is a balancing act in which they must deal with contracts, egos, organizational expectations and direction, incredible specialization, and, oh yes, managing the team and motivating the players.

Years ago, Philadelphia Phillies Hall of Fame third baseman Mike Schmidt jokingly said of his situation in a media-hyped city, "Philadelphia is the city where you enjoy the thrill of victory and the agony of reading about it the next day."

Today's collection of big-league managers have every move they make—and don't make—examined, criticized, scrutinized, and debated from the moment the game ends until the moment the next game begins. ESPN, numerous other national outlets, local and national newspapers, blogs, and local TV affiliates have managers looking over their shoulders. And every fan has access to a litany of opinions from a wide variety of baseball pundits.

No wonder they hardly ever vary from baseball's book. The latest edition, that is.

CHAPTER 10

Set-Up Men and the Hold

The casual baseball fan knows the names of most of the big-name starting pitchers on the hometown pitching staff. The average fan knows not only his or her own team's pitching staff but a number of other starters throughout the game. And both of these groups can name a big-time closer in the mold of a Mariano Rivera, a Brad Lidge, or a Jonathan Papelbon. But it is only the die-hard fans who know the names of the middle-relief specialists and the set-up men who act as the bridges to the Lidges.

It is an important part of the game. Starters have fame and fortune, and closers have increasing fame and fortune. But with starters leaving early and closers appearing late, there is a gap that needs to be filled between the fifth or sixth inning and the ninth inning owned by the closer.

Your closer is your best relief pitcher on the team. The set-up man is normally the second-best relief pitcher on the team. He's the best of the rest. It used to be that middle-relief and set-up pitchers were not that highly thought of. They were sort of an unnecessary evil, a redheaded stepchild to get you to the back of the bullpen. But with the advent of the new style of managing the pitching staff, middle relief has become a vitally important part of the game. Every team has starters, and every team has a closer. To be successful, the front part of the game and the finishing part of the contest need to be quality. But getting from point A, the starter, to point C, the closer, now necessitates additional quality, dependable pitchers.

Thanks to the new game of baseball with relation to starting pitching—with starters often hitting the showers before the home team hits in the sixth inning—a new role has opened up in baseball. This speaks to the incredible specialization in the game. When a player gets plugged into a specific role on a pitching staff, that's his job. But much like in the business world, in baseball, there is the opportunity for advancement as well as demotion.

It has been said that because of the glut of new teams caused by expansion, major league pitching has become diluted. That may not be the case. Because there are more teams than there have ever been before, there are more spots on the pitching staffs that need to be filled and thus more opportunities for young pitchers to audition for the major leagues. Although there are some examples of the Peter Principle who will no doubt fade after their weaknesses are exposed, there are also countless other pitchers quite adequately filling middle-relief and set-up roles who might not have enjoyed that opportunity without expansion. Are there some slugs out there? Of course there are. But there are also a number of fine pitchers who have fairly earned their major league roster spot.

If earned-run averages aren't as low as some parochial purists would like to see, some of that might be the cause of lesser talent on the mound. But it also could very well be that there are simply just a lot more good hitters out there. The knock-down pitch never occurs anymore, and most pitchers can't pitch effectively inside. To an aggressive, hungry hitter, today's game is a smorgasbord of opportunity.

"When I pitched, the offensive part of the game was different," said Dennis Eckersley. "They can really hit now. There were so many lambs in the lineup when I broke in. Suppose the second baseman, shortstop, and catcher couldn't hit. You had outs galore. The levels of hitters are better now. Guys are bigger, stronger, better, and they hit better. And parks are smaller now, let alone the steroid era."

With improved offensive players, there are now different roles and more pitchers to choose from to try to shut them down. Young guys, pitchers stuck in another role, and pitchers who come out of nowhere are auditioning for the closer's role, the set-up role, and middle relief. If you fail to succeed in an early opportunity to move up to a different role, you may not get the chance to move up the ladder again. You might be perceived as not having the right stuff.

There are a plethora of pitchers who can pitch the seventh and eighth innings. Other guys can be counted on to eat up innings by relieving an ineffective starter in the second or third inning. But getting a seventh- or eighth-inning guy to be effective in the ninth inning is a whole new ballgame. Many set-up and situational relievers can make the transition to the closer's role. It is sort of a Manifest Destiny kind of thing. They pay their dues as the set-up man, and then when the closer's contract is up, it's time to move up the ladder to that corner office in the bullpen with all the windows.

But by no means can they all make that transition. Whether a set-up man can make the transition or not, he is an incredibly valuable member of the pitching staff on current big-league rosters. Without a great set-up man, there can be no great closer.

"I believe that great relievers have good set-up men," said Jim Gott. "My pitching coach with the Dodgers, Ron Perronoski, used to rag us about how easy it is to be a closer now. When he was a closer, it was common to have three-inning saves. Holding a one-run lead for three innings for a save was a true save. It sure was nice for me to pitch one or less for a save!

"Pedro Martinez was my set-up guy in '93. That was awesome. He would blow people away for two innings, and I would get three outs and it was all the high fives. Jeff Robinson would baffle people with his Roger

Craig split finger when I was the closer in Pittsburgh. Again, the manager and pitching coach play an important role nurturing [a] psyche."

In the new millennium of America's Game, the makeup of a pitching staff is different, and the types of pitchers have changed as well.

"Just going back into the 1970s, most of the staffs were made up of nine or 10 pitchers," said former general manager Pat Gillick. "Now you seldom see a staff with less than 11 or 12. You can even see a 13-man staff now. So certainly the depth of the pitching staff has changed. Starting pitchers just pitched further into the game then. The one thing in the '70s that most teams had was a four-man rotation and a spot starter as a fifth starter. But he was not a true starter. If we didn't have an off day and needed someone, he'd start.

Pat Gillick knows a lot about the value of set-up men. As general manager of the Phillies, he built one of the best bullpens in baseball— one so good that it carried the team to the 2008 World Series title.

"Your starters would get 35 starts, and the fifth guy would get 20 or 22. You had a four-man rotation and six in the pen. Pitchers were encouraged to go further into the game. At least you were expected to get into the seventh inning. And usually a relief pitcher was a guy who wasn't good enough to be a starter. It wasn't as it is now. You weren't good enough to start, so to stay in the game and on the team, you had to assume a role in the bullpen.

"A lot of baseball is somebody following somebody else. Managers got into it. Gene Mauch was one of them. You'd get into a situation where they were using a right-handed pitcher against right-handed hitters and left-handed pitchers against left-handed hitters. Some managers saw others playing the percentages like that and didn't want to be viewed as being behind the times. So they started to develop specialists that assumed roles in the bullpen. So instead of having a multipurpose pitcher, you developed a specialist for the seventh inning, another one for the eighth inning, and then your closer in the ninth. It just evolved, and like a lot of sheep, the rest of the herd following didn't want to get left behind."

Although Gillick understands what has happened, the closed-mindedness of some players and managers about players being in specific roles with no opportunity or desire to expand on that role is annoying to the longtime GM. To a baseball lifer, the concept of a ballplayer dictating his role on a team is a little disconcerting at best.

"I get frustrated from the standpoint that guys will tell you that they can't pitch certain innings," he said. "We get a little too smart and try to overmanage. Just because some guy pitches in the seventh inning some night and doesn't do well doesn't mean he can't do it. He just needs more opportunity. We are overspecializing and overmanaging the situation from the sixth inning on. Once you get into that rut, it's hard to get out of it. That is something that needs to be changed in our game. There are just too many specialists, guys who can pitch only one inning and only pitch certain innings and throw only 20 pitches. I think most pitchers are capable of pitching more.

"But unless you can get into the head of the manager and the player and let them know that a guy *can* pitch the seventh, eighth, or ninth, it becomes difficult. It's hard to get it out of their head once it's built in there. Certainly getting the right ingredients for the bullpen is now a challenge."

And one of the most important of these ingredients is the set-up man. These pitchers are sort of like old-time middle relievers but with a specific role. You have the long men who come in if a pitcher is injured early in a game or roughed up to the point where he needs to come out even earlier than the fifth or sixth. Then the successful teams have a succession of pitchers to get you to the closer. There is a sixth, and seventh-inning guy. There is the eighth-inning guy, the prototypical set-up man in today's game. Don't forget to throw into the mix the left-handed specialist who comes into the game to go head-to-head with a tough left-handed hitter or a weaker right-handed hitter. He may not be the closer, but he helps get his team to the closer. The respect given to middle-relief and set-up pitchers has been a work in progress, much like the evolution of the closer's role.

"It changed with different decades," said former manager Jim Fregosi. "In the '80s, a lot of times a guy would come in and get a three-inning save. Then to try to protect the arm of the closer, who was usually a power guy, they tried to get roles for guys in the seventh or eighth innings, so that they could use the closer for just one inning, and he'd be available. That's when you always tried to have a left-handed guy and a right-handed guy to pitch the eighth inning."

These set-up and middle-relief pitchers don't always get the headlines, and they aren't making the kind of money that the closer makes. Sure, most of these hurlers earn less than the average major league salary. But the role has grown in importance. And let's face it, the set-up guy is the heir apparent to the closer. If your ninth-inning guy goes down with an injury or becomes suddenly ineffective, oftentimes it is the eighth-inning, or set-up, man who is given the first chance to come to the team's rescue. If he succeeds, he is the heir apparent. If not, he is the set-up man.

The evolution of this role is clear. When starters became more and more apt to leave a game early on, and once Dennis Eckersley revolutionized the end game with his manager Tony La Russa in Oakland using him for one inning only, there was a glaring hole between innings six and nine. Home runs and high-scoring affairs bring in the fans, but it is defense and pitching that bring in titles. The teams that address the middle-inning role are the ones that succeed.

As a generation earlier, when the closers could not solely be judged by won-loss records and ERA, the value of the middle reliever and set-up man cannot be judged that way either. To make matters more difficult, you can't add a second save for every win.

The concept of a team having a defined set-up pitcher is still a relatively new one. Much like in the 1960s when Jerome Holtzman began tracking how many "saves" pitchers had, even though it was an unofficial baseball term at the time, history is repeating itself with the "hold." As yet, baseball has not acknowledged the validity of the hold as a viable statistic. The term is still relatively undefined, or underdefined. Set-up pitchers often enter the game with their team losing or with the game all tied up. Closers rarely come into a game when the team is losing and will seldom come into a tie game. Although the idea of the hold is a step in the right direction, it may not be a finished work of art just yet. But if baseball needs a stat as the precursor to the save when a team wins, the hold seems more than acceptable. It flat-out makes sense.

Most serious baseball fans are statisticians when it comes to their game. Although not all are members of the Society for American Baseball Research (SABR), most have an understanding of the statistical value that is often put on a particular player or position. In years past, even though saves were not part of the official baseball statistics, they were recorded and eventually awarded retroactively. To paraphrase the words of the great Yogi Berra, although the hold is a relatively new baseball stat, it might very well be a case of déjà vu all over again.

Invented in 1986 by John Dewan and Mike O'Donnell, the hold statistically measures the effectiveness of relievers who normally don't close games. A hold is different from a save in that a hold provides your closer a save opportunity. Technically, all pitchers who earn a hold enter the game with an opportunity for a save.

A hold is credited anytime a relief pitcher enters the game in a save situation, records at least one out and leaves the game never having relinquished the lead. Unlike wins, saves, and losses, more than one pitcher per team can earn a hold for a game. A pitcher can receive a hold by protecting a lead, even if that lead is lost by another pitcher who enters the game after he exits the tilt. So if Team A is leading 3–1 in the sixth inning and relief pitcher B throws a scoreless seventh inning with Team A still in the lead, even if pitcher C gives up 10 runs in the eighth inning, pitcher B still earns a hold for that game.

Will the hold become an official baseball statistic much like the save did? No decision is currently looming from Major League Baseball, but because such numbers give value to certain roles, it seems a fairly safe bet that at some point the hold will become an official stat. How soon that will happen is difficult to surmise, as baseball is not known for reacting rapidly to various situations. It took years for the game to accept the save. Fans and stat hounds would like to see the hold become official—and an even smarter bet is that middle relievers would, too.

Love them or hate them, the New York Yankees have a proud tradition in the game of baseball and have on more than one occasion helped lead America's Game to new areas. Such was the case in their use of the bullpen. In the late 1970s they instituted a sort of bullpen by committee but with each committee member having a specific role. The tandem of Hall of Famer Goose Gossage and his set-up man, Ron Davis, was particularly effective. Setting the stage for today's game, Davis would enter a contest in the seventh or eighth inning before turning the reins over to Gossage in the ninth. During one particularly effective streak, the Yanks won 77 of 79 games where they led going into the seventh inning.

From 1979 through 1981, Davis appeared in 142 games for the Yankees with a 27–10 record, 22 saves, and an ERA that never exceeded 2.95. As is often the case, Davis moved on, going to the Minnesota Twins where he parlayed his success as a set-up man into the closer's role, saving 106 games over the next four years.

In fact, the great Mariano Rivera spent the first year and a half of his stellar career setting up for John Wetteland. He is not the only closer to earn his stripes as a set-up man. Brad Lidge had 57 holds with Houston. Cardinals closer Ryan Franklin accumulated 52 holds over his career. Solomon Torres had 74, and Tom Gordon has 109 holds in his long career. While with the Angels, Francisco Rodriguez had 133 holds. The odds are that he won't increase that total very much in his tenure with the New York Mets.

Another Yankee hurler who enjoyed success in the Ed McMahon role was Ramiro Mendoza. A master of all trades, Mendoza was a starter and reliever during his tenure in pinstripes. On three separate occasions he appeared in more than 53 games, winning championships in 1998 and 2000 in New York. He is also the first player in the last 76 years to win championships with both the Yankees and the Boston Red Sox (2004).

Topping the list of all-time hold leaders is southpaw Mike Stanton with 266, as of the end of 2008. Another lefty, Arthur Rhodes, is second on the list with 192 holds. Alan Embree ranks third with 188, followed by Dan Plesac and Mike Jackson, who are tied with 179. A pair of righties, Paul Quantrill and Jeff Nelson, have 177 holds. Mike Timlin recorded 172, and Buddy Groom has earned 171.

The idea of middle relievers, set-up men, and closers can put the leadership abilities of the manager and pitching coach, who need to keep their charges in line, to the test. Baseball is a game with a tremendous competition for prime spots. Some guys are team players who will gladly go wherever they are told. And others are looking out for themselves, desiring fame and a fat paycheck. At the end of the day it is performance

Mike Stanton was the classic set-up man. The hard-throwing Texan finished his 19-year major-league career as the all-time leader in holds (266) and second in games pitched. Despite his 1,178 appearances, he accumulated only 68 wins and 84 saves.

that counts. It is the job of the manager and his staff to put players in positions where they can succeed. It's a very defined process when handling pitchers in the pen. And during the course of a season, pitchers will move up and down the depth chart, depending on performance or lack thereof.

"When the roles in the bullpen work, the team wins and the personalities in the pen are calm and confident," said Jim Gott. "When it doesn't, mutiny is at hand, and the role becomes like a totem pole. Pitch well, and you climb to the top. One bad outing, and you crash to the bottom, holding everybody up.

"I remember being a Dodger and going through a period of no established roles, which was the fault of the players. I began to climb the totem pole, and I finally made it to the top. Playing in many close games in one stretch, I was called into my sixth game of the last eight. My arm was hanging. I threw my warm-ups and didn't have much. My catcher, Mike Scioscia, came to the mound and made a funny comment about my lack of nastiness. As he walked away he reminded me that a bad outing was my only chance for rest. Of course I knew that, but I was enjoying being at the top of the totem pole.

"The bottom line is that the bullpen is a very important line of defense. There needs to be defined roles, and everyone's goal is to protect the closer. He needs to be as fresh as possible."

The closer may get pretty much all of the publicity and fame, as well as a bigger paycheck. But make no mistake, it is the middle relievers and set-up men who help make them successful. Baseball is a team sport played by individuals. That truth is especially evident in the bullpens, where the team of relievers acts in concert.

Most times, if a closer earns a save during a game, the odds are that he was not the only member of the pen who contributed to the victory.

CHAPTER 11

Closing the Deal: Seasons Worth Saving

Ballplayers can come of out nowhere and have career seasons that were completely unexpected. Or a fine ballplayer can kick it up a notch one year and exceed his career stats for that single season before reverting back to his regular level of accomplishment.

Position players are one thing. They are out there every day with regular opportunities to keep a good streak going or get into a little funk. Guys who play 162 regular-season games and put up fantastic efforts just seem as though they are in a trance for the entire season. Pitchers are different. They can burst onto the scene, getting everyone's attention and confounding the experts who didn't think they had it in them. But after the league sees them a couple of times, hitters adjust, the hot streak is over, and they are often soon gone from the majors and destined to spend the rest of their lives as answers to trivia questions.

Relief pitchers are a breed inside a breed. Even the most talented starter with a long history of 20-win seasons might not have the right stuff to pitch out of the pen and become a closer. It's a different mind-set that separates the closer from his other pitching mates.

The National League Most Valuable Player in 1950 was Phillies right-hander Jim Konstanty. The bespectacled relief specialist appeared in 74 games with a 16–7 record, 22 saves, and a 2.66 ERA. Konstanty was one of the earliest pitchers to throw almost exclusively out of the bullpen. Ironically, because the Phillies were shorthanded for Game 1 of the Fall Classic, with Curt Simmons in the service and Robin Roberts unavailable because he pitched the pennant-clinching game three days earlier, Konstanty was the Game 1 starter in the World Series.

Elroy Face had his famous season in 1959, going 18–1 for Pittsburgh with 10 saves and a 2.70 ERA. His .947 winning percentage lead the league. Always a steady performer, this one season stood out among the rest.

At the same time that Face was confounding National League hitters with his forkball, lanky Lindy McDaniel was having similar success with the same pitch. A former starting pitcher who had gone 15–9 in 1957, he became a reliever in 1959, going 14–12 for the St. Louis Cardinals with a league-leading 15 saves. But he had an All-Star season in 1960 when he appeared in 65 games, boasting a 12–4 record with a league-leading 26 saves and a 2.09 ERA. A decade later, in 1970, McDaniel was still going strong when he contributed 29 saves as a New York Yankee. His career spanned 21 years, and he amassed a 141–119 record and 172 saves.

Right-hander Don Elston, formerly a spot starter, became a full-time reliever with the Chicago Cubs in 1958 and enjoyed newfound success. He led the league with 69 appearances that season with a 9–8 record, 10 saves, and an ERA of 2.88. But he had perhaps his best season in 1959 when he again led the league with 65 appearances, sporting a 10–8 record with 13 saves and an ERA of 3.32.

Ryne Duren bounced around during his 10-year major league career, with a modest 27–44 career record with 32 saves and a 3.83 ERA. But "Blind Ryne," as he was known because of his poor eyesight, used to have five different pairs of glasses to help him try to find home plate. His 95-mph fastball made facing him a difficult task for many hitters. The fact that he also always uncorked a wild pitch back to the screen behind home plate on his first warm-up could also cause some tension for the hitter.

In 1958 with the Yankees, Duren appeared in 44 games and had a 6–4 record, leading the league with 20 saves with a fine 2.02 ERA. Although he never quite matched those marks on the field, he certainly deserves credit off the field for overcoming alcoholism.

Los Angeles Dodgers right-hander Larry Sherry had an 11-year big-league career that also included stops in Detroit, Houston, and California. But his greatest accomplishment may have been the 1959 World Series, in which the Dodgers defeated the Chicago White Sox in six games. Sherry was named the Most Valuable Player of the Series, as he completed all four Los Angeles wins, getting credit for two victories and eventually getting credit for saving the other two. It was his World Series play that led to the statistic of the save being introduced to baseball.

In the Series he was 2–0 with a 0.71 ERA in 12⅔ innings pitched. He followed up his postseason MVP with another fine season in 1960, going 14–10 with seven saves. He had his career high in saves with 20 in 1966 while pitching for the Tigers.

Previously mentioned was the stunning season put together by New York Yankees left-hander Luis Arroyo in 1961. Using his screwball and a sneaky fastball, he led the league in appearances with 65 and saves with 29, sporting a 15–5 record with a 2.19 ERA.

Because of his size and demeanor on the pitcher's mound, Boston reliever Dick Radatz was nicknamed "the Monster." And he put together a couple of monster seasons in Beantown. As a rookie in 1962 he led the league with 62 appearances and 24 saves, good enough to earn him *The Sporting News* Fireman of the Year Award. Radatz continued his fine work in 1963 when he went 15–6 with 25 more saves, becoming the first pitcher in history to have consecutive 20-save seasons.

But 1964 was perhaps Dick Radatz's best and final great season. Using his flaming fastball, he had a 16–9 record in 79 games with a 2.29 ERA and a league-leading 29 saves. He fanned 181 batters in 157 innings and was once again *The Sporting News* Fireman of the Year as well as a member of the American League All-Star team. But in that game, he surrendered a dramatic three-run home run by the Phillies' Johnny Callison in the bottom of the ninth to bring the Senior Circuit the victory. The big right-hander suffered elbow and shoulder injuries the following season and was never the same pitcher.

Another right-hander who made quite a mark during that era was Phil Regan, who had enjoyed limited success as a starter with the Detroit Tigers. Converted to a relief specialist in 1966 with the Los Angeles Dodgers, Regan appeared in 65 games with a 14–1 record, a league-leading 21 saves, and an ERA of 1.62. As a result of his fabulous season, Regan was named *The Sporting News* Fireman of the Year as well as Comeback Player of the Year.

He once again received Fireman of the Year status in 1968 after being traded to the Chicago Cubs. He went 10–5 in Chicago in 68 games, saving a league-leading 25 games with a 2.27 ERA.

Wayne Granger was traded to Cincinnati after spending a nondescript rookie season with the St. Louis Cardinals. He responded to the Queen City by setting a new record for appearances by a pitcher in 1969 with 90, going 9–6 with 27 saves and a 2.80 ERA, good enough to capture *The Sporting News* Fireman of the Year Award.

The following season he won the award again, appearing in 67 games with a 6–5 record and a league-leading 35 saves. The tall, skinny right-hander, whom a teammate once said could "shower in a shotgun barrel," injured his arm and was never quite the same dominating pitcher. But he did save 19 games for Minnesota in 1972.

Another top pitcher of that era was southpaw Ron Perranoski, who experienced most of his success as a key member of the Los Angeles Dodgers' and Minnesota Twins' bullpens. He led the league in appearances three times while with the Dodgers, pitching in 70 games in 1962, 69 games the following year, and 70 in 1967. In 1963 his 16–3 season with a 1.67 ERA with 21 saves helped Los Angeles advance to the World Series. He had two outstanding seasons with the Twins, where he led the league in saves two times, with 31 in 1969 and 34 in 1970.

Mike Marshall's 1974 season earned him the National League Cy Young Award while pitching for the Los Angeles Dodgers. He appeared in an incredible 106 games, a record that still stands, winning 15 and losing 12 with 21 saves and a 2.42 ERA. But Marshall also threw 208 innings and finished 83 games. He was baseball's first relief pitcher to win Cy Young honors.

One of Marshall's top competitors for the award was his Dodger team-mate, starting pitcher Andy Messersmith, who went 20–6 that season. Ironically, Messersmith the starter threw just 84 more innings than Marshall the reliever. Marshall pitched more often and for longer periods of time than any closer even comes close to in today's game. He clearly took the role of the reliever to new heights.

Three years later, in 1977, a second reliever earned Cy Young honors, the New York Yankees' stellar southpaw Sparky Lyle. He appeared in 72 games, sporting a 13–5 record with 26 saves and an outstanding 2.17 ERA. Although pitching nowhere near the number of innings that Mike Marshall did, Lyle still was one of the relievers of his era who averaged multiple innings per appearance. He also finished 60 games.

Unlike so many closers of today who consider the ninth inning their own, Lyle not only pitched multiple innings but also came into games where there was immediate pressure, as he regularly inherited difficult situations. Of his 72 games, he entered the game with no base runners just 13 times. And yet he succeeded.

As did Marshall's, Lyle's winning of the Cy Young Award had a large influence on the game. Sporting a good fastball and a devastating slider, his success on Broadway with the Yankees gave his craft, closing baseball games, credibility that it had not enjoyed before.

One of the newest members of the Baseball Hall of Fame had an outstanding season among a number of outstanding seasons with his 1979 performance with the Chicago Cubs. Bruce Sutter used his split-finger fastball to dazzle hitters en route to a Cy Young Award. Sutter appeared in 62 games with a 6–6 record and a 2.22 ERA with 37 saves.

In 1977 the Yankees' Sparky Lyle put together one of the greatest relief pitching seasons in MLB history: 72 appearances, a 13–5 record, 26 saves, and a 2.17 ERA. New York won the World Series, and Lyle became the second reliever to win a Cy Young Award.

He finished 56 games and also averaged two innings per appearance. Unlike his two predecessors who won the Cy Young Award out of the bullpen, Sutter's 37 saves led the league. He came within one save of breaking John Hiller's previous single-season save record of 38 with the 1973 Detroit Tigers.

A native of Toronto, Ontario, Hiller pitched for 15 seasons with the Tigers. A spot starter and reliever, Hiller was a nondescript left-hander until he nearly died in 1971 after suffering a heart attack at the age of 28. The following season, Hiller was designated as a coach for Detroit and was the team's batting practice pitcher. With his teammates unable to do much with him, he was activated in July 1972, going 1–2 with three saves in 24 games with an ERA of 2.03.

In his record-setting season of 1973, Hiller appeared in a league-leading 65 games, going 10–5, setting the league save record with 38, and sporting an ERA of 1.44. Hiller was the first Detroit pitcher to lead the league in saves since Al Benton did the trick in 1940 with 17 and the first Tiger to lead the league in appearances since Harry Coveleski pitched in 50 games in 1915. Hiller's 38 saves remained the league's best until Dan Quisenberry broke it with 45 in 1983. The first left-hander to break Hiller's mark was Dave Righetti with 46 saves with the 1986 New York Yankees.

After the season, John Hiller won the Hutch Award, emblematic of fighting spirit and competitive desire, the American League *The Sporting News* Fireman of the Year and the Comeback Player of the Year.

Right-hander Bill Campbell came into his own out of the Minnesota Twins bullpen in 1976 when he went 17–5 in 78 games with 20 saves and a 2.96 ERA. His timing was impeccable, as he was able to parlay that big season into a big free-agent contract with the Boston Red Sox. And in 1977, he did not disappoint.

Campbell was 13–9 in 69 games out of the Red Sox's bullpen, leading the league with 31 saves and a 2.96 ERA. His season was good enough to gain an All-Star berth as well as being named American League *The Sporting News* Fireman of the Year and Rolaids Relief Man of the Year. Injuries limited his effectiveness after that breakout season, but Bill Campbell was still an effective relief pitcher through the 1986 season.

One of the finest seasons out of the bullpen belonged to the afore-mentioned Rollie Fingers, who won the Cy Young Award and the Most Valuable Player Award for his efforts in the strike-shortened season of 1981. Fingers appeared in 47 games with a 6–3 record, 28 saves, and a stunning 1.04 ERA in 78 innings pitched. That he saved 28 games in a 109-game season is also extraordinary.

For a guy with a three-quarter submarine delivery, Dan Quisenberry had quite a run during his 12-year career with Kansas City, St. Louis, and San Francisco. When he was throwing his fastball or outstanding slider, his pitches looked as if they were coming out of the rosin bag on the pitcher's mound. But when it got to the plate, hitters never looked entirely comfortable against Quiz.

He led the American League three separate times in appearances with 75 in 1980, 84 in 1985, and 69 in perhaps his best season in 1983 with the Royals. In those 69 games, he accumulated a 5–3 record with 45 saves and a stellar 1.94 ERA. During the next two seasons, Quisenberry saved 44 and 37 games respectively. Dan Quisenberry passed away September 30, 1998, at age 45 of cancer.

The 1984 Detroit Tigers were the toast of the town. They breezed to a division title, swept the Kansas City Royals in the American League Championship Series, and defeated San Diego in the World Series. Although the core of the team remained the same for a number of years, the most important addition to the '84 squad was Willie Hernandez.

Teaming up with "Señor Smoke," the late Aurelio Lopez, in 1984, Hernandez was a key reason the Tigers were 96–0 when leading in the ninth inning. Hernandez appeared in 80 games with a 9–3 record, 32 saves (in 33 attempts), and an ERA of 1.92. He finished 68 games, and much like pitchers of that era, he averaged just under two innings per appearance. There was little in Willie Hernandez's season to consider him anything less than the Cy Young Award winner and the American League Most Valuable Player. It was the year of years.

Steve Bedrosian won the Cy Young Award with the Philadelphia Phillies in 1987. The hard-throwing right-hander appeared in 65 games with a 5–3 record, 40 saves, and a 2.83 ERA. He finished 56 games and threw 89 innings. He accumulated more saves and fewer wins than any previous Cy Young Award winner. Bedrosian did have saves in 13 consecutive appearances, a major league record. He was able to outpoint Rick Sutcliffe of the Chicago Cubs for the award. While Sutcliffe earned four first-place votes and 55 total points, Bedrosian received nine first-place votes and a total of 57.

Southpaw Mark Davis was a journeyman pitcher who had started as many as 27 games in a season, which he did in 1984 with the San Francisco Giants en route to a 5–17 record. The following season he became primarily a reliever. It took a few seasons for him to reach his potential. But in 1989, Mark Davis had a season that nobody had any right to expect.

He appeared in 70 games for San Diego, going 4–3 with a league-leading 44 saves and an ERA of 1.85. He also finished 65 games. He was the National League *The Sporting News* Fireman of the Year and won the league's Cy Young Award. In the final month of the season, he pitched nearly 25 innings and stranded every one of the 19 base runners he inherited. He was signed to a $10-million free-agent contract with Kansas City following his big season but reverted to his former form with a 2–7 record, just six saves, and a 5.11 ERA.

Dave Righetti was an up-and-coming left-handed starting pitcher in the New York Yankees' organization. Making the team for good in 1981, he went 33–22 over the next three years, including a 14–8 season in 1983 that featured a no-hitter against the Boston Red Sox on July 4 at Yankee Stadium. When Goose Gossage left the team there was a void in the bullpen, and manager Yogi Berra tabbed "Rags" for the job.

In his first year as a reliever in 1984, Righetti went 5–6 in 64 games but saved 31 contests. But his standout season among standout seasons as the Yankees closer occurred in 1986. He appeared in 74 games with an 8–8 record and set a single-season major league save record with 46. Over his seven-year career as the Yankees' closer, Righetti went 41–38 with 223 saves. He later had three years with San Francisco before finishing up with Oakland, Toronto, and the Chicago White Sox.

Another White Sox pitcher, right-hander Bobby Thigpen, put up some impressive numbers during the mid to late 1980s. From 1986 to 1989 he established himself as a fine closer with a 16–19 record and 91 saves. But what he did in 1990 defied logic. Thigpen appeared in a league-leading 77 games and had a 4–6 record and an outstanding 1.83 ERA. He also set the major league record for saves when he notched 57, a mark that stood until Francisco Rodriguez eclipsed it in 2008 with 62.

"Bobby had a great deal of confidence," said his former manager with the White Sox, Jim Fregosi. "He was a very good athlete who liked the limelight. There are certain guys who have that makeup. They want the ball in the ninth inning with the game on the line. Bobby had a great attitude and was a great kid.

"I remember when we got Barry Jones to set up for Thigpen. We had a game in Toronto where Jones had pitched the eighth inning, and we had gotten a few more runs. It wasn't a save situation, so I sent him out for the ninth. He went out there and gave up base hit, base hit, base hit. So I had to bring in Thigpen. Jones looked at me, smiled, and told me that he set up a save situation for Thigpen."

Although he enjoyed two more successful seasons with Chicago, saving 30 and 22 games, Bobby Thigpen never again reached those heights. He then pitched for Philadelphia and Seattle before his big-league time ended in 1994.

Dennis Eckersley's incredible success in the bullpen after being a premier starter has already been chronicled here. But his 1992 season is one for the record books. Or in his case, one *more* season for the record books. He appeared in 69 games with a 7–1 record and a league-leading 51 saves with a 1.91 ERA. Eckersley won the American League Cy Young Award as well as the American League Most Valuable Player honors.

Blown saves have become a statistic of interest in the game. It should be noted that in 1992, Dennis Eckersley saved 51 games with just three blown saves.

Another pitcher who had an incredible season was Los Angeles Dodgers right-hander Éric Gagné. After three years of struggling as a spot starter and reliever, he was converted to a closer full time in 2002 and responded with a 4–1 record with 52 saves and a 1.97 ERA in 77 games. The following season, in 2003, Gagné earned the Cy Young Award, appearing in 77 games again, finishing with a 2–3 record with 55 saves. He did not blow a save that entire season and finally reached 84 consecutive saves. During his Cy Young season, Gagné also fanned 137 hitters in 82 innings.

There are countless examples of players who put together a big season in the last year of their contract, thus earning a big-time new contract. Francisco Rodriguez certainly qualifies. Already an outstanding closer with the Los Angeles Angels, K-Rod earned 45, 47, and 40 saves in three consecutive years, leading the league twice. But in his contract year of 2008, he led the American League with 78 appearances, setting a new save record with 62. His reward was a three-year, $37-million free-agent contract with the New York Mets—proof that in baseball, as in life, quite often it's all about timing.

CHAPTER 12

A New Era:
The 1990s and 2000s

Although the year 2000 ushered in the new millennium, it was the 1990s that debuted a new era in baseball. Things were different, and to be blunt, stuff happened: expansion, realignment, tragedy, and something that even world wars did not produce. It all started when two new teams necessitated a different alignment. In 1993, the National League added two new teams to the lineup, the Florida Marlins and the Colorado Rockies. As a result, each league had three divisions, the Eastern, Central, and Western divisions.

The postseason also changed. Each of the division champions advanced to the playoffs along with a wild-card team in each league. The wild-card was a new concept in baseball but had been an accepted opportunity to earn a playoff appearance in the National Football League. Now in America's Game, in addition to the three division champions in each league, the best second-place team in each league was added to the opening round, best-of-five playoff series. After the winners of those series are decided, the winners meet in a best-of-seven series to decide the league champions, and those two teams meet in the Fall Classic.

Two new teams meant two additional rosters full of big-league talent that would not be there were it not for expansion. People will complain about the dilution of talent that comes with expansion, but although there is some truth in that, expansion also gives deserving players a chance to perform on the big stage.

The big-league stage makes players appear like supermen, almost larger than life. But every now and then something happens that makes fans and athletes seem alike—revealing that athletes are, in fact, people. And as people they are subject to the same dangers as the rest of us, regardless of what they can accomplish on a baseball field.

The 1993 season in Cleveland was supposed to be a good one for the Tribe. Blessed with good hitting, a fine starting pitching staff, and a strong bullpen, Cleveland had high hopes for its chances to make the postseason. But the Indians' season was lost before it even began. Baseball, in fact, became insignificant.

Cleveland had but one single off-day during spring training of 1993. On that day, pitcher Tim Crews invited his fellow Indian bullpen mate, closer Steve Olin, and starting left-hander Bob Ojeda to his ranch just outside of Orlando, Florida. The Olin and Ojeda families joined Crews and his family for a day of fun and good cheer. As darkness fell, the three teammates went on a boat ride together. Crews owned an 18-foot open-air bass boat that could motor along at nearly 50 mph. While riding at a high rate of speed, the boat rammed a new dock that extended some 250 feet out into the lake. Olin was killed instantly. Crews died a short time later. Ojeda survived and was hospitalized, no doubt wondering why he had been spared. An autopsy later revealed that Crews was legally drunk at the time of the accident.

After a number of seasons with the Los Angeles Dodgers, Crews had signed a free-agent contract with Cleveland. He was expected to be a strong set-up man for Olin. But the plan never had a chance to be tested. As news spread of the tragedy, former teammates of those involved in the tragic accident remembered their friends.

"It was an incredible shock," said Jim Gott, an outstanding reliever with four teams, including the Dodgers, where he and Crews became the best of friends. Relief pitchers pass countless hours together in the bullpen waiting for the call to action. "We became friends when we were both pitching with the Dodgers, hanging out in the bullpen together with our buddy, Jay Howell. We got to know each other and each other's families. 'Crewser' was a cowboy. He loved country and western music and had just finished building their dream house. He was so excited that he'd bring blueprints to the bullpen and show us. The place looked great, and it was on a lake.

"We were sad to see him move to another team when he signed with Cleveland. Right after the accident, Tim was alive for a short time. It was an incredibly sad time.

"Tommy Lasorda [the Dodgers manager] had a team meeting, and all of the bullpen guys were crying. The O'Malley family, who owned the Dodgers at the time, chartered a bus for us all to go to the memorial service."

It was certainly no easier for friends of Steve Olin. Coming off a dominant year in 1992 with Cleveland, he appeared in 72 games with an 8–5 record with 29 saves and a 2.34 ERA. While many successful closers either blow hitters away with heat or have an unhittable specialty pitch, Olin kept hitters' feet in the bucket with his three-quarter underhanded delivery. In each of his four big-league seasons, he saw his workload and success ratio increase and improve. He was an up-and-coming star in the American League when he died at the age of 27.

"It was really tough," said his teammate Derek Lilliquist. "Mike Hargrove was in his first year as manager of the Indians, and he was really big on making us all feel like family. That was a day off, and I remember that I was scheduled to pitch the next day in Port St. Lucie against the Mets. We were supposed to go to that cookout, but my wife suggested that we spend the day at home instead. So I could have been right there with them. That night at around 2 AM, my mother called me. She couldn't believe that I wasn't on the boat with them.

"We had to pull through it. In a sense, we used it to motivate ourselves. As a professional, Steve would have wanted us to move forward. It was a really tough year. But I'm sure he was up there smiling at us the whole time. He was just a class act."

Ojeda, who had also come over from the Dodgers, recovered from his injuries and returned to the Indians later that season, pitching in nine games and going 2–1. He pitched two games for the Yankees in 1994. He has never discussed publicly the tragic day of March 22, 1993.

The years of 1904 and 1994 have something in common. They are the only seasons since the first World Series in 1903 that there was no Fall Classic. The 1994 season stopped on August 12. The remainder of the season, the playoffs, and the World Series were lost when the players walked out after owners demanded a salary cap to ease financial hardships. It was the eighth work stoppage in the history of baseball and probably the most damaging.

After future Supreme Court justice Sonia Sotomayor issued an injunction against the owners the following spring, the 1995 season got underway on April 25 with a 144-game schedule, rather than the usual 162 games. The game was severely damaged, as millions of fans were disgusted with the perceived greed involved in the game on the part of players and owners.

On the field, the trend away from complete games continued as the 1990s saw fewer than 10 percent of starting pitchers complete games. Relief pitching, specialization, and the one-inning save all continued to be the rule in the game rather than the exception. There was no shortage of fine pitchers manning the roles of closers as well as set-up men.

A number of closers who made a name for themselves in the 1980s continued to perform their magic in the 1990s. Dennis Eckersley, Lee Smith, John Franco, Bobby Thigpen, Rick Aguilera, Tom Henke, Mitch Williams, and others kept putting up big save numbers. In addition, a number of new names began to surface in box scores with regularity.

Doug Jones

Mustachioed right-hander Doug Jones had a good amount of success in the late 1980s with the Cleveland Indians. In the last two years of the decade, he went 10–14 with 69 saves and a fine ERA under 2.35. In 1990 he had an outstanding season, going 5–5 with 43 saves and a 2.56 ERA. Unlike closers who threw heat or a specialty pitch, Jones used changing speeds to fool hitters. As a guy who threw a screwball when he first came up to the major leagues, he achieved success when he used his slow fastball and two different change-ups in his arsenal. He kept hitters off balance with slow, slower, and even slower change-ups that also had movement.

After an off year in 1991 in which he went 4–8 with just seven saves and a high ERA of 5.54, Jones was dealt to the Houston Astros, where he revived his career. He went 11–8 in 80 appearances in 1992 with 36 saves and a 1.85 ERA. He had a 26-save season with the Astros in 1993 before being traded along with big right-hander Jeff Juden to Philadelphia in exchange for Mitch Williams, who Phillies brass thought needed a new address after serving up Joe Carter's walk-off, World Series–winning home run.

Jones had an excellent season in Philadelphia, winning two games and saving 27 more in 29 opportunities with a 2.17 ERA. Jones had two more big seasons, earning 22 saves in 1995 with Baltimore and 36 in 1997 with the Brewers. In 16 seasons Jones accumulated a 69–79 record with 303 saves and a 3.30 ERA.

Jeff Montgomery

Right-hander Jeff Montgomery earned one more career save than Doug Jones. Another nonprototypical closer, Montgomery actually pitched like a starter. Unlike most closers who throw two pitches, he used a fastball, slider, curve, and change-up.

"My best pitch was a strike," he told Bob Dutton of the *Kansas City Star*. "I don't know that I had one pitch that was better for a strike than any other. If I had to narrow it down, I got more quality outs over my career on a slider."

After coming up in the Cincinnati organization, Montgomery was traded to the Kansas City Royals prior to the 1988 season. He had a 7–2 record with the Royals in his first full big-league season in 1988. The following season, he went 7–3 with 18 saves. Over the next 10 seasons he saved at least 24 games eight times. Montgomery's best season came in 1993 when he appeared in 69 games with a 7–5 record, had a league-leading 45 saves, and sported an ERA of 2.27. He also had 36 saves in 1998.

When Jeff Montgomery was done for good following the 1999 season, he finished his 13-year career with a 46–52 record with 304 saves and a 3.27 ERA. But he spent most of his career in relative obscurity playing for a small-market team in Kansas City that did not have much national attention.

José Mesa

Much like Doug Jones and Jeff Montgomery, veteran right-hander José Mesa surpassed the 300-save mark, earning 321 during his 19 big-league seasons. With a 95-mph-plus fastball as well as a two-seamer that had great sinking action, Mesa pitched for Baltimore, Cleveland, San Francisco, Seattle, Philadelphia, Pittsburgh, Colorado, and Detroit during his two-decade stint in the majors. His 112 saves with the Phillies is a team record. He also saved 104 during his years with the Indians.

A starter early in his career, Mesa went 10–12 with Cleveland in 1993. The following season he was converted to the role of a reliever. He appeared in 51 games, going 7–5 with two saves. But 1995 saw Mesa have his best season in the big leagues. He appeared in 62 games, going 3–0 with a league-leading 46 saves and an outstanding 1.13 ERA. Based on his outstanding season, Mesa won *The Sporting News* Fireman of the Year Award and the Rolaids Relief Man of the Year Award. His efforts helped Cleveland reach the World Series for the first time in 47 years. He was 1–0 with one save in two games, but his efforts were in vain, as the Tribe lost to the Atlanta Braves in six games.

Mesa had 39 saves with the 1996 team and then went 4–4 in 66 appearances for the '97 Cleveland team with 16 saves. That team also made it to the postseason with Mesa pitching well in the American League Championship Series but blowing a lead in the seventh game of the World Series.

With their second World Series appearance in three years, Cleveland took on the Florida Marlins in Game 7. With the Indians clinging to a 2–1 lead, Mesa was brought into the game in the home half of the ninth inning, three outs away from helping the Indians win their first World Series title since 1948. But unfortunately for Mesa and his teammates, it was not to be.

Moises Alou led off the bottom of the ninth with a single, and one out later he advanced to third base on a single by Charles Johnson. Craig Counsell then hit a sacrifice fly to score the tying run. Florida eventually won the game and the Series by scoring the winning run in the eleventh inning.

Ever the supportive teammate, Cleveland shortstop Omar Vizquel ripped Mesa in his book, *Omar! My Life On and Off the Field,* writing in part, "The eyes of the world were focused on every move we made. Unfortunately, Jose's own eyes were vacant. Completely empty. Nobody home. You could almost see right through him. Not long after I looked into his vacant eyes, he blew the save and the Marlins won the game."

Not surprisingly, Mesa was incensed with Vizquel's comments, vowing to hit him with a pitch every time he faced him. Although he drilled his former teammate only twice, he buzzed his tower on more than one occasion, telling reporters, "I want to kill him."

Although Mesa's 5.40 ERA in the 1997 World Series was below his expected level, Omar Vizquel's eyes may have been a little vacant as well, as he hit just .233 in the Series and was only 1-for-5 in the pivotal Game 7.

Mesa put the disappointing game behind him. He helped the Mariners reach the playoffs in 2000 as a set-up man but took over his more familiar closer's role the following season. He ended his long career in 2007 with an 80–109 record with 321 saves.

Gregg Olson

Gregg Olson burst onto the scene with the Baltimore Orioles in 1989. There are no guarantees in life or in baseball, but it seemed a sure thing that Olson would have a long and fruitful major league career. Although he certainly did, as his 217 saves indicate, had he not been hit with numerous injuries, he probably could have achieved much more.

Olson went 5–2 in 64 games for the '89 O's with 27 saves and a 1.69 ERA, good enough to earn him American League Rookie of the Year honors. He also set a league record for the most saves by a rookie pitcher.

Things only got better for Olson in 1990 as he went 6–5 with 37 saves and was elected to the American League All-Star team. Using a fastball in the 90s and what he called "Uncle Charlie," a deep dropping curveball that baffled batters, he saved 96 games over the next three seasons, including 36 in 1992. But things started to go sour for him in August 1993 when he suffered a torn ligament in his pitching elbow and missed the remainder of that season. The Orioles chose to let Olson go and signed Lee Smith as their closer.

Olson fought injuries and bounced around from Atlanta to Cleveland, Kansas City, Detroit, Houston, Minnesota, and Kansas City again before landing in Arizona in 1998. He rebounded with a 3–4 record with 30 saves and a 3.01 ERA. The following season he was 9–4 with 14 saves.

Olson spent the next two years with the Los Angeles Dodgers, primarily as a set-up man. He finished his injury-plagued 14-year major league career with a 40–39 record with 217 saves and a 3.46 ERA.

Billy Wagner

Left-hander Billy Wagner could light up a radar gun with the best of them. The diminutive flamethrower regularly delivered heat in excess of 100 mph. But just as much of a rarity, he had the ability to throw strikes.

Wagner had his first full season in "The Show" with the Houston Astros in 1996, winning two games and saving nine more. But in 1997, he

Billy Wagner is on the short side as far as closers go, but he's one of the toughest the game has ever seen. Starting in 1997, he recorded at least 20 saves in 11 out of 12 seasons; by the end of 2009 he ranked No. 6 on the all-time saves list with 385.

went 7–8 with 23 saves and a 2.85 ERA. He also fanned 106 hitters in 66 innings. He had some serious cheese.

Dealing with an occasional stint on the disabled list during his career in Houston, Wagner continued to put up big numbers. He had seasons of 30, 39, 39, 35, and 44 saves with the Astros through 2003. But the emergence of Brad Lidge in Houston made Wagner expendable, and he was traded to Philadelphia in November 2003 in exchange for Brandon Duckworth, Taylor Buchholz, and Ezequiel Astacio.

Wagner's serious heat and competitive nature made him an instant fan favorite in the City of Brotherly Love. In his two seasons in Philadelphia, which included one 10-week stint on the disabled list, Wagner went 8–3 with 59 saves. But he was not only competitive with the opposition, he could also be critical of his team and teammates, making his act wear a little thin. Following the 2005 season, Wagner signed a free-agent deal with the New York Mets.

He had two fine years with the Mets, notching a combined 74 saves in 2006 and 2007, but the Mets blew a late-season lead to the Phillies in '07. Determined not to let the same thing happen in 2008, Wagner and the Mets played well. Wagner pitched in 45 games with an 0–1 record, 27 saves, and a 2.30 ERA before a serious arm injury that required surgery shut him down on August 3. The Mets stumbled again, and the Phillies took the division, pennant, and World Series. With Wagner slated to miss most of the 2009 season, the Mets signed Francisco Rodriguez as their new closer.

Wagner recovered and made two relief appearances for the Mets in August 2009 before being traded to the Red Sox. He made a solid impression in Boston in 15 middle-relief appearances, posting a 1–1 record and a 1.98 ERA. Boston did not need a closer with Jonathan Papelbon in the bullpen, but the Atlanta Braves were willing to pay Wagner $7 million to be their closer in 2010. Over his first 15 seasons, Wagner went 40–38 with 385 saves and a 2.39 ERA. He also fanned 1,092 batters in 813 innings.

Jeff Brantley

Although Jeff Brantley didn't come close to the number of saves that other pitchers of his era did, he was a real fighter on the pitcher's mound. He used a split-finger fastball, or forkball, along with a sinker, slider, and curve. He broke in with the San Francisco Giants in 1988 and 1989 and he pitched in 59 games with a 7–1 record. Moved into the closer's role the following season, he went 5–3 with 19 saves and had a 5–2 mark with 15 saves in 1991. He struggled over the next couple of seasons, and the Giants chose not to offer him a contract for 1994. That's where the Cincinnati Reds got into the act, and that is also where Brantley came into his own, having his two best seasons in the big leagues.

Brantley got off to a good start with the Reds in '94 with a 6–6 record and 15 saves in 50 games. The following season was better as the right-hander had a 3–2 record in 56 games with 28 saves. But Brantley saved the best for his third year in Cincinnati, when he appeared in 66 games with a 1–2 record, a league-leading 44 saves, and an ERA of 2.41.

But injuries bit into his 1997 season as two stints on the disabled list limited Brantley to 13 appearances. He moved on to St. Louis in 1998, where he saved 14 games, and had one final good year with Philadelphia in 2000, where he saved 23 games.

In 14 years, Jeff Brantley had a 43–46 record with 172 saves.

Tom Gordon

Standing at 5'9" and 180 pounds, Tom "Flash" Gordon is not an intimidating presence in the same manner as a Dick Radatz, but armed with an outstanding fastball and deep-breaking curveball, Gordon has spent more than 21 years in the major leagues and may not be done yet.

An entire group of non-sports fans also know of Gordon because he was mentioned in the 1999 Stephen King novel, *The Girl Who Loved Tom Gordon,* a psychological thriller about a girl who idolizes and dreams about Gordon while lost on a hiking trip.

Much like other relief studs such as Dennis Eckersley, Gordon began his career as a starting pitcher for the Kansas City Royals as a 20-year-old in 1988. He went 0–2 that year, but he won a career-high 17 games against just 9 losses the following season, striking out nearly a hitter per inning. He won 12 games three times and 11 games once over the next six seasons.

Gordon was dealt to the Boston Red Sox prior to the start of the 1996 campaign, and he responded with much of the same, a 12–9 record. But in 1997 the Red Sox needed a closer and turned to Tom Gordon part of the way through the season. He saved 11 games in 17 outings out of the bullpen.

Gordon had perhaps his best season in 1998, with a 7–4 record in 73 games and a league-leading 46 saves. He spent time with the Cubs, Astros, White Sox, and Yankees either setting up, closing, or a combination of the two. He signed with the Phillies in 2006 and closed in 59 games, going 3–4 with 34 saves, the second-highest single-season total of his career.

He fought elbow and shoulder injuries over the next few years, saving just eight games, and spent most of the 2009 season on the disabled list with the Arizona Diamondbacks. Gordon has pitched 21 seasons with a 138–126 record and 158 saves.

John Wetteland

Here's a trivia question that could get the better of your average baseball fan: who preceded Mariano Rivera as the closer of the New York Yankees? It was right-hander John Wetteland, who put together nine solid seasons in which he never had fewer than 25 saves.

Wetteland broke in with the Los Angeles Dodgers as a sport starter, going 5–8 in 1989 and 3–4 over the next two years. Following the 1991 season, the young, hard-throwing right-hander was a hot commodity, as he was traded twice, from the Dodgers to the Reds and then from the Reds to the Montreal Expos. When he landed north of the border, he became a full-time closer and made his mark immediately.

Using a fastball, curve, slider, and cutter, he appeared in 67 games in 1992 with a 4–4 record and 37 saves with a 2.92 ERA. He only got better the following season as he pitched in a career-high 70 games with a 9–3 record and 43 saves (his career high, which he matched two other times) and a 1.37 ERA.

Following another good season with Montreal when he won four and saved 25 more games in 1994, Wetteland was traded to the New York Yankees in exchange for Fernando Seguignol. He responded to the Bronx Zoo with a 1–5 season and 31 saves, helping the Yankees to the postseason against Seattle. But his 1996 season was one for the ages. Wetteland appeared in 62 games with a 2–3 record and 43 saves with a 2.83 ERA. The Bronx Bombers advanced to the World Series against the Atlanta Braves, and Wetteland saved all four victories in the Series, which tied a record. But he also saved seven total postseason games, which set an all-time record. He was the World Series Most Valuable Player as well as the recipient of the 1996 Rolaids Relief Man of the Year.

With Rivera waiting in the wings, Wetteland signed a big four-year contract with the Texas Rangers and didn't miss a step. He went 20–12 over four years with 150 saves. At the end of the 2000 season (when his contract expired), following a 6–5 campaign with 34 saves, he retired at the age of 34.

John Wetteland certainly went out at the top of his game. He was given the Rolaids Reliever of the Decade Award for the 1990s, had the most saves of any pitcher in the decade, and became the all-time saves leader for the Texas Rangers. In his 12-year career, he was 48–45 with 330 saves.

Rod Beck

Rod Beck was a bulldog of a right-handed pitcher who toiled for 13 seasons in the big leagues. A sinker, slider, split-finger pitcher, he was known for his competitiveness out on the mound and quite-often flowing hair and a thick mustache. Like many successful relievers, he began his career as a starter in the minor leagues in the Oakland A's organization.

Rod Beck's wild hair and mustache made him a memorable sight on the mound, but batters were more fearful of his nasty sinkers and sliders. In the 1990s he was one of baseball's top closers, averaging 38 saves per season over a six-year stretch.

He was dealt to the San Francisco Giants in a March 1988 minor league deal in exchange for Charlie Corbell and began a swift journey up through the Giants' farm system. He was promoted to the big club in 1991 and went 1–1 with his first big-league save in 31 appearances.

Beck supplanted Dave Righetti as the closer the following season, appearing in 65 games with a 3–3 record and 17 saves. He earned his first of three All-Star selections in 1993 when he went 3–1 in 76 games with 48 saves and a 2.16 ERA. He continued his upward arc in 1994 when he went 2–4 in 48 games with 28 saves and no blown saves. He was once again an All-Star and also was the National League Rolaids Relief Man of the Year.

Beck's effectiveness waned a bit over the next couple of seasons in San Francisco, but he rebounded nicely by going 7–4 in 73 games in 1997 with 36 saves. The Giants made the decision not to re-sign him after the season, deciding instead to go with young fireballer Robb Nen in the team's closing role. As a result, Beck signed a free-agent contract with the Chicago Cubs, where he led the league with his personal-best 81 appearances, going 3–4 with his career-high 51 saves and a 3.02 ERA.

Struggling due to injuries the following season, Beck was traded to the Boston Red Sox after making 31 appearances for Chicago. He pitched well for the Bosox, going 0–1 in 12 games with three saves. After two seasons in Boston, in which he accumulated just six saves combined, he had Tommy John surgery performed on his pitching arm and missed the 2002 season.

He hooked on with the Chicago Cubs' Triple A team in Iowa and pitched well enough to be picked up in a trade by San Diego. With Trevor Hoffman out due to an injury, Beck filled in admirably in 2003, going 3–2 in 36 games with a perfect 20-for-20 record in save situations. But when he was moved back into a set-up role in 2004, Beck struggled and was released in August.

Sadly, Rod Beck's story does not end with a long life after baseball. He was found dead in his Phoenix home on June 23, 2007, at the age of 38. Police found cocaine and drug paraphernalia at his home. His wife,

Stacey, released a statement following Beck's death in which she admitted her husband's addiction to drugs.

"While we were all deeply saddened by the death of Rodney, he suffered from a debilitating, degenerative brain disease called addiction," she said. "The last three years we have seen this disease progress and destroy the person we knew. Unfortunately, the details of his death are not pretty or palatable, but those details are merely symptoms of this devastating brain disease. Rodney overcame other illnesses and injuries, but sadly this brain disease got the best of him."

In his 13-year career, Rod Beck had a 38–45 record with 286 saves and an ERA of 3.30.

Mark Wohlers

Mark "Bay City" Wohlers burst onto the scene with the Atlanta Braves and seemed like the answer to years of prayers by fans and the organization alike for a dominant closer. He was brought along slowly by manager Bobby Cox, who used him primarily in a set-up role for his first four years with the Braves, during which he accumulated a 17–7 record and seven saves.

But in 1995 both Wohlers and the Braves had a magical season. He appeared in 65 games with a 7–3 record, 25 saves, and a 2.09 ERA. In 65 innings he fanned 90 hitters and walked just 24. During spring training of that year, he became the baseball pitcher with the fastest-recorded fastball, which was clocked at 103 mph. That record was broken by Tigers pitcher Joel Zumaya, who was clocked at 104 mph.

Not only was Mark Wohlers fast, but he also was good. Following his breakout season as a closer, he continued his dominance in the playoffs, helping the Braves win the World Series. He was an All-Star selection that season and looked on as one of the best young closers in the game.

He pitched well the following season, going 2–4 in a career-high 77 games with 39 saves, a 3.03 ERA, 100 strikeouts, and just 21 free passes in

77 innings. Again the Braves advanced to the World Series in 1996 but lost to the New York Yankees in six games. In Game 4, Wohlers surrendered a three-run home run to Jim Leyritz to tie the game at 6–6 in a momentum-shifting game.

He was not quite the same pitcher in 1997, but he was certainly still an outstanding closer. In 71 games he was 5–7 with 33 saves. His strikeouts were down, and his walks increased slightly. But what happened to Mark Wohlers in 1998 surprised everyone. He came down with what baseball people know as "Steve Blass disease." Suddenly, much like the Pirates' ace pitcher of the early 1970s, Wohlers was unable to throw strikes. With the Braves in 20 innings, he walked 33 batters and had an ERA of 10.18. Sent to Triple A Richmond to try to work through his problems, he walked 36 batters in 12 innings. Steve Blass disease is believed to be a psychological block that occurs when players overthink the act of throwing the baseball and become unable to control their pitches.

Things got only worse for Wohlers in 1999, even though Atlanta fans roared their support for the World Series–winning closer. In two-thirds of an inning, he walked six hitters and had an ERA of 27.00. Feeling that he needed a change of scenery to continue what had been a successful career, the Braves dealt him to Cincinnati in exchange for John Hudek. The day after joining the Reds, Wohlers was placed on the disabled list with anxiety disorder. While undergoing treatment, he also needed Tommy John surgery on his elbow.

He returned to the Reds in 2000 and then went 3–1 in 30 games in 2001, in which he was not used as the closer. His ERA was 3.94, and in 32 innings he fanned 21 and walked just seven. He was then dealt to the New York Yankees, where he went 1–0 in 31 games and seemed to have solved his wildness.

Although he was nowhere near the same pitcher that he was in his big years with Atlanta, Wohlers had a fine comeback season with Cleveland in 2002. He went 3–4 in 64 games with seven saves and a 4.79 ERA. In 71 innings, he struck out 46 and walked 26. But fate was not kind to Mark Wohlers. The following spring training he needed to have surgery to remove bone chips from his pitching elbow. Attempting to make it back to the Indians, in his second rehab game with Akron, he ruptured the tendon graft he had had in his elbow in 1999, requiring a second Tommy John surgery.

After the surgery, he called it quits. In 12 seasons he went 39–29 with 119 saves. Even with the control problems and injuries, he struck out 557 hitters in 533 innings. He also walked 272.

Robb Nen

Whenever Robb Nen trudged in from the bullpen to enter a home game for the San Francisco Giants at AT&T Park, the music of Deep Purple's monster hit "Smoke on the Water" would greet the big right-hander. It wasn't necessarily Nen's favorite song, but the park is on the water, and Robb Nen threw some serious smoke.

With a fastball that regularly hit the high 90s on the radar gun, Nen also possessed a slider that looked just like a fastball, coming in to the plate at a white-hot 92 mph until it broke straight down. His slider was known as "the Terminator." Make no mistake, Robb Nen terminated the hopes of a huge majority of his opponents.

Originally signed by the Texas Rangers, Nen made his major league debut with the team in 1993. But after making just nine appearances, he was dealt to the Florida Marlins with Kurt Miller in exchange for Cris Carpenter. Nen didn't make much of an impression that year in Florida, but that all started to change in 1994. He appeared in 44 games with a 5–5 record and a perfect 15 saves in 15 opportunities with an ERA of 2.95.

After a difficult 1995 season in which he was 0–7 with 23 saves, he rebounded nicely the following year with a 5–1 record in 75 games with 35 saves and a 1.95 ERA. But 1997 may have been his greatest season (9–3 record, 35 saves), because it ended with the Marlins winning the World Series.

Although it would have seemed normal for a dominant closer on a World Series championship team to be part of that organization for many years, that was not the case for Nen with Florida. In an effort to keep payroll low following its title game, the team held what amounted to a fire sale in which the better players were traded away for young prospects. A month after winning the Fall Classic, Nen was dealt to the San Francisco Giants in exchange for Mike Villano, Joe Fontenot, and Mick Pageler.

Replacing a popular San Francisco closer in Rod Beck, Nen not only met Beck's high standards but even exceeded them. He introduced himself to Giants fans in 1998, pitching in 78 games with a 7–7 record and 40 saves with an ERA of 1.52. Rod who?

Over the next few years he saved 37, 41, a league-leading 45 in 2001, and 43 in 2002. That was also the year that the Giants played in the Fall Classic against the Anaheim Angels. By this time, San Francisco fans were calling the ninth inning the "Nenth" in honor of their outstanding closer.

The 2002 edition of the San Francisco Giants advanced to the World Series against their neighbors in Anaheim. Nen had an All-Star season in 68 games with a 6–2 record, the aforementioned 43 saves, and a 2.20 ERA. But he also had a sore shoulder that had labrum damage and a torn rotator cuff.

"A few weeks before the [All-Star] break, in Toronto, I felt something wrong," Nen told ESPN.com's Eric Neel. "I'd pitched an inning and a third that night, and I remember sleeping on the plane going home and waking up with the top of my shoulder just aching."

Ache or not, he kept pitching, kept taking the ball, even though his velocity wasn't what it was before. He was still effective, and he still went out and did his job in spite of the pain. His dad, former major league infielder Dick Nen, had often given him the same advice.

"He told me, it must have been a thousand times, 'Let everything you do show respect for the game. Don't cheat yourself, and don't cheat your teammates.'"

Robb Nen did exactly that and pitched well in the postseason, garnering two saves in the National League Division Series against Atlanta, three in the National League Championship Series against St. Louis, and two more against the Angels in the Fall Classic. But it was not enough, as the Giants fell to the Angels, and Nen's shoulder just fell. He had three surgeries over the next two seasons to try to fix his shoulder and rehabilitate it enough to get back to the Giants. But the tear in his rotator cuff went through 40 to 75 percent of his shoulder. His contract with San Francisco expired after the 2004 campaign. He filed for free agency but could not muster interest from any big-league club and retired in February 2005.

Robb Nen remains the all-time save leader for the San Francisco Giants with 206. In 10 seasons, he had a 45–42 record with 314 saves and a 2.98 ERA. He struck out 793 batters in 715 innings. He also more than met his dad's challenge about respect for the game, himself, and his teammates.

Troy Percival

Troy Percival became one of the greatest closers in the game, but he began his career as a catcher in the California Angels' organization. A funny thing happened during his one season as a catcher, when he hit just .200. The coaches noticed that he was throwing the baseball back to the pitchers faster than they were throwing it to him. As a result, Percival was converted to a pitcher in 1991 with Boise in the Northwest League and went 2–0 with 12 saves and a 1.41 ERA. Apparently the coaches made the right decision.

He made the Angels' roster in 1995 as a set-up man for Lee Smith and responded with a 3–2 record in 62 games with three saves and a 1.95 ERA. Promoted to the closer's role the following year, he never looked back, again appearing in 62 games in 1996, with an 0–2 record, 36 saves, and a 2.31 ERA. Percival became one of only six pitchers in the history of the Angels to strike out at least 100 batters in a season without starting a game. The others were Mark Clear, De Wayne Buice, Bryan Harvey, Scott Shields, and Francisco Rodriguez.

With a good fastball in the high 90s, a curveball, and a slider, Percival quickly made his mark in the Angels' bullpen. He continued his streak of effectiveness in 1997 when he went 5–5 in 55 games with 27 saves and an

Troy Percival was a catcher in the minor leagues when coaches noticed his arm strength and converted him to a pitcher. With the Angels, he became one of the dominant closers in the game, racking up 358 saves over 14 seasons.

ERA of 3.46. He became the epitome of consistency, saving no fewer than 31 games over the next seven seasons. But the Angels had a young star in the making in Rodriguez. So when Percival's contract expired at the end of the 2004 season, the Angels chose not to re-sign him.

Although his fastball had lost a bit of its zip in his 10 seasons with the team, he was still 29–38 with 316 saves. But the business part of baseball entered into the decision making, and a young, hard-throwing set-up man again replaced the former closer. Percival signed a contract with the Detroit Tigers prior to the 2005 season, looking to continue his history of consistent excellence.

That consistency was gone as Percival struggled mightily in the Motor City. In 26 games he was 1–3 with eight saves and a 5.76 ERA. He suffered a serious arm injury in early July, missing the remainder of the season. He reported to spring training in 2006, but in his first outing he reported significant pain in his pitching arm and was disabled for the entire season. When his contract expired at the end of the season, Percival was left without a team and with a history of arm problems. To say the least, his career was in jeopardy.

In January 2007, the Angels hired him as a special-assignment pitching instructor. But he believed that his arm had healed, was released from his coaching contract, and signed with the St. Louis Cardinals. After six games with the Cardinals' Memphis Triple A affiliate, Percival was brought back to the major leagues with St. Louis. In his first big-league appearance in nearly two years, he fanned the first batter he faced, David Ross, and got the win against the Cincinnati Reds. In 34 games with the Cards, he was 3–0 with a 1.80 ERA.

In November 2007 Percival signed a two-year, $8 million deal with the Tampa Bay Rays. He went 2–1 in 50 games with 28 saves. But he visited the disabled list three times and had a high ERA.

In 2009 Percival returned to the disabled list after getting six more saves for the Rays. It is doubtful he will pitch again. In 13 big-league seasons, Percival was 35–43 with 358 saves.

Jason Isringhausen

Back in the mid-1990s the New York Mets felt sure that their pitching future was bright because of a trio of top-notch prospects who were considered can't-miss real deals: Paul Wilson, Bill Pulsipher, and Jason Isringhausen. Injuries had a profound effect on all three hurlers, and the only one of the three to enjoy a moderately long big-league career has been Isringhausen—but it has not been without plenty of challenges and a great amount of desire to overcome adversity.

After getting off to a 9–1 start with Triple A Norfolk of the International League in 1995, Isringhausen was brought up to the big club as a starter and responded with a 9–2 record. But in 1996, things got a whole lot more difficult. Off to a troublesome start with a 6–14 record, he then became a regular visitor to the disabled list. His statistics for the next part of his career read like this:

On disabled list from August 13 to September 1, 1996

On disabled list from March 24 to August 27, 1997

On disabled list from March 21 to September 28, 1998

An assortment of issues included a bout with tuberculosis, an altercation that his pitching hand had with a trash can in the dugout that the trash can won, and three major arm surgeries. He pitched in six games for the Mets in 1997 with a 2–2 record and an ERA of 7.58. He missed the entire 1998 season. To say the least, the career of Jason Isringhausen was in serious peril. But he stuck with it, got healthy, and earned a relief role on the club in 1999.

After getting off to a mediocre start with a 1–3 record in 13 games, he was traded to the Oakland A's, along with Greg McMichael, for Billy Taylor. Fate had finally smiled on Jason Isringhausen. He saved eight games during the balance of that year and then became a stand-out closer. He greeted the new millennium in 2000 by appearing in 66 games and going 6–4 with 33 saves. He had another outstanding season in 2001 with 34 saves, good enough to earn him a free-agent contract with the St. Louis Cardinals.

While still having to endure the occasional stint on the DL, Isringhausen became a valuable and dependable performer out of manager Tony La Russa's bullpen. For the Cards, he notched 32, 22, 47, 39, 33, and 32 saves from 2002 to 2007.

But the injury bug bit Isringhausen again in 2008, and he signed a free-agent deal with Tampa Bay in 2009. Nine ineffective games into the season he broke down again, tearing a ligament in his pitching elbow that required Tommy John surgery. Needless to say, his career was in serious doubt. In 14 big-league seasons, Isringhausen was 45–50 with 293 saves.

Derek Lowe

Right-hander Derek Lowe is one of those rare breed of pitchers who has had great success both as a starter and reliever. Armed with an outstanding hard sinker, along with a curve change, and most recently a cut fastball, he is the epitome of a ground-ball pitcher who keeps the ball in the park. Early in his career with Seattle and later with Boston, Lowe had little success as a spot starter and reliever, as his 5–15 record after two seasons would indicate. But in 1999 he was converted into a full-time reliever, and his stats improved. He had a 6–3 record that year in 74 games with 15 saves.

In 2000 he again appeared in 74 contests, recording a 4–4 record and a league-leading 42 saves. He fell to 5–10 the following season with 24 saves and was switched to a starting pitcher. It was obviously the correct call, as in the ensuing eight years he won 121 games as a starter. But one wonders how much more success he would have had as a reliever, already with 85 career saves.

John Smoltz

Another pitcher who took a similar detour is the great Atlanta Braves right-hander John Smoltz. Part of the rotation that included Greg Maddux and Tom Glavine, Smoltz put up big numbers as a starter in Atlanta. His outstanding fastball and big-dropping curve made him one of the best pitchers of his era and will undoubtedly see him, Maddux, and Glavine as teammates in a few years in Cooperstown.

Coming off another in a long line of arm miseries, Smoltz became the Braves' closer in 2001, earning 10 saves. Over the next three seasons, he saved a league-leading 55, 45, and 44 games. But Smoltz felt he was better suited to be a starting pitcher and was moved back into the rotation for the 2005 season. At the end of 2009, Smoltz signed with the Boston Red Sox, was released, and then signed with the St. Louis Cardinals. But his 21-year career boasts a record of 213–155 and 154 saves.

Brad Lidge

Brad Lidge broke onto the scene with Houston in 2002 for a cup of coffee. He appeared in 78 games in 2003 as a set-up man, earning one save during a 6–3 season. But after taking over the closer's role from Billy Wagner in 2004, he had consecutive seasons with 29, 42, and 32 saves.

After losing and then regaining the closer's role with the Astros in 2007 when he went 5–3 with 19 saves, he was dealt to Philadelphia where he helped lead the Phillies to the 2008 World Series title, appearing in 72 games with a 2–0 record, and achieving a perfect 41-for-41 record in save opportunities during the regular season. That perfection continued in the postseason when he went 7-for-7 in save chances to finish the year a perfect 48-for-48.

Largely because of a lingering knee injury, he fell back to earth in 2009, although still finished with 31 regular-season saves. But when healthy, he remains one of the best closers in baseball, with a mid-90s fastball and a devastating slider. Following the 2009 regular season, Lidge had a career record of 25–28 in eight seasons with 195 saves.

Francisco Rodriguez

Francisco Rodriguez, better known as "K-Rod" because of his propensity to gain strikeouts, was a 20-year-old rookie when he broke into the majors with the Anaheim Angels for five games in 2002. But he had an

Francisco "K-Rod" Rodriguez was groomed by the Angels for future greatness by serving as set-up man for Troy Percival. He became California's closer in 2005 and led the league in saves three of the next four seasons before moving on to the Mets.

eye-popping postseason, going 2–0 out of the pen in the American League Division Series, 2–0 in the American League Championship Series, and 1–1 in the World Series.

In 2003 and 2004, serving as a set-up man for closer Troy Percival, he had a combined 12–4 record with 14 saves in 128 games. He was being groomed for the closer's role, which he took over in 2005 when Percival inked a free-agent deal with Detroit. He and the Angels never looked back.

In 2005 he saved 45 games. The following year, 47. Forty more saves followed in 2007, but he saved his best for 2008. Rodriguez appeared in 76 games with a 2–3 record, setting a major league record with 62 saves and an ERA of 2.24. He struck out 77 batters in 68 innings. His seven-year total with the Angels was a 23–17 record with 208 saves.

Armed with a mid-90s fastball, Rodriguez primarily uses his two curve-balls to confound hitters. One is thrown very hard, which resembles a slider. The other is a slower, big-breaking, looping pitch that often buckles the knees of the hitter. He could not have picked a better time to have the best season of a collection of great seasons as he was in the final year of a contract and on December 10, 2008, struck it rich by signing a three-year, $37 million contract with the Mets. New York had suffered consecutive disappointing seasons in 2007 and 2008, and their bullpen was identified as one of the major culprits.

K-Rod finished the 2009 season (a hugely disappointing campaign for the Mets) with a 3–6 record and 35 saves. After eight big-league seasons, his career mark is 26–23 with 243 saves.

Joe Nathan

Joe Nathan began his career as a starting pitcher with the San Francisco Giants. The right-hander went 12–6 in parts of two seasons. But after a number of seasons split between the Giants' Triple A team in Fresno and the City by the Bay, he was switched to a reliever in 2003 with immediate success. In a career-high 78 games he went 12–4 in a set-up role with the Giants.

Following the season, Nathan was traded, along with Boof Bonser and Francisco Liriano, to the Minnesota Twins for catcher A.J. Pierzynski. Given an opportunity to compete for the closer's role in Minnesota, he beat out J.C. Romero and Jesse Crain. Appearing in 73 games, he had a 1–2 record with 44 saves and a 1.62 ERA. He followed his first year as a full-time closer with a series of more outstanding seasons. In 2005 he came out of the bullpen 69 times with a 7–4 record, 43 saves, and a 2.70 ERA. That was the highest ERA that Nathan would have through the 2009 season.

During the next four seasons with the Twins, Nathan went a combined 12–4 with 159 saves and ERAs of 1.58, 1.88, 1.33, and 2.10. He is a four-time All-Star and was the winner of the Joseph W. Hayes Award as the Twins Pitcher of the Year in 2008 when he went 1–2 with 39 saves and a 1.33 ERA.

After 10 seasons in the big leagues (at the end of 2009), Nathan had a 46–22 record with a 2.75 ERA and 247 saves.

Jonathan Papelbon

A new fan favorite over the last four years in Boston has been right-handed fireballer Jonathan Papelbon. A relative unknown, he advanced quickly through the Red Sox farm system and made his debut in 2005, going 3–1 in 17 games as a reliever and spot starter. He was expected to compete for a starting job in 2006, but when Keith Foulke pitched ineffectively due to a series of injuries, Papelbon was made the Boston closer. Appearing in 59 games with a 4–2 record, he had 35 saves and an incredible 0.92 ERA. Papelbon surrendered only seven earned runs in 68 innings with 75 strikeouts. His 35 saves that season were the most ever by a rookie.

In 2007, he again pitched in 59 games, going 1–3 with 37 saves and a 1.85 ERA. He helped the Red Sox win a second world championship in four years by pitching seven scoreless innings in the postseason with one save in the American League Championship Series against Cleveland and three in the Fall Classic against Colorado.

Colorful fan favorite Jonathan Papelbon was a surprise choice to take over as Red Sox closer in 2006, but by the next season he cemented his reputation as one of the best by posting three saves in Boston's World Series victory over Colorado.

In 2008, Papelbon achieved career highs in games (67), wins (5), losses (4), saves (41), and games finished (62). He also struck out 77 in 69 innings. Even though the Red Sox eventually fell to Tampa Bay in the playoffs, Papelbon continued his spotless record, pitching seven more scoreless games with three more saves. In 2009, he was 1–1 with 38 saves and a 1.85 ERA.

In five major league seasons (at the end of 2009), Papelbon is 14–11 with 151 saves and an ERA of 1.84.

Trevor Hoffman

Numerous pitchers made their mark in the 1990s and the first decade of the new millennium. But there are two relief pitchers who began their big-league careers in the last decade of the 20th century, have

Conversations about the greatest closers in history always include Trevor Hoffman. At the end of 2009—after 17 seasons and still going strong—he ranked first all-time in saves (591) and games finished, 820 of the 985 contests he had appeared in.

extended quite well into the new century, and are head and shoulders above the rest. You never know what Hall of Fame voters are thinking. Some votes made by those voters, as well as the Veterans Committee, have left many baseball fans shaking their heads over the years. But if these next two closers are not guaranteed first-ballot Hall of Famers, they might as well close the doors at Cooperstown. In 1993 Trevor Hoffman made his debut with the Florida Marlins, and two years later Mariano Rivera broke in with the New York Yankees. They are simply the best of the best of the one-inning closers. They are the Top Guns of the one-inning save.

Which of the two pitchers is better could be debated for decades. But it also seems true that these two right-handers are destined to be No. 1 and No. 2 in career saves for many years to come. The one difference in their career marks is the incredible postseason career that Rivera has enjoyed.

For a while, Trevor Hoffman was known as the younger brother of Glen Hoffman, a utility infielder who played nine years in the major leagues with the Boston Red Sox, Los Angeles Dodgers, and California Angels during the 1980s. Younger brother Trevor was originally drafted by the Cincinnati Reds as an infielder who hit just .212 in 103 games. Switched to a pitcher in 1991 by Charleston manager Jim Lett, Hoffman embraced the switch with a 1–1 record and 12 saves with a 1.87 ERA. Glen Hoffman's younger brother was well on his way to becoming Trevor Hoffman the closer.

Hoffman was selected from the Reds' organization by the Florida Marlins in the expansion draft of 1992. In 28 games with the Marlins in 1993, he had a 2–2 record and the first two saves of his illustrious career. But on June 25 of that year, Hoffman was traded to the San Diego Padres, along with Andres Berumen and Jose Martinez, in exchange for Gary Sheffield and Rich Rodriguez. That is a trade the Marlins' organization would no doubt like to take back.

Hoffman earned three more saves that season with the Padres but took over the closer's spot from Gene Harris in 1994. Appearing in 47 games in that strike-shortened season, he had a 4–4 record with 20 saves. Although the 1995 season was a successful one statistically, it was a landmark season for Hoffman, who changed his pitching style as a result of the season in which he went 7–4 with 31 saves in 55 games. He spent most of the season pitching with a torn rotator cuff, which he had surgically repaired following the season. The arm injury forced him to master his combination change-up/palm ball. The pitch was so deceptive that hitters could not pick up the difference between that pitch and his average fastball until after the pitch was released.

Hoffman helped the Padres to the National League Division Series in 1996 with a 9–5 record, 42 saves, and a 2.25 ERA in 70 appearances, his career high, which he would equal two more times. He led the league in saves the following season with 53 and had another 40 in 1999.

He continued his mastery out of the bullpen with 43, 43, and 38 saves. But his career was in doubt following the 2002 season, when he had two surgeries on his shoulder, limiting him to nine games in 2003. Rod Beck did an outstanding job as his replacement. But come 2004, it was the same Trevor Hoffman, who never skipped a beat. He appeared in 55 games with a 3–3 record and 41 saves.

Hoffman was the picture of consistency with San Diego. From 1994 to 2008 he saved at least 20 games 14 times, at least 30 games 13 times, at least 40 games 9 times, and 53 games once. He was a six-time All-Star in that time frame, was the 2008 Branch Rickey Award winner, and was twice named the National League Rolaids Relief Man of the Year. He appeared in 902 games for San Diego, a major league record for games pitched for any one team. He was the first pitcher to accumulate 500 saves. Following the 2009 season, he seemed secure in his spot as the all-time save leader with 591.

Although two of those saves came when he pitched for Florida and 552 came with the Padres, the rest have come as a member of the

Milwaukee Brewers. At the end of the 2008 season it was announced that Hoffman would not come back to the Padres. In January 2009, Hoffman signed a one-year deal with the Brewers. After a solid campaign in which he posted 37 saves, Hoffman was signed by Milwaukee to another one-year deal for 2010.

At the end of the 2009 season (his 17th in the big leagues), Hoffman had a 59–68 record and a 2.73 ERA. A trip to Cooperstown and the Hall of Fame seems only five years away after his eventual retirement.

Mariano Rivera

Although Mariano Rivera may never reach or surpass the all-time save record of Trevor Hoffman, he is firmly ensconced as the pitcher with the second-most saves (526) in major league history. Both he and Hoffman have more than 500 saves, and their closest neighbor in the 500-save club is Lee Smith, who retired with 478. The two closest active hurlers to that mark are Billy Wagner (385) and Troy Percival (358). Suffice it to say that the chances are good that Hoffman and Rivera may never be caught as the two greatest save leaders in the history of the game.

While it seems reasonable to assume that Rivera may not catch Hoffman in saves, there is absolutely no doubt that Rivera is by far the best postseason closer in the history of the game. He has been lights out whenever the Yankees turn the lead over to him in the postseason. In 88 games, he has an 8–1 record with 39 saves and an ERA of 0.74. In 133⅓ innings, he has surrendered just 82 hits while striking out 107.

Rivera came up to the Yankees in the 1995 season and appeared in 19 games with a 5–3 record as a spot starter and reliever. At the tender age of 25 he saw his first postseason action, appearing in three games against the Mariners in the American League Division Series without surrendering a run. Spending the entire season with the big club in 1996, he appeared in 61 games as a seventh- and eighth-inning set-up man for John Wetteland. The duo were so successful that the Yankees were 70–3 when leading after the sixth inning that year. Basically, if you didn't get to

It is unlikely that Mariano Rivera will surpass Trevor Hoffman for the all-time saves lead, but the Yankees closer may be remembered as the best ever because of his excellence come October: in 77 postseason games, Rivera is 8–1 with 34 saves and an incredible 0.76 ERA.

the Yankee starters, you were not going to catch them. Rivera was 8–3 and recorded his first five career saves, with an ERA of 2.09.

Rivera's postseason success continued as the Yankees won the World Series. He pitched eight-and-two-thirds scoreless innings in the playoffs against Texas and Baltimore before pitching five-and-two-thirds innings in the Fall Classic against Atlanta, yielding only one earned run.

The Yankees were so impressed with their hard-throwing set-up man that they chose not to re-sign Wetteland, who signed a generous free-agent deal with Texas. Rivera slid up smoothly into the role of closer in 1997, appearing in 66 games with a 6–4 record, 43 saves, and a 1.88 ERA. The Yanks once again made the playoffs but were upset by Cleveland.

Rivera combined a mid-90s rising fastball, slider, and change-up and then separated himself from mere humans with his devastating cutter. When batters hit his cutter, as Chris Wheeler explained, they just don't make good contact on Rivera. His easy, fluid motion is the calm before his explosive storm. While many relief pitchers, especially closers, rely on the strikeout to finish off games, Rivera is not afraid to pitch to contact.

"I want ground balls," he said in an article in *Sports Illustrated* in March 2003. "They're better than strikeouts. I'll throw the cutter the first pitch of the at-bat or the last pitch. It doesn't make a difference to me."

Not only did Rivera revolutionize the closer's role, but he also gave value and attention to the set-up role that was never there before. Earlier, when closers became a more prominent and respected entity, set-up men were the variety of guys who weren't good enough to start or close. But the new importance to the closer's role and the increase in the use of pitch counts to monitor how long starters should pitch made the set-up and middle-relief roles much more important.

"A good set-up man holds a lead and in many instances is more important to the victory than the guy who gets the last out," Tim McCarver wrote in *Baseball for Brain Surgeons and Other Fans*. "Mariano Rivera was the set-up man for John Wetteland on the Yankees in 1996, and people were talking about a middle reliever who should have been on the All-Star team and who was a legitimate MVP candidate. It was unheard of. Because of Rivera, the Yankees revolutionized baseball because they played six-inning games. If they were ahead for six innings and Rivera came in for two innings and Wetteland for one inning, they won. It showed everybody that you can shorten games—you can win if you grab an early lead—if you have strong middle relief.

"In today's game, middle relief is so important, yet only a few teams today have quality middle relievers. That's because if a quality set-up man like Rivera breaks onto the scene, he will want to switch to the more glamorous and better-paid closer role the year after his lowly paid set-up success. So his manager must revert back to putting the most important part of the game—the sixth, seventh, and eighth innings—in the hands of the weakest, lowest-paid part of the staff."

It is exactly because of that problem that teams are spending more time and money finding and keeping quality set-up pitchers such as Ryan Madson in Philadelphia.

Rivera continued his domination over American League hitters like few before him, not to mention his mastery over National League hitters in any World Series opportunities they had against him.

Since taking over the closer's role in 1997, with the exception of the 2002 season where he spent three intervals on the disabled list, he has never appeared in less than 54 games, appearing in at least 60 games 11 times. In that same time span he has saved a minimum of 30 games 12 times, saved at least 40 games seven times, and reached the 50-save plateau twice. He's led the league in saves on three different occasions, 1999 (45 saves), 2001 (50 saves), and 2004 (a career-high 53 saves). And he has a good chance to build on those impressive streaks. For the 2009 regular season he appeared in 66 games, saving 44 of them, at the age of 39. His career totals at the end of that season: 71–52 record, 526 saves, and an ERA of 2.25.

Rivera is a 10-time American League All-Star, a four-time World Series champion, was voted four times as the American League Rolaids Relief Man of the Year, and was the World Series Most Valuable Player in 1999, the Most Valuable Player of the American League Championship Series in 2003, the two-time DHL Delivery Man of the Year, and the 1999 Babe Ruth Award winner.

Whether or not Rivera plays long enough to surpass Hoffman is irrelevant. He is a close second, and the 500-save plateau may never be reached again. This record may be right up there with Cy Young's 511 victories and Joe DiMaggio's 56-game hitting streak.

Can anyone catch them? Two interesting names are Francisco Rodriguez and Jonathan Papelbon.

CHAPTER 13

Snubbed by Cooperstown—The Struggle for Recognition

Baseball is a game for debating. Two seemingly intelligent, die-hard fans can watch the same play or the same player and have a completely different opinion. It's part of what makes baseball America's Game. The interesting thing is that both fans could be absolutely correct.

One fan might feel that the best baseball has to offer is a 1–0 or 2–1 pitchers' duel, in which every pitch means something, that climaxes in the final at-bats of the contest. Another might prefer a slugfest in which one team beats another by a 12–11 score with balls batted all over the ballpark and pitchers going through a revolving door throughout the game as the best way to spend three-plus hours.

Some baseball debates cross generations. There are those who know beyond a shadow of a doubt that players of a past generation were far and away better players than the soft, coddled players of today. Others will swear that today's players are much better athletic specimens. But discussions about the game itself transcend what happens on the field. And those "hot stove" debates occur all year long, even when baseball is on its winter sabbatical.

If you ever feel like starting a heated debate, open up the subject of the Baseball Hall of Fame. Baseball fans of all levels have opinions about the hallowed hall. Have some fun with it. Tell a baseball purist that Joe Jackson and Buck Weaver of the 1919 Chicago White Sox belong in the Hall of Fame. You have a 50-50 chance that the purist will agree with you wholeheartedly or lecture you about baseball's golden rule about consorting with gamblers, which can hurt the credibility of America's Pastime.

Bring up the subject of Peter Edward Rose. What a player! No one played the game with such determination, energy, and a fierce desire to succeed and win. During his 24 seasons in the major leagues, Rose hit for a .303 average and left the game as the all-time hits leader with 4,256. On the field there was little doubt that Pete Rose was a first-ballot Hall of Famer. But allegations of gambling on baseball, which he admitted after years of denials, have forever shaded his statistics. That he accepted a lifetime ban from baseball has also made attempts to be reinstated and to ultimately be elected to the Hall of Fame fruitless. The debate about Pete Rose may last as long as the Jackson/Weaver debates.

There are a plethora of players who can make a strong case for admittance to the hall who have not, as yet, gotten there. Andre Dawson slugged 438 home runs and drove in 1,591 runs during his illustrious 21-year career with a solid .279 batting average. "The Hawk," as he was known, also possessed one of the strongest arms from right field of his generation and won eight Gold Gloves. But he still is on the outside looking in when it comes to baseball's hallowed hall.

Another great Chicago Cub player was third baseman Ron Santo, who patrolled the hot corner for 15 years in the Windy City, 14 of which were with the Cubs. He had a career .277 average with 342 homers, 1,331 RBIs and five Gold Gloves. One of the real good guys in the history of the game, he has maintained a presence as an announcer for the Cubs, even though crippled by diabetes.

Another one of the good guys of the game who has always fallen short in Hall of Fame balloting is former Atlanta Braves outfielder Dale Murphy, who also played for Philadelphia and Colorado. In his 18 seasons he hit for a .265 average but belted 398 homers and drove in 1,266 runs.

The oft-injured Tony Oliva hit .304 in his 15 seasons with the Minnesota Twins, leading the league in hits five times and in hitting three times. Boston fans will argue that their outstanding right fielder Dwight Evans has earned the right to induction to the hall. In his 20 big-league seasons, he hit .272 with 385 homers and 1,384 RBIs and won eight Gold Gloves.

Had he been a little more of a conformist during his playing days, Dick Allen may have been able to increase his already impressive 15-year stats that include a .292 average with 351 homers and 1,119 RBIs. A guy who would have been left alone in today's game, baseball's strict codes of conduct during his career made him an outcast at times, even though he was one of the most dynamic players of his era. Had he played for Chuck Tanner during his entire career, he might have replicated his 1972 Most Valuable Player year with the Chicago White Sox in which he hit .308 with 37 homers and 113 RBIs in a strike-shortened season.

Although there are many other position players who merit consideration for Cooperstown, fans from previous generations look to Brooklyn Dodger great Gil Hodges as someone who has been unfairly locked out of the hall. During his 16 years as a Dodger and two as a Met, Hodges hit .273 with 370 home runs and 1,274 RBIs and won three Gold Gloves.

Pitchers have also been left waiting for the phone call. A starting pitcher whom many feel deserves a spot in the Hall of Fame is Minnesota, Texas, Pittsburgh, Cleveland, and California right-hander Bert Blyleven. Blessed with a great fastball and a big, dropping curveball, Blyleven went 287–250 during his stellar 22-year career. He struck out 3,701 hitters and was the model of consistency. While he won 20 games only one time, he won at least 15 games 10 times.

To fans of this generation, Tommy John is a type of arm surgery that salvages pitcher's careers. But to those who have earned a few veteran stripes, the aforementioned left-hander was an outstanding pitcher for 26 big-league seasons. John had a 288–231 record pitching for the Chicago White Sox, Los Angeles Dodgers, New York Yankees, California Angels, and the Oakland Athletics. He won 20 games on three occasions and won at least 10 games 17 times during his career. He's never received a nod from Hall of Fame voters.

Neither has another left-hander, Jim Kaat. During his 25-year career, he posted a 283–237 record with the Washington Senators, Minnesota Twins, Chicago White Sox, Philadelphia Phillies, New York Yankees, and St. Louis Cardinals. Much like Tommy John, Kaat won 20 games three times and at least 10 games 15 times. He added an impressive 16 Gold Gloves.

Suffice it to say that Hall of Fame votes are one of the great topics of baseball debates throughout the years. Numerous position players and starting pitchers have certainly put up what most consider Hall of Fame numbers. But the voters have their own ideas of what merits that great honor.

Just what does it take to gain entrance to Baseball's Hall of Fame? Players are inducted into the Hall through an annual election by the Baseball Writers Association of America (BBWAA) or the Veterans Committee, which includes some Hall of Fame members. Five years following his retirement, a player who had at least 10 years of major league experience is eligible to be elected by BBWAA members with membership of at least 10 years.

From a ballot that could include as many as 20 to 40 candidates for election to the hall, each writer can vote for up to 10 players. Any player named on 75 percent or more of all ballots cast is elected. Conversely, any player who is named on fewer than 5 percent of the ballots is dropped from future elections. However, in 2001 the election procedures were changed so that these dropped players could be considered and elected by the Veterans Committee.

Players also considered by the Veterans Committee are those who have not been elected by the BBWAA for a 20-year period following retirement.

There are 289 members of the Baseball Hall of Fame. The breakdown by position is interesting. There are 68 infielders, 58 outfielders, 13 catchers, and 62 pitchers. If you consider the four infielders and three outfielders, the Hall averages 17 players for each position, slightly more than the 13 catchers who have gained entrance to Cooperstown. Of course, the physical toll of being a backstop has slowed the career of many a fine player. A Hall of Fame member who began his minor league career as a catcher, the late Richie Ashburn often called the catcher's equipment the "tools of ignorance."

But of the 62 pitchers enshrined, only five are relievers. Until Hoyt Wilhelm was inducted in 1985, there was not a single relief pitcher in the Hall. Wilhelm was followed by fellow relievers Rollie Fingers in 1992, Dennis Eckersley in 2004, Bruce Sutter in 2006, and Rich "Goose" Gossage in 2008. And in truth, part of the reason for Eckersley's induction was not only his powerful role in revolutionizing the game with his clear dominance as a one-inning closer, but also that he was a premier starting pitcher for the first half of his career.

Eckersley has an interesting slant on relievers finally getting some Hall of Fame respect and recognition. "I do think that relievers are getting more respect now," Eckersley said. "The only reason I'm in the Hall of Fame is because I did both, started and relieved. The two guys who most recently got in, Sutter and Goose, I don't think my election had anything to do with. They both threw more than one inning.

"I don't think I have anything to do with the new-age closer. Nobody has gotten in yet. John Franco is sitting out there. Lee Smith did two innings and then one inning. He's sitting there. What about Trevor Hoffman? What will happen with him? The over-300 saves guys came and went. [Jeff] Reardon and [Randy] Myers didn't stay on the ballot. Mariano [Rivera] will be a slam dunk. It's not even a question. I think it

Relief pitchers don't get much love from Hall of Fame voters. Consider Lee Smith, still waiting for induction despite ranking third all-time in saves and boasting a save conversion percentage higher than HOF inductees Goose Gossage, Rollie Fingers, and Bruce Sutter.

has a lot to do with the postseason. But is it Trevor Hoffman's fault he didn't have as much postseason experience as another guy?

"If I came up today as a closer and played 20 years, would I have made it? These pitchers did the job they were supposed to do for 20 years. What else are they supposed to do?"

An interesting question. Players become eligible for induction five years after their career is over. But many times they will hang helplessly on the whim of voters who suddenly find more or less value in their careers, years after their final game. It's comical in a way, because debates will be going on about players 20 years after they've played their last game. Suddenly, a player's stock will rise as if he just went 6-for-8 in a Sunday afternoon doubleheader. The only thing not comical about the situation is that players deserving of serious consideration wait and age, hoping to enjoy one last day in the sunshine celebrating their induction into the Baseball Hall of Fame.

Then, after years of waiting, the player finally gets the congratulatory call, even though he was no more or less qualified or deserving that year than he was 20 years prior. One wonders what discussions can sway a voter from one year to the next. There are those who compare Baseball Hall of Fame voting to the election of a new pope in the Roman Catholic Church.

"I think part of the Hall of Fame voting is who else is on the ballot at the same time," said Maury Allen. "If there were four or five big home run hitters on the ballot at the same time, they can get most of the attention. A lot of it is publicity and attention."

Perhaps former players should hire a Madison Avenue public relations whiz to muster the type of advertising campaign that will reach and affect voters. Because baseball writers are the voters, there have been times when sullen and moody players who were not particularly kind or understanding of the scribes may have suffered during their early years of eligibility. Payback can be a bitch.

Questions will always resonate about seemingly deserving players who have been excluded from Cooperstown to date. There are countless position players and starting pitchers who can make a case for inclusion who were not mentioned here. But there also has been a lack of appreciation for the efforts of many pitchers who have excelled as closers. There is no doubting the validity of Wilhelm, Fingers, Eckersley, Sutter, or Gossage. They were all among the best who have ever toed the rubber on the pitcher's mound. But there is also an alarming case of a closer who is absolutely deserving of election to the Hall of Fame who has been mysteriously snubbed thus far by voters.

Although two active pitchers, Trevor Hoffman (591 saves) and Mariano Rivera (526), seem to be locks for their day in Cooperstown, there is another pitcher who has more career saves than any of the relievers who have been inducted in the hall to date. Lee Smith retired as the all-time saves leader with 478, and he held that honor until he was passed by Hoffman nine years after his retirement.

Wilhelm has 227 saves, Fingers finished with 341, Eckersley earned 390, Gossage has 310, and Sutter has 300. Smith amassed 88 more saves than his closest comrade in Eckersley. He was a seven-time All-Star and a three-time Rolaids Relief Man of the Year. A power pitcher with great command, Smith struck out 1,251 hitters in 1,289⅓ innings.

In his best 14 seasons as a closer, Smith saved 42 percent of his team's wins. Combining wins and saves, he represented 47 percent of his team's wins. He also was a pitcher with a low percentage of blown saves compared with four of the five relievers already in the Hall. There are no records to indicate a reliable figure of blown saves for Wilhelm, as the idea of a save came into being long after his career ended. But compared to the other four Hall of Famers, Smith is nearly the best of the bunch.

Lee Smith had 478 saves with 103 blown saves. So he blew 21 percent of his save opportunities, or, in a more positive light, he converted 79 percent of his save opportunities. The only pitcher in the hall with a better mark is Eckersley, who blew 18 percent of his opportunities, saving 82 percent. Fingers blew 31 percent of his save chances, Sutter 33 percent, and Gossage 36 percent.

Smith was a dominating pitcher who led baseball in all-time saves and is still third on the list now. Not only is it doubtful that anyone will ever top the total saves that Hoffman and Rivera will end their careers with, the chances of anyone ever catching Smith seem very doubtful. Francisco Rodriguez is a young phenom of a closer with the Mets, but he is nearly 250 saves shy of Smith's total. Not only is it a lock that no closer will ever catch Hoffman and Rivera, but it seems certain that Lee Smith will always be third in career saves. And in his career, Smith had 155 six-out saves while Rivera has only five. Lee Smith clearly deserves to be in the Hall of Fame.

Those who have been close to the game certainly appreciate Smith's career and readily endorse his candidacy for baseball's hallowed hall.

"There is no question that Lee Smith deserves to be in the Hall of Fame," said former Dodgers GM Fred Claire. "When you think of the greatest relief pitchers of all time, you have to think of Lee. He was a dominant force. If you took a vote of his former teammates, there is no question but that Lee would be a lock for the Hall of Fame."

One of the former trammates was Ferguson Jenkins, who hopes they will be teammates again in Cooperstown. He said of Smith's qualifications: "All of the relievers in the Hall of Fame deserve to be there. But nobody deserves to be there more than Lee Smith. He should have been the first one voted in."

A contemporary of Lee Smith was another right-handed reliever, Jim Gott, who has a real appreciation for all that Smith was able to accomplish during his 18-year career. Gott was right there in the opposing bullpen.

"Hey, you're talking to a reliever," Gott said. "Why isn't Lee Smith in the Hall of Fame? He should be in the Hall of Fame. He was so consistent and so dominant for so many years. I loved to watch his slow-moving, methodical pace. The way he dominated big-league hitters was amazing. I'd hear my teammates as he loped into the game. They'd complain about the shadows of Wrigley Field, defeating themselves before they even stepped into the batter's box. Then after their at-bat, some saying how tough it was to see or that they just missed the ball.

"Anyhow, he got them out. Another point was that he wasn't on consistently winning teams either. I struggle with the fact that the Hall of Fame should be there to celebrate the best of the best. Lee Smith should be in, [as should] Tony Oliva. Let's celebrate the game and its stars, and let's see Lee Smith elected to the Hall of Fame."

Certainly the fact that Smith pitched for much of his career with teams that were either right around or slightly below the .500 mark may have had a negative effect on his candidacy for Cooperstown. He appeared in just two postseasons in his career. Although baseball fans often saw Goose Gossage on center stage with the Yankees, Rollie Fingers and his handlebar moustache starring for the Oakland A's, Bruce Sutter with the Cardinals, and, of course, Dennis Eckersley dominating with the A's, Lee Smith was not a regular on the postseason rosters.

During the playoffs and World Series, teams get national attention. And big-market teams that get national attention help a marginal candidate get more credibility. But spending 16 of his 18 big-league seasons out of postseason play, Lee Smith was seldom on the big stage. When baseball had its highest ratings and most interest, through no fault of his own, he was sitting at home. But the fact that he amassed such an incredible number of saves for teams that were not always in contention for the postseason makes his record even more impressive. The fact that he so seldom blew a save, less often than three of his four contemporaries, speaks to his consistency. But to date, for some reason he has not been more than a marginal Hall of Fame candidate. That fact is one that countless stewards of the game question. Among them is Goose Gossage, who is a member of the hall.

"Lee Smith belongs in the Hall of Fame, period," Gossage said. "Just as an opposing player watching him come in, you saw that your teammates were disheartened because they knew the game was over. One of the things that might hold him back is that he didn't have the flair that an Eck had. I had a little something extra with the power thing. Guys should be like Goose was, be mean. But Lee was an imposing pitcher on the mound first of all just because of his size. He was a great relief pitcher, and he absolutely belongs in the Hall of Fame.

"He's a tremendous person. He had size, a great fastball, a great breaking ball, a great slider, and great command. He had imposing command. Lee was a pitcher with great stuff. He could locate and was not afraid of failing. He had everything it took to be a great relief pitcher, and he was. Plus, he just didn't do one inning. He started out doing two or three innings. I really don't understand why he's not in. I guess the biggest knock is that he did it with the least amount of flair, you know, big, easygoing Lee. He didn't jump around or have the antics that Eck used to. But you can't be jumping around when you're going more than one inning. If you do that, you'll fire those guys up, and you have to go back out there.

"Why are people not voting for him? What is the knock against him? With all the exposure you get today with the press and everything going on in terms of the news media all being involved, it's out of hand. During the time I was trying to get elected I really tried to point out how the role of relief pitching changed. Hall of Fame voting is a fickle thing. C'mon, he led the world in saves before Mariano and Hoffman. I am one of the many people who don't understand the voting. I think a lot of guys play games with their vote. But quite simply he belongs in the Hall of Fame."

Lee Smith doesn't need to be inducted into the Baseball Hall of Fame to give his career meaning. He is thrilled to have been in the major leagues for as long as he was and to have made so many friends while doing it. But that doesn't mean that finally being recognized as one of the best of the best wouldn't be a great way to cap off a career.

"The teammates I had were like family," Smith said. "Ozzie Smith and Fergie Jenkins were like brothers. Those guys were an elite group. When you look at the names in the Hall of Fame, and to have your name mentioned in the same breath gives you goose bumps. I don't know that getting in is the top priority of my career. I'd like to be remembered as a good player and a good human being. But being elected to the Hall of

Fame would be the topping on the cake. To be up there on stage, sitting beside Fergie, would be tops.

"When I was playing in the major leagues, all I heard about was people telling me I'd be a first-ballot Hall of Famer. I thought my numbers were good, but now you start to wonder. I look at Sutter and Gossage, who were great. But I thought the reason you go in are the numbers you put up, and I put them up. I can't believe that [Bert] Blyleven and [Tony] Oliva aren't in. Maybe it's the number of years you are on the ballot, and you just have to wait. I look at myself and Ron Santo and wonder why. Why were Jim Rice's numbers better now than they were 15 years ago? I don't understand why you have to wait.

"I'm not really frustrated. I've seen guys go off the deep end over this. I would absolutely love to be in there. But it's not life or death with me. It's not like my career would mean nothing if I didn't go in. But to get in? Man, that would be something.

"All you can do is wait and hope that someone who never played the game says you were good enough."

Smith was good enough much more often than he wasn't. But up to this point, Hall of Fame voters have not found it the correct time to make Lee Smith a member of baseball's most exclusive club. As we have seen with other pitchers, and position players as well, sometimes, with the passage of time, a player's career is more respected by Hall of Fame voters.

When looking at the numbers and remembering the pitcher, it seems only right for Lee Smith to be elected to Cooperstown. If Rollie Fingers, Dennis Eckersley, Bruce Sutter, and Goose Gossage earned a place in the Hall of Fame, there is no way to exclude Lee Smith. He's earned the honor every bit as much.

CHAPTER 14

Warming Up—
The Future

Times have changed over the past decade, not to mention over the past 100 years or so. Baseball has changed with the times, and pitching has represented one of the biggest changes in the game. And a big part of the biggest changes in baseball have occurred 60 feet, 6 inches from home plate—on the pitcher's mound late in the game. Pitchers used to finish what they started. It was not just what was expected; it was a machismo thing that they expected from themselves. Relief pitchers were the excuse-me players on the roster. But then the game began to change.

Relief pitchers started to make solid contributions. It turns out all they really needed was a chance to prove themselves. Not every reliever was a washed-up starter. Some of these guys were actually talented pitchers who were best suited to pitch out of the pen in short bursts, rather than starters who would try to pitch deep into games. It took some time, but relievers actually became appreciated members of the team.

Then the likes of Wilhelm, Arroyo, Face, and Baldschun revolutionized the game. Using specialty pitches, these pitchers assumed specialized roles, coming out of the bullpen and closing out ballgames. Now the pitch count has further revolutionized the game and the way that relief pitchers contribute to a team. Successful teams have a pitching staff that consists of hurlers who pitch in very specific roles after the starter is out of the game. Some have made the switch to the pen from starting roles. And a whole new generation of pitchers is being groomed to pitch in relief from early on.

Even in recent times, there are examples of relievers who began their careers as starting pitchers and then made the switch to relieving. Dennis Eckersley made it to the Hall of Fame because of his expertise in both roles. John Smoltz will no doubt be there as well, a player with a long history as a successful starter who also made the switch to the pen and back again. Joe Nathan is as accomplished a closer as there is in the game. But he began his career spending two seasons as a starter. Even Mariano Rivera started 10 games early in his illustrious career. Brad Lidge and Jonathan Papelbon each started just one game in their careers. But the trend is toward even more specialization.

Most big-name relief pitchers in the game today have never started a single contest in the major leagues, and many have not even started in the minors. Some of the best closers have pitched out of the bullpen only since making it to The Show. The names include Trevor Hoffman of Milwaukee, Francisco Rodriguez of the Mets, Brian Fuentes of the Los Angeles Angels, Heath Bell of the Padres, Joakim Soira of Kansas City, Bobby Jenks of the White Sox, Francisco Cordero of Cleveland, and Jonathan Broxton of the Dodgers.

One of the game's bright new stars, Andrew Bailey of the Oakland A's, was a spot starter and reliever in 2008 at Double A Midland. But during his rookie year in Oakland in 2009, he pitched strictly out of the bullpen and did so well enough to earn a spot on the American League All-Star team.

The game has gone from a place where everyone wanted to be a starter to where players are willing to pitch out of the bullpen. Some pitchers will go back and forth between roles, but more and more relievers are trained for their role from the early stages of their careers. The impact of relief pitching has been felt throughout all levels of the game.

In the minor leagues, college ball, and even high school baseball, closers are already pitching in relief roles, hoping to climb up the ladder to the major leagues. It goes even further than that.

One of the best players in the Cresskill (New Jersey) Alpine Baseball Association is a member of the Cresskill Cardinals, 10-year-old Jagger Kushner. The young right-handed pitcher doesn't start any games. He doesn't come in as the first alternate. Jagger has the nickname of "the Closer." The specialization in baseball has filtered down all the way to Little League, where this young player throws a fastball that comes in at 45 mph. He has become the "go-to guy" with the game on the line.

On three different occasions during the 2009 season, Jagger came into the game with runners on base in the sixth and final inning. Cool as a cucumber, Kushner was able to pitch out of trouble. His manager, Frank DeCarlo, understands his young pitcher and helps harness his intensity. DeCarlo calms him down and manages to get the best out of him.

"I like the excitement of being the closer," Jagger Kushner said. "I pitch at the end of the game. I usually pitch two innings, the fifth and the sixth. But if our pitcher gets in trouble, I'll come in with the bases loaded and zero outs. I just throw my fastball and get out of trouble and win the game."

Sometimes it's just that simple. Throw your fastball and get out of trouble and win the game. But sometimes successful players use alternative ways to succeed. Sometimes the game produces the visionaries who dictate what the future will hold. To see a fine young man like Jagger Kushner, who loves the game of baseball, pitching in a closer's role in Little League shows just how influential the game really is. As has been mentioned, baseball is composed of followers, sheep who follow the shepherds who seem to have the right idea. It's come to this point in the evolution of baseball. From early on, pitchers are being taught to pitch out of the pen and even close games.

There are followers in baseball, but there are also renegades. They are the ones, like a Tony La Russa, the designer of the one-inning save, who are brave enough to swim against the tide and try something different. If it works, they will be like the Pied Piper of Hamelin, soon to be leading most other organizations down their renegade path.

Strange as it may seem, the one true renegade in baseball these days is Hall of Famer Nolan Ryan of the Texas Rangers organization. If his experiment of encouraging and expecting his starting pitchers to pitch deep into games, in direct opposition to the idea of pitch counts, is successful, there might be a new trend for other organizations to follow. If Texas pitchers start to complete games and are successful and healthy, there could be a legion of followers adopting the same techniques.

Should Nolan Ryan or someone else come up with a new idea or concept that seems to work, there will be a shift in the game. Those who have played the game still appreciate it, even with the changes. Some, in fact, welcome change to the game.

"I've gotten to like the changes over the years," said Dennis Eckersley. "I still don't really like National League baseball. I'm just not a traditionalist. But I love the game. I had two careers, one as a player, and now I can broadcast. I've been very fortunate because I have a chance to do something in the game after playing ball. Baseball is your whole life, and I respect the game."

Baseball has changed remarkably over the last couple of generations. But what makes baseball so great is that even with all of the changes, it is still the same wonderful game that we all grew up with. People relate to baseball and its players so well because it's the game we all played as kids. We've done exactly what today's major league players do—just not quite as well or nearly as consistently.

There are those who scoff at the changes in the sport, the specialization and 21st-century strategy now part of baseball's "book," but if you truly appreciate the game for what it is, it is much easier to accept the changes. Specialization is part of all sports, and baseball is just following suit, though the game's basic concept hasn't changed. It doesn't matter who gets the 27th out of the game and earns a complete game or a save or a hold. All that really matters is that the team that has scored the most runs when the last out is tallied wins the game. In this brave new world, that is a comforting idea.

Were Alexander Cartwright or Henry Chadwick able to see how the game has evolved in the last century or so, they would probably marvel at the changes and fall in love with the game all over again.

"I just love the game," said Fred Claire. "For me, it's just recognizing that the changes are there. It's all been part of an evolution in the game. I must say that I certainly enjoy the game as much today as I ever have in my life."

Fred Claire isn't just a baseball lifer. He is a lifetime baseball fan. It's pretty difficult not to be.

Appendix

Fran Zimniuch's Top 20 Closers of All Time

After researching and writing about the evolution of the closer in baseball, it seemed only appropriate for me to create a list of the best of the best. Compiling a list of the Top 20 anything opens up the possibility for disagreement, debate, and criticism—sounds like a plan to me! Let's face it, during the long, cold winter, debates and discussions are a baseball fan's best source of entertainment until the start of spring training.

My criteria for creating this list included a combination of things. Initially I considered longevity, the total number of saves, postseason success (or lack thereof), and a general determination of whether or not each pitcher dominated games in his era. Then I went a step beyond these (mostly) measurable qualities. I acted like a manager who plays the book most of the time but every now and then goes on a complete hunch. Supporting my list of the 20 best closers are some hunches that readers might disagree with.

Placing these great pitchers in a particular order also was challenging, because it's difficult to compare a Mariano Rivera with a Goose Gossage—they pitched in different eras, were different types of pitchers, and their job descriptions were different. Rivera is the prototypical closer of the modern era, usually pitching just one inning. Gossage was the prototypical closer of his era, meaning he pitched as many as three innings.

But because they were both responsible for getting the final out, their jobs were similar and provide common ground for comparing them.

1. Mariano Rivera
Although he'll probably never surpass Trevor Hoffman in total saves, Rivera closed out the 2009 season with 526. He has dominated his era and has been as close to a sure thing as you'll ever see in the postseason. Even when he lost the deciding game of a World Series, it was on a bloop hit against a drawn-in infield. He's simply the best.

2. Dennis Eckersley
Eckersley had two successful careers. His first was as a starter, and his second was as a closer. Had he been a reliever for his entire career, his statistics would have been even more phenomenal. He dominated and was overpowering. Plus, he was the pitcher who created the one-inning save with the help of his manager, Tony La Russa.

3. Trevor Hoffman
Hoffman's career save totals may never be touched—he closed out 2009 with 591 and planned to return to the Brewers to pitch in 2010. Mr. Consistency out on the mound, he also has had some postseason success. He is the thinking man's closer, using guile rather than heat.

4. Lee Smith
Smith is the best closer not in the Hall of Fame—in fact, he might be the best closer among those already in the Hall of Fame. He saved 478 games, which might be a nearly untouchable third on the all-time list. He was a dominating, intimidating closer. Playing through different eras, he succeeded both in pitching multiple innings and pitching just one inning. He belongs in Cooperstown, plain and simple, end of discussion.

5. Rollie Fingers

Fingers is another one of the closers from a different era, when they were expected to pitch more than an inning. He began his career as a starter but was switched to the bullpen after being ineffective. Today, 341 saves and a handlebar mustache later, he is enshrined in Cooperstown as one of the best ever. Well deserved.

6. Goose Gossage

Gossage was an overpowering pitcher who dominated his era and earned a place in the Hall of Fame. He was one of those multiple-inning guys who had an intimidating presence on the mound. Although it's tough to compare different generations of players, you get the feeling that Gossage would have thrived as a one-inning closer as well.

7. Bruce Sutter

Sutter was a very steady pitcher who used his split-finger fastball to confound hitters for years. He was not a guy who could knock the bat out of a hitter's hands but rather was a craftsman who pitched—and thanks to that fact, he earned his way into Cooperstown.

8. Troy Percival

Percival lasted long enough to amass 358 career saves, but an injury-plagued 2009 might have marked the end of the road for this outstanding closer. He enjoyed most of his success with the Angels, a team he helped win a World Series title. Hall of Fame material? Doubtful.

9. John Wetteland

Wetteland was the guy who preceded Mariano Rivera as the Yankees' closer, and he had quite an impressive run himself as his 330 saves would attest. He notched a World Series–winning save with New York and was a steady, if not spectacular, pitcher.

10 (tie). Hoyt Wilhelm, Elroy Face, Jack Baldschun

The critics might have a field day with this pick. Although Wilhelm has been inducted into the Hall of Fame and amassed 227 saves in his career, I feel that his place in history should be shared with Face (193 saves) and Baldschun (60 saves). These contemporary pitchers changed the game by being the first full-time closers who succeeded largely thanks to a trick pitch: Wilhelm mastered the knuckleball, Face the forkball, and Baldschun the screwball. All three hurlers were a huge influence on the evolution of the closer's role.

13. Randy Myers

This lefty had a fine career with 347 saves and a World Series win. Myers displayed both steadiness on the mound and longevity—he was a very good closer for a very long time.

14. Tom Henke

Henke was a big, hard-throwing guy who looked more like a teacher than a pitcher, thanks to the glasses he wore. Despite his spectacled presence, he could be very intimidating on the mound. He enjoyed considerable success in Toronto, ending up with 311 saves.

15. John Franco

Franco was one of the most popular players in the history of the New York Mets. A hometown boy made good, he earned 424 saves over the course of his long career. He could have been ranked higher, but he wasn't outstanding in the postseason and didn't play on a championship team.

16. Billy Wagner

Wagner is a hard-throwing southpaw who could break the 100-mph mark early in his career, but he has also developed a fine breaking pitch to complement his speed. He closed the 2009 season with 385 saves and has been a strong, consistent closer, but he has a 10.32 ERA in the postseason and has had some difficulty in big games.

17. Sparky Lyle

In the multipl -inning–closer era, the mustachioed Lyle was a typical left-hander in the true baseball sense. But his success on the big stage in New York with the Yankees changed the way relief pitching and relievers were looked at. For that reason, he belongs on this list. He had a great screwball.

18. Johnny Murphy

Murphy, who pitched from 1932 to 1947 (all but one season for the Yankees) was one of the earliest closers. He collected 107 saves over 13 seasons and helped define the role of reliever.

19. Firpo Marberry

Marberry pitched from 1923 to 1935 and was one of baseball's groundbreaking relievers. He started 187 games in his career but came on in relief in 364 others, earning 101 saves.

20. Jim Konstanty

Konstanty was another closer who looked more like a teacher than a ballplayer. He was as dominating out of the bullpen for the 1950 Philadelphia Phillies' "Whiz Kids" as Robin Roberts was as a starter; as a result, Konstanty won the NL MVP that season. He used an array of off-speed pitches to keep hitters off balance.

Top 100 All-Time Saves Leaders

(As of end of 2009 regular season; active players in bold; 2009 saves in parentheses)

1.	**Trevor Hoffman (37)**	591
2.	**Mariano Rivera (44)**	526
3.	Lee Smith	478
4.	John Franco	424
5.	Dennis Eckersley	390
6.	**Billy Wagner**	385
7.	Jeff Reardon	367
8.	**Troy Percival (6)**	358
9.	Randy Myers	347
10.	Rollie Fingers	341
11.	John Wetteland	330
12.	Roberto Hernández	326
13.	José Mesa	321
14.	Todd Jones	319
15.	Rick Aguilera	318
16.	Robb Nen	314
17.	Tom Henke	311
18.	Goose Gossage	310
19.	Jeff Montgomery	304
20.	Doug Jones	303
21.	Bruce Sutter	300
22.	**Jason Isringhausen**	293
23.	**Armando Benítez**	289
24.	Rod Beck	286
25.	Bob Wickman	267
26.	Todd Worrell	256
27.	Dave Righetti	252
28.	**Francisco Cordero (39)**	250

61.	**Tom Gordon**	158
	Dan Plesac	158
63.	Jay Howell	155
64.	Stu Miller	154
	John Smoltz	154
66.	Don McMahon	153
67.	**Jonathan Papelbon (38)**	151
68.	Greg Minton	150
69.	Ted Abernathy	148
70.	Willie Hernández	147
71.	**Bobby Jenks (29)**	146
72.	Dave Giusti	145
73.	Jesse Orosco	144
	Mike Williams	144
75.	Clay Carroll	143
	Darold Knowles	143
77.	Mike Jackson	142
78.	Mike Timlin	141
79.	Gary Lavelle	136
80.	Jim Brewer	132
	Steve Farr	132
	Bob Stanley	132
83.	Joe Borowski	131
84.	Ron Davis	130
85.	Antonio Alfonseca	129
	Kazuhiro Sasaki	129
	Huston Street (35)	129
88.	**Chad Cordero**	128
89.	Terry Forster	127
90.	Bill Campbell	126
	Dave LaRoche	126
	Mel Rojas	126

Top 100 All-Time Holds Leaders

(As of end of 2009 regular season; active players in bold)

1.	Mike Stanton	266
2.	**Arthur Rhodes**	217
3.	**Alan Embree**	194
4.	Jesse Orosco	185
5.	Paul Assenmacher	180
6.	Mike Jackson	179
	Dan Plesac	179
8.	Paul Quantrill	177
	Jeff Nelson	177
10.	**Bobby Howry**	175
11.	Mike Timlin	172
12.	Buddy Groom	171
13.	Steve Reed	168
14.	Rick Honeycutt	165
15.	Mike Myers	163
16.	Mike Remlinger	158
	Steve Kline	158
	Dave Weathers	158
19.	**Julian Tavarez**	155
20.	**Scot Shields**	154
	Mark Guthrie	154
22.	**Kyle Farnsworth**	145
23.	**Scott Linebrink**	144
24.	**J.C. Romero**	143
25.	**Scott Eyre**	141
26.	Ricardo Rincon	139
27.	**Chad Bradford**	136
	Ray King	136

29.	Felix Rodriguez	134
30.	**LaTroy Hawkins**	132
31.	Rheal Cormier	129
	Damaso Marte	129
33.	Tony Fossas	128
34.	**Justin Speier**	126
35.	Jim Mecir	125
36.	**Eddie Guardado**	122
37.	**Tom Gordon**	121
38.	Tim Worrell	120
39.	Rob Murphy	117
40.	**Octavio Dotel**	116
41.	Paul Shuey	115
42.	**Doug Brocail**	113
43.	Scott Radinsky	112
	Eric Plunk	112
45.	Scott Sullivan	111
46.	Dan Miceli	109
	Guillermo Mota	109
48.	**Russ Springer**	107
	Scott Sauerbeck	107
	Dan Wheeler	107
51.	Dennis Cook	106
52.	Larry Andersen	105
53.	**Luis Vizcaino**	102
	Bob Patterson	102
55.	Jason Christiansen	101
56.	**Dennys Reyes**	100
	Jason Grimsley	100
	Todd Jones	100
59.	Rich Rodriguez	99

60.	Brian Shouse	97
	Chad Qualls	97
62.	**Rafael Betancourt**	96
63.	**Ryan Madson**	95
	Graeme Lloyd	95
	Brendan Donnelly	95
	Jamie Walker	95
67.	**Ron Villone**	93
	Trever Miller	93
	Stan Belinda	93
70.	Ricky Bottalico	91
71.	Mike Fetters	90
	Juan Rincón	90
	Terry Adams	90
	Luis Ayala	90
	Scott Schoeneweis	90
	Bob Wickman	90
77.	Norm Charlton	89
	Ron Mahay	89
79.	Greg McMichael	88
80.	Jay Powell	87
	Alan Mills	87
	Mike Muñoz	87
83.	Dave Veres	86
	Jeff Fassero	86
85.	Rudy Seanez	85
	Shigetoshi Hasegawa	85
87.	**Matt Thornton**	84
	John Grabow	84
89.	Curt Leskanic	83
	Hector Carrasco	83
	Mike Trombley	83

92.	Mike DeJean	82
93.	Cliff Politte	81
	Chuck Crim	81
	Greg Swindell	81
	Chuck McElroy	81
97.	Kent Mercker	79
	Brandon Lyon	79
	Gabe White	79
	Roberto Hernández	79

Sources

Books

Bissinger, Buzz. *Three Nights in August: Strategy, Heartbreak, and Joy Inside the Mind of a Manager.* Boston: Houghton Mifflin, 2005.

Chadwick, Henry. *Haney's Baseball Book of Reference: Rules of the Game for 1867.* Bedford, MA: Applewood Books, 1866.

Cooperstown: Hall of Fame Players. Lincolnwood, IL: Publications International Ltd., 2002.

Felber, Bill. *The Book on The Book: A Landmark Inquiry Into Which Strategies in the Modern Game Actually Work.* New York: Thomas Dunne Books, 2005.

James, Bill, and Rob Neyer. *The Neyer/James Guide to Pitchers: An Historical Compendium of Pitching, Pitchers, and Pitches.* New York: Simon & Schuster, 2004.

Johnson, Lloyd. *Baseball's Book of Firsts.* North Dighton, MA: World Publication Group, 2005.

Kaufman, Alan S., and James C. Kaufman. *The Worst Baseball Pitchers of All Time: Bad Luck, Bad Arms, Bad Teams, and Just Plain Bad.* New York: Citadel Press, 1995.

Mathewson, Christy. *Pitching in a Pinch: Baseball from the Inside.* New York: Putnam, 1912.

McCarver, Tim, and Danny Peary. *Baseball for Brain Surgeons and Other Fans: Understanding and Interpreting the Game So You Can Watch It Like a Pro.* New York: Villard, 1998.

McCarver, Tim, and Ray Robinson. *Oh, Baby, I Love It!* New York: Dell Publishing, 1987.

Morris, Peter. *A Game of Inches: The Stories Behind the Innovations That Shaped Baseball.* Chicago: Ivan R. Dee, 2006.

———. *But Didn't We Have Fun: An Informal History of Baseball's Pioneer Era, 1843–1870.* Chicago: Ivan R. Dee, 2008.

Murphy, Cait. *Crazy '08: How a Cast of Cranks, Rogues, Boneheads, and Magnates Created the Greatest Year in Baseball History.* New York: HarperCollins, 2008.

Musial, Stan, and Bob Broeg. *Stan Musial: The Man's Own Story.* New York: Doubleday, 1964.

Palmer, Pete, and Gary Gillette. *The 2005 ESPN Baseball Encyclopedia.* New York: Sterling Publishing, 2005.

Peary, Danny. *We Played the Game.* New York: Black Dog & Leventhal Publishers, 2002.

Vizquel, Omar, and Bob Dyer. *Omar! My Life On and Off the Field.* Cleveland, OH: Gray & Co., 2003.

Votano, Paul. *Late and Close: A History of Relief Pitching.* Jefferson, NC: McFarland & Co., 2002.

Will, George, F. *Bunts: Curt Flood, Camden Yards, Pete Rose, and Other Reflections on Baseball.* New York: Scribner, 1998.

Zimniuch, Fran. *Phillies: Where Have You Gone?* Champaign, IL: Sports Publishing LLC, 2004.

———. *Shortened Seasons: The Untimely Deaths of Major League Baseball's Stars and Journeymen.* Lanham, MD: Rowman & Littlefield, 2007.

———. *PH-Antastic! The 2008 World Champion Philadelphia Phillies.* Chicago: Triumph Books, 2008.

Periodicals

Baseball Magazine, 1950

Baseball Monthly, 1962

Boston Globe, 2005

Philadelphia Inquirer

Saturday Evening Post, 1929

Spalding Base Ball Guide, 1892

The Sporting News, 1933

Washington Post, 1904

Sporting Life, 1908

Time, November 1950; June 1959

Websites

BaseballHallofFame.com

Major League Baseball statistics & history (Baseball-Reference.com)

Major League Baseball (www.mlb.com)

Society for American Baseball Research (www.sabr.org)

Suggestions for Further Reading

Asinof, Eliot. *Eight Men Out: The Black Sox and the 1919 World Series.* New York: Henry Holt and Company, 1963.

Bouton, Jim, and Leonard Scheter. *Ball Four.* New York: World, 1970.

Casway, Jerrold. *Ed Delahanty in the Emerald Age of Baseball.* South Bend, IN: University of Notre Dame Press, 2004.

Claire, Fred, and Steve Springer. *My 30 Years in Dodger Blue.* Champaign, IL: Sports Publishing LLC, 2004.

Colton, Larry. *Goat Brothers.* New York: Random House, 1995.

Conlin, Bill. *Batting Cleanup, Bill Conlin.* Philadelphia: Temple University Press, 1997.

Feinstein, John. *Living on the Black: Two Pitchers, Two Teams, One Season to Remember,* New York: Little, Brown and Company, 2008.

Giles, Bill, and Doug Myers. *Pouring Six Beers at a Time, and Other Stories from a Lifetime in Baseball,* Chicago: Triumph Books, 2007.

Gruver, Edward. *Koufax.* Lanham, MD: Taylor Trade, 2003.

Jacobson, Steve. *The Pitching Staff: A Basic Portrait of Baseball's Most Unique Fraternity.* New York: Thomas Y. Corwell Company, 1975.

James, Bill. *The New Bill James Historical Baseball Abstract.* New York: Free Press, 2001.

Jenkins, Ferguson, and Lew Freedman. *Fergie: My Life from the Cubs to Cooperstown.* Chicago: Triumph Books, 2009.

Kahn, Roger. *The Head Game: Baseball Seen from the Pitcher's Mound.* Orlando, FL: Harcourt Inc., 2000.

Leavy, Jane. *Sandy Koufax: A Lefty's Legacy.* New York: HarperCollins, 2002.

Schmidt, Mike, and Glen Waggoner. *Clearing the Bases: Juiced Players, Monster Salaries, Sham Records, and a Hall of Famer's Search for the Soul of Baseball.* New York: HarperCollins, 2006.

Vecsey, George. *Baseball: A History of America's Favorite Game.* New York: Modern Library, 2006.